W9-AQF-824

WITHDRAWN

Gloria Naylor's Early Novels

Gloria Naylor's

University Press of Florida

Gainesville · Tallahassee · Tampa · Boca Raton · Pensacola · Orlando · Miami · Jacksonville

Edited and with an Introduction by Margot Anne Kelley

Early Novels

04 03 02 01   6 5 4 3 2

Library of Congress Cataloging-in-Publication Data
Gloria Naylor's early novels / edited and with an introduction
   by Margot Anne Kelley.
p. cm.
Includes bibliographical references and index.
ISBN 0-8130-1649 (alk. paper)
1. Naylor, Gloria—Criticism and interpretation. 2. Women and
literature—United States—History—20th century . 3. Afro-
American women in literature. 4. Afro-Americans in literature.
I. Kelley, Margot Anne.
PS3564.A89Z684   1999
813'.54—dc21   98-47244

The University Press of Florida is the scholarly publishing agency
for the State University System of Florida, comprising Florida
A & M University, Florida Atlantic University, Florida Interna-
tional University, Florida State University, University of Central
Florida, University of Florida, University of North Florida,
University of South Florida, and University of West Florida.

University Press of Florida
15 Northwest 15th Street
Gainesville, FL 32611–2079
http://www.upf.com

For Robert, who has the best qualities

of Willie and of George

Contents

Preface   ix

Introduction   xi

Gloria Naylor's Poetics of Emancipation: (E)merging (Im)possibilities
in *Bailey's Cafe*
    Karen Schneider   1

Women's Screams and Women's Laughter: Connections
and Creations in Gloria Naylor's Novels
    Jenny Brantley   21

"Weapons Against Women": Compulsory Heterosexuality
and Capitalism in *Linden Hills*
    Kimberly A. Costino   39

Good Housekeeping: Domestic Ritual in Gloria Naylor's Fiction
    Maxine Lavon Montgomery   55

Metaphor and Maternity in *Mama Day*
    Amy K. Levin   70

Africana Womanist Revision in Gloria Naylor's *Mama Day*
and *Bailey's Cafe*
    Dorothy Perry Thompson   89

"Into the Midst of Nothing": Gloria Naylor and the *Différance*
Philip Page   112

Framing the Possibilities: Collective Agency and the Novels
of Gloria Naylor
Margot Anne Kelley   133

Selected Bibliography   155

List of Contributors   160

Index   162

Preface

Making connections. One of the major concerns in all of Gloria Naylor's novels is making connections in different ways, among disparate elements, at different levels: from individuals who are schismatized and want to create a sense of wholeness or unity for themselves, to men and women who seek loving partners, to groups of people struggling to become communities, the characters are involved in quests for connection. Naylor reproduces those efforts by deploying details from African, African-American, Anglo-American, and European literary and cultural traditions in the novels to link her texts with others already in the world. Equally important, she has connected her novels to one another, through resonances loud and soft.

Like the novels by Naylor that are discussed in the essays gathered here, the act of creating a collection, and perhaps the act of creating this kind of collection in particular, is about finding, making, and coming to know the value of connections. As this book began to take shape, links began to be forged. Ideas of one writer began to resonate with those of another, as nearly always happens when one pursues scholarly research. But as happens less often, the intellectual interactions, the connections on the page, led to ties (both intellectual and personal) being created among the contributors, most of whom had not previously met. Several of the authors have enjoyed this opportunity to discover and correspond with an intellectual kindred spirit—to begin to build relationships based on shared concerns, despite being geographically distant from one another. And so as I think about the troubling geographies and the struggling communities that recur in Naylor's novels, or about the persistent efforts of characters not at all sure that they can forge the connections they ache to have, I see us as engaged in an enterprise that has much in common with the sort Naylor depicts: an effort to imagine ourselves into worlds that are less confining, more liberating, and more joyous; an attempt to use our minds and our hearts to connect more fully to others and to the world. I am delighted to be part of such an effort.

Therefore, I want to thank both the contributors and the other people who have been involved in making this collection possible. I would like to thank my family for giving me an early appreciation of the pleasures that connections can enable. Many thanks to my colleagues at Ursinus College, at conferences, and in on-line discussions for their intellectual enthusiasm and support. I appreciate the generosity of the Ursinus Faculty Development Committee, without whose assistance this book would have taken much longer to complete. My gratitude to my students for their excitement about life and literature is immeasurable. Thank you all, and thanks especially to the members of the 1998 seminar on Gloria Naylor's novels who brought fresh ideas and incredible passion to every discussion. Thanks to Jared Rakes, my research assistant, for wit and energy as we edited this manuscript, and to Margie Connor, for never being annoyed when I needed something typed *right away.* Thank you to Fred Schreiber, my *sensei,* for gentle insight at many uncertain moments, and—as always—to Robert Kelley.

Introduction

With this last novel, *Bailey's Cafe,* I have done the quartet that I had dreamed about. As I look back, I wasn't keeping stock of time or anything, but this is 1991, and I finished *Brewster Place* in 1981, and now I have finished the quartet. This was to lay the basis or the foundation—I saw it like this little square foundation—for a career I was going to build. So I now believe that I will have the kind of career I want.

—Gloria Naylor

Near the middle of *Mama Day,* George Andrews is whitewashing a chicken coop for Miranda Day, while Miranda watches him and hopes that he and Cocoa (who is his wife and her grandniece) can get past the nasty fight they had the night before. She worries a little that they might "go the way of so many of these young people nowadays. Just letting things crumble apart, 'cause everybody wants to be right in a world where there ain't no right or wrong to be found" (*MD,* 229–30). Moreover, she sees the impulse behind this desire to be right as the desire to have one's "side" validated, to be not only listened to but also agreed with. The latter strikes Mama Day as problematic because "just like [a] chicken coop, everything got four sides: his side, her side, an outside, and an inside. All of it is the truth" (230). One of the distinctions that Gloria Naylor draws here, between there being "no right and wrong," on the one hand, while "all of it" is "the truth," on the other hand, is crucial to her fictions and is relevant to the essays in this collection.

Not only in her novels but also in the ways that she writes and talks about authorship, Naylor attends to the importance of multiple truths, of moving past unduly simplified notions of what constitutes the truth, the right way. She connects this need to challenge received truths to her childhood search for literature that acknowledged her existence as a racialized and gendered being, as a black woman who could be a writer. In describing her childhood and adolescence, again and again she notes that she read voraciously, but that her readings "told [her] that black people did not write books." Even though she read "to the tune of a book a day . . . there was nothing about black Americans or by black Americans . . . on the shelves in the public libraries in New York City, and they definitely weren't on my standard junior high school or high school curriculum" (Naylor 1995, 172); and so it was not until she was a student at Brooklyn College that she read a novel by a black woman, *The Bluest Eye* by Toni Morrison. Discovering that it was not "true" that black Americans did not write books was a catalyzing experience, one that provided her with an image in the mirror, an acknowledgment that she existed. This confirmation of her self and of her possibilities for artistry "reverberated enough to give me the courage to pick up the pen" (173).

Sometimes when Naylor recounts this journey to writing professionally, she also notes that the works she did read during her adolescence, works by Faulkner, Hemingway, the Brontës, Dickens, Thackeray, Emerson, Melville, Poe, and Hawthorne, were "wonderful and fine" (Carabi 1992, 37). The problem, as she explains it, was not that the texts were wanting; it was that the authors wrote from their own historically and culturally specific moments. And these moments were not her moment; these specific cultural contexts were not her context. In the same way that "Shakespeare wrote about Elizabethan Englishmen" (even, she explains, if these Englishmen lived in the Caribbean, Denmark, or Verona) and that "Joyce wrote about the Irish [and] Philip Roth writes about the Jews," Gloria Naylor wanted to read and write about African-American women (Naylor 1995, 175).

And so she began to write the sort of books she wanted to read. In writing such novels, Naylor participates quite deliberately in the widespread efforts occurring during the 1980s and 1990s to address and redress the limited representations of women and people of color within the literature that is regularly published and taught in the United States. Like others who are labeled multicultural writers, Naylor is working to make a space for her own visions, while couching those visions in terms of ethnicity and gender, as well as to indicate the richness of her insights. In fact, as the century draws to a close, black women are often perceived as the most successful American group in conveying one community's particular visions in new and compelling ways. Naylor attributes this success both to black women's entrance into the publishing industry itself and to the richness of black women's lives as subject matter, for "the black woman brings both her history as a black person and her living reality as a female . . . [which means that] their portrayal of what it has been like to have a dual existence in this country becomes a celebration of the self, a transcendence" (Carabi 1992, 37). Moreover, the attention to both race and gender allows black women to respond to the historical privileging of not only white, but also male, versions of the American experience. Such attention is especially important now, for, as Henry Louis Gates, Jr., observed in *Loose Canons*, "we might well argue that the problem of the twenty-first century will be the problem of ethnic differences, as these conspire with complex differences in color, gender, and class" (1992, xii).

The problems associated with "difference" have made the literary theoretical concerns about multiculturalism and identity politics significant and available to a wider population than is usually concerned with literary theory. Nevertheless, this concern has not made the complex negotiations that a woman literary writer must make any more straightforward as she strives to highlight previous silences within the canon and to offer her own voice. The task still involves defining a metaphorical space to speak from, a site that is contiguous with existing spaces without being subsumed by or entirely predefined by them. A persistent awareness of this need to carve a niche, to make a space, may be one of the reasons that the novels of Gloria Naylor (along with those of Toni Morrison and other black American women) routinely offer highly particular accounts of space—be they architectural spaces, geographical spaces, psychic spaces, or communal spaces.

While such indications of new regions work well within the texts, many authors feel the need, also, to clarify the ways in which their works carve out a new terrain at the level of the literary canon, that is, how they relate to preexisting texts. Naylor has made her desire to talk to her precursors a prominent element in her novels. Thus, in *The Women of Brewster Place*, Naylor invokes Shakespeare's *A Midsummer Night's Dream*, as well as Ann Petry's *The Street*, among other works. In *Linden Hills*, she conspicuously creates a community whose construction and spirit recall Dante's *The Inferno*. In *Mama Day* she again emphasizes Shakespearean plays—most obviously *Romeo and Juliet*. And in *Bailey's Cafe*, she rewrites five biblical stories and reminds us of Chaucer's *The Canterbury Tales*. Through this process of allusion and response, Naylor is able to articulate her own place within the canon, critically examine her precursors, and remind readers that diverse literary texts can represent the multiple truths of our lives in ways that can fruitfully, mutually exist.

Because Naylor's writing calls clear attention to its literary indebtedness, many critics have examined her allusions to the Western canon. Equally important have been other works that address her Africanist borrowings. The essays in this collection are beholden to these analyses, and several add specifically to those ongoing dialogues. But we are also engaged in a slightly different general project. What we are addressing are the ways in which Naylor's insistence on plurality, on multiple and contingent truths, and on highly particularized, culturally constructed identities matters throughout her first four novels. Such a focus requires that we recognize how her work relates to previous canonical texts and how she defines and presents her own vision. But it also demands that we couch that inquiry in terms of her narrative effort to foreground plurality, in terms of her choice to compose a foundation not simply of four novels, but quite specifically a set of interrelated texts.

In 1991 Gloria Naylor told interviewer Donna Perry that "for years and years" she had feared being a "one-book phenomenon" (Perry 1993, 239). She has also explained, on several occasions, that she had envisioned writing a "quartet" that would serve as the foundation for her career (224). In one sense, then, her choice to write a series of linked texts was governed by her desire to legitimate and validate herself as a serious writer. In another sense, describing these texts as a "quartet" enabled Naylor to accentuate the richness and variety that has come to be labeled, overly simply, as "the black experience." She explained to Angels Carabi that she drew so many women in *The Women of Brewster Place* because she was "attempting to create a microcosm of the black female experience in America. . . . People tend to talk about 'the black experience,' lumping it all as one mass searching but there is no one thing that can stand for that experience because it is indeed so rich and so varied" (Carabi 1992, 38). And across the novels, Naylor presents men and women, single and partnered, financially stable and in dire need, young and old, urban and rural, American and international—people whose very beings represent the variety she deems it essential to chronicle. As important as acknowledging this range of identity attributes is acknowledging and exploring the range of forces that work to limit these identities and the opportunities available to African-American women and men. This latter range is also chronicled in her first four novels—and we see that capitalism, heteronormativity, and conventional gender roles work in concert with racial and racist assumptions to define and, all too often, limit the opportunities available to characters. Thus, a second reason that the entwining of these works is significant is that it allows Naylor to explore the consequences of a wider variety of cultural forces than she could have examined within a single work. Because we regard the works as intertwined, we also regard the cultural forces as intertwined—even though we cannot attend to them all at once.

In principle one could imaginatively consider these varied cultural and personal issues in texts that are not interconnected, although the suggestion that the issues are interdependent would be lessened. Therefore, we do well to consider the ways in which a multiple-text universe allows an author to achieve effects that would be nearly impossible in a set of non-intertwined novels. First, like a metafiction, a multiple-text universe simultaneously foregrounds its fictive nature (it is an imaginary world; it is not "real") while challenging ontological boundaries (ultimately unconfined, for its boundaries are redrawn with the publication of each successive novel). Thus, it cannot be as readily defined/demarcated as can a single text universe and can make us question the grounds for distinguishing between "fictive" and "real" worlds. But unlike in a metafiction, the ontological challenge occurs by prompting the reader to shift *position,* or vantage point, rather than to shift between *levels*—between the "real" and the "fictive." A short example can illustrate this difference: when Kurt Vonnegut has a character named Kurt Vonnegut wander through a novel, we read that character as both "real" and "fictive," as disrupting a hierarchical distinction between the corporeal world and the imaginative world; that is metafiction. But when Cocoa Day mentions that her cousin died in a fire in Linden Hills, the line between two apparently self-contained fictive universes is transgressed. This permeability of the worlds violates realist convention and forces us to consider that the ontologies of those fictive universes must, somehow, be reconcilable. But because the two worlds—while perhaps ontologically distinct—are both fictive, the transgression is not metafictional.

Moreover, we should note that this permeability is also different from traditional allusion, and different from parody, in that it exceeds the capacity of those techniques. Wallace Martin notes in *Recent Theories of Narrative* that devices like parody, satire, and irony, which one can think of as "internal devices" (because they function within the fictive level), work to disrupt the "one-to-one relationship between convention and meaning." By enabling the reader to "look at prevailing literary and social conventions from another position," these devices also permit the reader to question "the validity or authenticity of the norm." Like these devices, cross-referencing within a multiple-text universe can "call attention to the formal and ideological frameworks that govern literature and society." But at the same time, it accomplishes an aim typically associated with metafictional devices: cross-referencing puts the fictional world temporarily "in quotation marks, so to speak, stepping beyond its boundaries" (Martin 1986, 179–81). Thus, when George Andrews is born at the close of *Bailey's Cafe* and the reader realizes that Andrews is unequivocally not a "son of a bitch" (the label he had vehemently resisted in *Mama Day* because he believed it held some truth), he or she puts the reading of this novel momentarily on hold, allowing *Mama Day* to inhabit the consciousness for a period of time and rethinking his or her understanding of that novel, before completing *Bailey's Cafe*. Such intertextual reference moves one beyond the boundaries of the novel and changes ontological parameters but not the ontological level.

What distinguishes this response from that of traditional parody or allusion is that the reader does not believe he or she has simply a new perspective on a situation but rather believes he or she has a new understanding based on an increase in knowledge about that situation. Once the reader knows the new information, the reader sees his or her former understanding as impoverished and also sees the characters as operating with an obviously limited perspective. For example, when Naylor "revises" a biblical story, we regard the revision as providing a new slant, a new perspective. But when Naylor revises Naylor, we regard the revision as a supplement. Like the Derridean *supplement*, Naylor's supplement alerts us to the incompleteness of our earlier vision and thereby encourages us to examine the commitments we held that prompted us to believe it was sufficient. Further, this particular example about George Andrews illustrates that such textual transgressions can accomplish another significant task that metafictional devices permit: they enable an author to explore "the whole system of traditional distinctions between reality and fiction on the one hand and truth and falsity on the other" (Martin, 181). Establishing a multiple-text universe, then, enabled Gloria Naylor to employ intertextual links that accomplished some of the same things "internal devices" and metafictional devices can, but without reinscribing the real/fiction, true/false dichotomy that she has consistently described as problematic.

Naylor's decision to make her multiple-text universe a world composed, at least initially, through four novels allowed her to achieve two further narratological ends that are consistent with major African-American literary traditions: she participates in the tradition of signifyin(g) in significant ways and she does so using repetition cycles. Henry Louis Gates, Jr., describes signifyin(g) as "a trope that subsumes other rhetorical tropes, including metaphor, metonymy, synecdoche and irony" (1984, 286). A signifyin(g) structure, he goes on to point out, is one that includes "intertextual revision, because it revises key tropes and rhetorical strategies," and it is significant to African-American literary history because "black writers read and critique other black texts as an act of rhetorical self-definition" (Gates 1984, 290). Certainly, Naylor's intertextual deployment of other authors' texts is part of this tradition, a point that has been noted by many critics. In addition, her cross-referencing of her own universes can be discussed within this framework. I believe, though, that still another aspect of the way signifyin(g) structures use repetition and reversal illuminates her choice to think of her first four novels as a quartet.

Gates observes that there are many interrelated descriptions of signifyin(g), and Thomas Kochman defines it by saying "that signifying depends upon the signifier repeating what someone else has said about a third person in order to reverse the status of a relationship heretofore harmonious; signifying can also be employed to reverse or undermine pretense or even one's opinion about one's own status. The use of repetition and reversal (chiasmus) constitutes an implicit parody of a subject's own complicity in illusion" (in Gates 1984, 289). Like Gates and Kochman, I want to focus on the capacity for signifyin(g) to challenge one's complicity in illusion through a narratological effort: by creating a structure marked by repetition and reversal, the "signifier" can challenge pretenses and disrupt assumptions. That the challenges might be at the level of narrative structure, rather than at the level of the "story," is made explicit when Gates describes signifyin(g) as "a theory of formal revision; it is tropological; it is often characterized by pastiche; and, most crucially, it turns on repetition of formal structures, and their difference" (Gates 1984, 285–86). Naylor's use of repetition is especially significant, for it allows us to comprehend her work in terms of repetition cycles, in the terms that James Snead has offered, at the same time that it allows us to see that she is creating a set of signifyin(g) texts, which instantiate a logic of repetition and reversal, creating a chiasmus, an aporia, between *Linden Hills* and *Mama Day*.

In many ways, *The Women of Brewster Place* and *Bailey's Cafe* complement each other, as do *Linden Hills* and *Mama Day*. The essays in this collection tease out some of the ways in which such counterpointing occurs and matters. But to give one example of the ways in which this repetition and reversal work, consider simply the contrast between enclosure and open-endedness at play across the four novels. Brewster Place is a dead-end, set off from the rest of the community by a wall. Linden Hills is a community unto itself, one to which entrance is strictly regulated in economic terms. They are reversals of each other in terms of the economic status of their residents, but are repetitions of each other in their emphasis on enclosure, separation, and economics. *Mama Day* enlarges the textual universe, introducing not one but two locales that are distinct from each other and from the locales in the first two novels. Juxtaposing Willow Springs and New York, Naylor widens the world appreciably; and *Bailey's Cafe* extends the universe beyond the east coast of the United States to, in principle, include the entire world. The latter novels reverse the former ones in terms of the emphasis on enclosure by employing images of openness—"the other place" and a door to the edge of infinity—as well as by examining the ways that people can try to come together (albeit often unsuccessfully) rather than remaining isolated. At the same time, *Mama Day* and *Bailey's Cafe* share with the earlier novels an emphasis on the stifling power of the economic order, thereby repeating a concern evinced in the first two books.

When we focus on reversal, we emphasize one attribute of signifying structures; when we focus on repetition, we see another—the one highlighted by Kimberly Costino in her essay in this volume when she argues that George's birth at the end of *Bailey's Cafe* "locks the novels into a cycle." The publication chronology and the event chronology of the novels differ, with the last published novel occurring first in narrative time. Through this play with time, Naylor draws our attention to the possibility that cycles might matter. James Snead has argued for the importance of cycles to black culture, saying that while repetition matters to all cultures, black cultures have acknowledged and foregrounded such repetition through an emphasis on cycles—biological, agrarian, ritual, and artistic. He posits this in contrast to what he calls the European tendency to emphasize linearity, that is, teleological progress. In making this distinction, Snead cites two attributes of repetition cycles that are especially relevant to our understanding of Naylor's texts. He notes:

> Black culture highlights the observance of such repetition, often in homage to an original generative instance or act. . . . In black culture, repetition means that the thing circulates . . . [that] there is an equilibrium. In European culture, repetition must be seen to be not just circulation and flow but accumulation and growth. In black culture, the thing (the ritual, the dance, the beat) is "there for you to pick it up when you come back to get it." If there is a goal (Zweck) in such a culture, it is always deferred; it continually "cuts" back to the start, in the musical meaning of "cut" as an abrupt, seemingly unmotivated break (an accidental da capo) with a series already in progress and a willed return to a prior series. (Snead 1984, 65, 67)

Through rituals like Candle Walk, we see the communities in Naylor's novel employing repetition in the first manner. And through the novels themselves—especially through Naylor's use of textual transgressions, or cross-references—we see a form of "cutting" that is especially effective in reinforcing the cycle.

In 1998 Gloria Naylor published her fifth novel, *The Men of Brewster Place*. As the title itself would suggest, this book revisits the locale she depicted in her first novel, but provides the vantage of some of the male inhabitants. For instance, the introduction to the new book is entitled "Dusk" and incorporates italicized passages from the conclusion (also entitled "Dusk") of *The Women of Brewster Place*. Interspersed between these passages are a first person narration by Ben, the janitor who appeared in the earlier novel. This book will certainly invite an intertextual reading, signifying as it does on Naylor's first novel, and is already prompting scholars to see the original quartet from a distinctly different vantage. Just as George's birth at the end of *Bailey's Cafe* forced us to rethink his rancorous reaction to the phrase "son of a bitch" in *Mama Day*, the new material about Ben, Basil, and the other men who interacted with the women of Naylor's first novel will prompt new considerations of *The Women of Brewster Place*. Interestingly, though, Naylor insists that she continues to regard the first four novels as working together in a relatively autonomous way. She says that *The Men of Brewster Place* is not meant to "change that [structure]" but is intended to "build on that foundation." She hopes her next novel, about Sapphira Wade (the Great, Grand mother to the people of Willow Springs), will serve as a "cornerstone" to the edifice she is constructing. Naylor frequently makes a metaphorical equation between the structure of the novels and her career, which is perhaps the reason she is quite adamant about continuing to see the first four novels as distinct from the successive works. She describes them as "an apprenticeship" that was necessary to her subsequent work (Naylor interview 1997). Thus, while both this new novel and the planned future novel will extend the textual universe that Naylor has constructed, challenging readers to discover still more ways in which she is utilizing the unique characteristics of a multiple-text world, they do not invalidate the varied connections she has already composed. Rather, they will further supplement our understandings, further signify upon existing notions, further encourage us to attend to the contingencies of our truths.

In thinking about the complex narrative devices and the other elements that link the first four novels, all of the contributors to this volume focused on Gloria Naylor's need to create a multiple-text universe, as well as on her desire to build a specific type of foundation. That focus led to the notion of multiple truths emerging in our analyses as frequently as it does in Naylor's novels. Therefore, almost all of the essays in this collection focus primarily on one text, but simultaneously note that the novel is part of a larger fictive universe, that the work Naylor is doing in one novel is inflected by and itself affects the other novels. Through that balance the authors of this book have tried to communicate insights that will help readers understand the individual texts and the wider aims we see as crucial to Naylor's work. Moreover, the essays themselves are juxtaposed in ways that allow readers to see that, like Naylor's work, this volume presents more than one truth. Contributors disagree about the significance of specific scenes (like George's death in *Mama Day*) and about the logic governing some of Naylor's narrative choices (like her emphasis on refiguring Western literary traditions). By encountering these divergent views in quick succession, the reader of this collection may come to appreciate more fully the complexity of Naylor's vision and her wisdom in maintaining that while "everything [has] got four sides . . . all of it is the truth."

Karen Schneider's essay on *Bailey's Cafe* opens this volume because she introduces a set of issues that many of the other contributors then develop. Attending to ideas given currency within poststructuralism, and counterpointing that understanding with concerns evinced by African-American feminist critics, she argues that Naylor strives to develop "a poetics of emancipation from within the booby-trapped field of Western/patriarchal discourse" by critically challenging linguistic and aesthetic images that have been used to disempower women and peoples of color. Demonstrating that the literary and religious allusions in *Bailey's Cafe* are complexly fashioned, that neither Shakespeare nor the Bible is used in a monovalent manner, she suggests that Naylor's achievement is, in part, that she has proffered a poetics that is itself a celebration of polyvalence and a move beyond a simple inversion of previously established terms. Doing so, she claims, has enabled Naylor to create a cyclic interaction among her novels, and the insights we gain from this novel encourage us to revisit the earlier texts and view them from a new, more liberatory, perspective.

Schneider notes that in *Bailey's Cafe* many of the women are subjugated by a sexual economy. In particular, she argues that Esther, who is sold into sexual servitude by her brother and ordered to be mute by her owner/ husband, is "subjected to/by a symbolic order in which she is 'unspeakable'." Jennifer Brantley explores the semiotic devices that Naylor uses to exceed the limits of this social order, which renders too much of women's lives unspeakable. In the second essay, "Women's Screams and Women's Laughter: Connections and Creations in Gloria Naylor's Novels," Brantley maintains that screams and laughter not only create patterns that "are essential in each novel separately, [but also they] . . . signal a narrative turn and serve as an essential connecting device among the novels." From Ciel's screams in *The Women of Brewster Place* to Willa's in *Linden Hills* to Cocoa's scream of revulsion and her great-grandmother's of anguish in *Mama Day* to the thin baby cry of George in *Bailey's Cafe*, outbursts of pain mark the novels as concerned with giving voice to the body. Concurring with Elaine Scarry that "physical pain does not simply resist language but actively destroys it . . . [reducing it] to the sounds and cries a human makes before language is learned," Brantley draws on French feminist considerations of the prelingual as a source for sounds and a language that will not be stifled by oppressive forces. She argues, further, that Naylor identifies laughter as one such sound, and traces the role(s) laughter plays in the four novels.

Schneider and Brantley have emphasized silencing of women within the symbolic order. In "'Weapons Against Women': Compulsory Heterosexuality and Capitalism in *Linden Hills*," Kimberly Costino argues that Naylor addresses another sort of silencing. She maintains that the relation between capitalism and heteronormative sexuality works to disallow a homosexual identity, effectively forcing characters to deny their sexuality (to silence themselves) in order to survive economically. She goes on to claim that Naylor is seeking to sever the link between these two ideological forces in order to explore the possibilities Adrienne Rich alluded to in "Compulsory Heterosexuality and the Lesbian Continuum." Costino argues that Naylor is extending the range that Rich considered by addressing the stifling consequences of heteronormativity for men and women, and showing the potential of the continuum for gay men as well as for lesbians.

In making these claims, Costino emphasizes the reproduction of conventional gender roles that reinforces heteronormativity both in *Brewster Place* and in *Linden Hills*. As dissimilar as those two sites are economically and socially, their shared acceptance of heteronormativity and of stereotypical gender roles makes them ideal for the inquiry Maxine Lavon Montgomery undertakes in "Good Housekeeping: Domestic Ritual in Gloria Naylor's Fiction." Counterpointing the efforts of the women of Brewster Place to form a family of choice to the almost unchallenged acceptance of the resolutely nuclear formations that dominate in Linden Hills, Montgomery examines the productive and stultifying roles that domestic rituals can play. In tracing the varied presentations (and critiques) of domesticity in these two novels, and in extending them to the rest of the quartet, Montgomery argues that "far from being a replica of domestic novels by white women writers, Naylor's texts mirror the unique realities of black women." With that perspective, she examines how Naylor does and does not present the home as what bell hooks has called "a site of resistance and liberation struggle."

Amy K. Levin, in her essay "Metaphor and Maternity in *Mama Day*," also focuses on women's activities, looking closely at the ways in which motherhood and midwifery are crucial to *Mama Day*. Levin situates her arguments, not in relation to American literary and cultural models of domesticity, but in the context of an African social one. Levin notes that *Mama Day* is among the many recent novels by African-American women that incorporates a significant focus on motherhood and maternity, and that these works have been considered in concert with European-influenced paradigms and/or African models that are, more accurately, gender-coded male. She argues that it is appropriate to regard these concerns through a framework that emphasizes both African and female elements. To do so, she discusses a variety of rituals and beliefs associated with West African women's secret societies, and maintains that although "the sources of such inherited rituals and beliefs have been largely forgotten by those who still practice them, . . . secret society traditions have gradually been woven into the fabric of African-American life." Showing the ways that these ideas pervade *Mama Day*, Levin argues for the value of "a multicultural angle of interpretation."

In the sixth essay, Dorothy Perry Thompson shares Levin's insistence on "a multicultural angle of interpretation," and formulates a revised understanding of Alice Walker's "womanism" to take Africanist considerations more fully into account. In "Africana Womanist Revision in Gloria Naylor's *Mama Day* and *Bailey's Cafe*," Thompson proffers a syncretic model of Africana (rather than African-American) womanism that functions in "a spiralytic relationship with Walker's original definition." By integrating African elements into her novels, Naylor is able, Thompson explains, to communicate a vision that moves beyond those of her precursors and to attain "levels of revision and refiguration that rest above the source of their energy by the magnitude or power of their difference." Moreover, she demonstrates that when this vantage is used to examine the biblical revisions in *Bailey's Cafe*, we can see that the work Naylor is doing is highly complex and takes into account a distinctively pluralistic set of concerns.

Thompson's model, which melds Euro-American, African-American, and African components, makes explicit Naylor's evasion of binary logic, her rejection of either/or systems. Philip Page, in "'Into the Midst of Nothing': Gloria Naylor and the *Différance*," explores the ways in which this rejection of simple either/or logic matters in Naylor's texts from a different vantage. Drawing on Derrida's idea that wells are typically "destructive," representing "a fixed, monologic entity," but that they can, in contrast, be seen as "beneficial if taken as part of a fluid and multivalent orientation toward the open-endedness of being," Page carefully illustrates the ways in which wells and well-like images work in Naylor's novels to elaborate a zone, at their edges, where neither the destructive nor the beneficial aspects entirely dominate. Instead, he argues, this zone is one characterized by the différance, by the Derridean notion that the well need not be understood as either positive or negative, but rather can be reconceived as "infinitely complex." Page demonstrates that Naylor's willingness to present images as multivalent is part of a more thoroughgoing attempt to move beyond the "traditional Western emphasis on fixed entities and the irreconcilable separations between binary opposites to a blurring of boundaries and an embrace of inclusiveness."

Moving from the edges of the wells to the edges of the novels, I look at the ways in which narrative frames function to create an undecided zone much like the ones Page describes. In "Framing the Possibilities: Collective Agency and the Novels of Gloria Naylor," I argue that the multiple, complicated frames in *Bailey's Cafe* are used to define a space within which new models of human agency can be tested. Likening the work done in "The Jam" section of *Bailey's Cafe* to that occurring in the middle two novels in the original quartet, I claim that one of Naylor's ongoing efforts is to formulate ways to escape debilitating interpellation into a capitalist identity while living in the contemporary United States. Such an escape may be possible for individuals who deploy what the sociologist Michel deCerteau has called "tactics." A tactic is "'an art of being in between,' an 'art of the weak . . .,' available to and often pursued by people living in disempowering situations. In contrast to a 'strategy,' which uses actions and culture products in their intended fashion . . . tactics work because individuals 'us[e] them with respect to ends and references foreign to the system they had no choice but to accept'" (deCerteau 1984, xiii).

With this final essay, we come full cycle—returning to Schneider's question as to whether Naylor has managed to imaginatively articulate emancipatory possibilities as well as returning to *Bailey's Cafe*. Shortly after George's birth at the end of that novel, "Bailey" laments that "when you have to face it [life] with more questions than answers, it can be a crying shame" (BC, 229). And while facing a life full of questions may be a "shame" in some ways, Naylor's ability to make us see that there can be debate and inquiry where once many people had presumed there was certainty, that there can be more than one side to the truth, is anything but a shame. It is the beginning of insight.

A Note on the Sources

In all of the essays in this volume, the following abbreviations are used for Gloria Naylor's first four novels: *BC* for *Bailey's Cafe*, *LH* for *Linden Hills*, *MD* for *Mama Day*, and *WBP* for *The Women of Brewster Place*.

Works Cited

Carabi, Angels. "Belles Lettres Interview." *Belles Lettres* (Spring 1992): 36–42.

deCerteau, Michel. *The Practice of Everyday Life*. Trans. Steven Rendall. Berkeley: University of California Press, 1984.

Gates, Henry Louis, Jr. "The Blackness of Blackness: A Critique of *The Sign and The Signifying Monkey*." In *Black Literature and Literary Theory*. Ed. Henry Louis Gates, Jr. New York: Routledge, 1984. 285–321.

———. *Loose Canons: Notes on the Culture Wars*. New York: Oxford University Press, 1992.

Martin, Wallace. *Recent Theories of Narrative*. Ithaca, N.Y.: Cornell University Press, 1986.

Naylor, Gloria. *Bailey's Cafe*. New York: Harcourt Brace Jovanovich, 1992.

———. "The Love of Books." In *The Writing Life*. Eds. Neil Baldwin and Diane Osen. New York: Random House, 1995. 167–75.

———. Telephone interview with author. Sept. 17, 1997.

Perry, Donna. *Backtalk: Women Writers Speak Out*. New Brunswick, N.J.: Rutgers University Press, 1993.

Snead, James A. "Repetition as a Figure of Black Culture." In *Black Literature and Literary Theory*. Ed. Henry Louis Gates, Jr. New York: Routledge, 1984. 59–79.

Gloria Naylor's Poetics of Emancipation

(E)merging (Im)possibilities in *Bailey's Cafe*

Karen Schneider

Even before the widespread dissemination of poststructuralist notions about the ideological constraints of language, many minorities and women were self-consciously engaged in a discursive struggle for meaning and authority from within a self-effacing or "othering" symbolic order. At one stage in the debate about what constitutes an efficacious form of that struggle for African-Americans, Larry Neal (among others) called for complete renunciation of the "western cultural aesthetic, a separate symbolism, mythology, critique, and iconology" (Neal 1972, 257). As notions of cultural identity, linguistic authority, and empowerment have evolved, theories of black aesthetic practice have proliferated accordingly. In his Nobel laureate address (1986), for example, Wole Soyinka proposed a paradoxical variation on "renunciation" of Western language and literature. His solution to the problem of how to use the oppressor's language without succumbing to its structural and tropic oppression—to avoid what Henry Louis Gates, Jr., has called "discursive indenture" (Gates 1989, 25)—entails a purposeful appropriation. Soyinka postulates that "when we borrow an alien language to sculpt or paint in, we must begin by co-opting the entire properties of that language as correspondences to properties in our matrix of thought and expression" (in Gates 1989, 24). No matter how one defines "alien language"—as the words themselves and/or as whole discursive systems (including, say, a culture's literary tradition)—agreement on what constitutes a successful appropriation and transformation of that "language" is hard to come by. African-American writers, for example, can still come under fire for too completely adopting or inadequately adapting Western plots and literary conventions.

Apropos of Shakespeare's having become a synecdochical figure for the Western literary tradition, Valerie Traub has dubbed the difficulties of using an "alien language" "Caliban's curse."[1] She also points out that the resulting discursive struggle is "doubly problematic" for black women, who must "negotiate a relationship to an Anglo-European language and tradition that doubly defines them as absence and lack—as black and as women" (1993, 151). In addition, as Deborah McDowell has observed, black women writers can still be censured for what some readers perceive as a misguided privileging of gender over race, and for unflattering, even damaging representations of black men. In response to such criticism, McDowell urges writers and critics to deconstruct the dualism at the heart of these overlapping dilemmas. That is, she suggests that they move away from a critical paradigm based on mutually determinant "oppositions" such as Western/African, female/male, and self/other. To avoid reduction of any identity to black and white or female and male "essences," McDowell champions a nonessentialist aesthetic, one that "comprehend[s]" experience "simultaneously in sexual, class, and racial terms" without privileging one at the expense of the others (1989, 53).[2] By definition, within such an aesthetic nothing and no one could be defined as essentially "Other."

Gloria Naylor's novels are among those criticized for disparaging representations of black male characters, reliance on Western cultural narratives, and even valorization of Western literary icons. A number of writers have responded to this criticism by arguing that Naylor's project is not simply a capitulation to alien discourse.[3] Discussing "The Role of Shakespeare in Naylor's Novels," for example, Peter Erickson argues that the "effect of *Mama Day*'s exploration of Shakespearean heritage is critically to revise and decenter it" (1993b, 241). More recently, Missy Dehn Kubitschek has remonstrated Naylor's critics, claiming that they "overemphasize the Euro-American sources" and consequently fail to see that *Mama Day* "simultaneously appropriates and signifies on earlier texts" from both the Western and the African-American literary traditions in order to forge a new "liberating social/sexual order" (1994, 75,77).[4] While Gary Storhoff optimistically declares Naylor has "rescue[d] the Shakespearean text for a gender-conscious, multicultural, multiracial audience" (1995, 37), Valerie Traub more problematically finds that *Mama Day* "embodies a . . . tension between adulatory and deconstructive impulses" (1993, 153). The resulting "structural ambivalence," Traub concludes, "maps . . . one possible strategy for negotiating the field of white Western aesthetic production" (1993, 161).

The problem with the sort of "repetition/mimicry/difference" (Traub 1993, 153) that Traub attributes to Naylor is articulated by Margaret Homans, who (writing about *Linden Hills*) nevertheless invokes Luce Irigaray's contention that "'mimicry' . . . is the best subversive strategy available to women given our embeddedness in androcentric culture" (Homans 1993, 180). But Homans also concedes that this self-conscious irony is itself bound by the irony that such a strategy positions women writers "within the frame of the . . . traditional female role, as transmitter and explicator of male culture" (1993, 176).[5] For African-American women writers, this irony is compounded by their analogous position within Anglo-American culture. To illustrate the consequences of this "double jeopardy," Teresa Goddu cites Naylor's inability to extricate herself from the dualistic metaphysics of that culture in *Linden Hills*. As Homans similarly notes, although Willa Nedeed literally uncovers women's lost histories and burns down the house of patriarchy, her act is suicidal. Moreover, by merely substituting a "female-centered, subjective" (Goddu 1993, 223) "model of history" for a "phallocentric, objective" one (1993, 222), as Goddu observes, Naylor is "merely flipping the binary oppositions of a patriarchal/matriarchal system" (1993, 226). In short, Naylor's strategies for developing a poetics of emancipation from within the booby-trapped field of Western/patriarchal discourse are fraught with peril.

Nevertheless, one cannot finally judge the success of Naylor's project until one takes into account *Bailey's Cafe*. Only then can we see how daringly and variously Naylor has met the challenge of avoiding "discursive indenture" and a reductive metaphysics. In *Bailey's Cafe* Naylor continues to appropriate familiar stories from Western culture, but by modifying content and/or form, she recasts them in ways that destabilize absolute ontological boundaries defined by genre, gender politics, class, and cultural/literary tradition. To this end, she deliberately foregrounds a reciprocal relation that potentially obtains among all texts—an incipient intertextuality, which she makes increasingly overt in her novels. Eventually, with the addition of *Bailey's Cafe*, the quartet of novels becomes self-reflexive and regenerative, their "meaning" and relation to one another, and to their

Western "precursors," constantly in flux, depending on one's point of (re)entry. Thus, the relationship of *Bailey's Cafe* to the quartet is exactly analogous to the relationship of the quartet to the Western literary tradition itself: belying established borders and signification, the parts reconfigure the whole. As a group the novels create a dynamic system of intertextuality that does not merely make room for the "Other" in the Western tradition but, rather, modulates the raw materials, reconfiguring the tradition itself. As if to follow Soyinka's advice, Naylor "co-opt[s] the entire properties of that language as correspondences to properties in . . . [her] matrix of thought and expression" as an African-American woman. Moreover, Naylor clearly conceives of the "entire properties of . . . language" as not only the word itself and the Western literary tradition at large, but, at the same time, any and all discourses integral to Western (especially American) culture.

Naylor has admitted to once having felt that she lacked the authority to write because the "masters" were "either male or white" (Naylor and Morrison 1985, 568). Then she read Toni Morrison's *The Bluest Eye*, which uses paradigmatic white middle-class cultural narratives against themselves to expose their disastrous consequences for an impoverished black family. From Morrison's disfigurement Naylor learned that literary "barriers were flexible," that "you can create your own genre" (Naylor and Morrison 1985, 568). While writing *The Women of Brewster Place*, her initial effort to create a genre of her own, Naylor was already conceiving of a "quartet of novels" that she believed "would be a foundation for [her] career" (Carroll 1994, 160). In one sense, then, their eventual interconnectedness seems to have been planned from the first. The interconnections encompass much more than the links between seemingly disparate characters and locales—Kiswana Browne's movement from Linden Hills to Brewster Place, for example, or George Andrews's dislocation from Bailey's Cafe to Willow Springs via New York, or the fact that Willa Prescott Nedeed and Ophelia "Cocoa" Day are cousins. For Naylor also weaves together the similarly disparate strands of her own complex heritage by relentlessly appropriating and "signifyin(g)" on Western narratives that have achieved the status of canon, history and/or myth—narratives of received Truth. In *Bailey's Cafe* she continues, modifies, and expands on her strategic interventions, extending her deconstructive impulse from the "Great Tradition" to the Bible and American popular culture, including, for example, Hollywood film and the history of baseball. Taken together, Naylor's discursive mergers and modifications self-consciously compel reconsideration of the "provisional nature of all fixity" (Gates 1988a, 622), by demonstrating that nothing is written in stone.

Much has been said about Naylor's fascination with Shakespeare and Dante, but *Bailey's Cafe,* with its variety of weary pilgrims, calls to mind *The Canterbury Tales* and its innkeeper (Harry) Bailly, who, like Naylor's narrator—mistakenly called Bailey—initiates the storytelling. However, Naylor modulates the formal design of her novel's distant kin (individual narratives within a frame tale) with the recursive suppleness of the blues ("Mood: Indigo"). By infusing her novel with musical rhythms and borrowing blues terminology ("The Vamp" and "The Wrap") as a structuring device, she effects a merger of two artistic forms.[6] The epigraph confirms that an affinity for the blues enables one to "hear" *Bailey's Cafe:* "needing the blues to get there / . . . look and you can hear / the blues open / a place never / closing: / Bailey's / Cafe" (n.p.).

Houston Baker describes the blues as the "multiplex, enabling *script* in which Afro-American cultural discourse is inscribed" (1984, 4). As Henry Louis Gates, Jr., points out, the musical phrases of the blues are "elastic in their formal properties"; they "stretch the form rather than articulate" it (1988b, 123). Naylor's modification of the novel form to express the "nonlinear, freely associative, nonsequential meditation" (Baker 1984, 5) known as the blues epitomizes what Michael Awkward calls the "denigration" of the novel: an appropriation that "successfully transform[s], by the addition of black expressive cultural features, Western cultural and expressive systems to . . . reflect . . . Afro-American 'intention' and 'accent'" (1989, 9). As a trope for African-American experience, the blues "matrix" shaping *Bailey's Cafe* renders the tales of its once silenced wayfarers powerfully audible. At the same time, it structurally signifies on its Western "origin," creating "intersections of experience where . . . the blues singer and his [sic] performance . . . absorb[ ] and transform[ ] discontinuous experience into formal expressive instances that bear only the trace of origins, refusing to be pinned down to any final, dualistic significance. Even as they speak of paralyzing absence and ineradicable desire, their instrumental rhythms suggest change, movement, action, continuance, unlimited and unending possibility" (Baker 1984, 8). Baker's characterization of a blues performance as transformative, indeterminate, and paradoxical perfectly describes one way in which Naylor's narrative endeavor exemplifies Soyinka's proposed appropriation.

Other methods of appropriation focus less on the form than on the nature of storytelling, the content of specific narratives, and language itself. Naylor ends *Mama Day* by having Cocoa comment that every time she and

George "meet" to talk over their story, their "versions will be different" because "there are just too many sides to the whole story" (*MD*, 311). This is a prelude to the several different "(im)possible" conversations, or discursive mergers, we find in *Bailey's Cafe,* and for which George and Cocoa assume an appropriately protean metaphoric status. To begin with, when George and Cocoa "talk" in *Mama Day,* George is dead. His stories should be unrevisable ("It has been written")—but they are not. Accordingly, George, although black, is aligned with the "dead white males" of the canon, as signaled by his adulation of Shakespeare and his identification with the "bastard son" (*MD*, 106) in King Lear. Thus, while George may figure the culturally dispossessed black man aligned with Western culture, at the same time he demonstrates the plasticity of narrative and the possible erasure of difference. Cocoa, who "brings back" Sapphira Wade, a slave of mythical proportions who freed herself and all her children in perpetuity, is equally polyvalent (*MD*, 48). Although her given name is Ophelia, Cocoa embodies the legacy of her Gullah culture; at the same time, however, in New York she is utterly alienated not only from her roots but from other people, all of whom she reductively—and racially—characterizes as some sort of food—"fudge sticks . . . bagels," "tacos," a "bonbon" (*MD*, 62–63), linguistically "othering" everyone she does not know. Although of the same race, George and Cocoa are of different worlds; thus, somewhat paradoxically, they embody absolute "difference." Significantly, as such, they each have something to teach the other, to give and to take, as they work toward a more perfect union.[7]

By virtue of their pronounced difference, George and Cocoa clash from the moment they meet and must constantly negotiate some common ground both for their relationship and, analogously, for the narratives they construct to make sense of it. George makes Cocoa feel at home in multicultural New York and with Shakespeare, even though at first she complains that "Shakespeare didn't have a bit of soul" (*MD*, 64). In return, Cocoa introduces George to the culture of Willow Springs, "a place . . . you can't find . . . on the map" (*MD*, 174), a place where belief in magic gives it power. Significantly, George's ignorance of his cultural roots combined with his inability to merge his "Western" rationalism and Mama Day's "magic" kill him in the end.[8] Nevertheless, his irrevocable connection to Cocoa enables them, even after George's death, to share their respective stories in an ongoing effort to find out "what really happened" (*MD*, 311) and to bridge the distance/difference between them. By (re)combining their different perspectives, together George and Cocoa keep seeing/telling their story differently—and keep narrative alive. As Cocoa explains to George, "each time I go back over what happened, there's some new development, some forgotten corner" (*MD*, 310). In this way, *Mama Day* prepares the way for the insistent renarration that constitutes *Bailey's Cafe*.

We are immediately reminded of this process when the unnamed opening narrator of *Bailey's Cafe* (whom I call Not/Bailey, in keeping with the notion of discursive paradox) gives us a lesson in line of vision and historical revision. His story about baseball, America's pastime, becomes a trope for Naylor's narrative project: She tells different versions of familiar stories, in the process illuminating the discursive mechanisms that reproduce "otherness" and thereby preclude deep change in the story of humankind. Having grown up watching segregated baseball, Not/Bailey decides that the "Negroes had separate teams" not because the whites considered the black players beneath contempt, but because the "Negroes were better players" (*BC*, 9). Thus, rather than thinking of Pop Lloyd as the "Black Honus Wagner," Not/Bailey considers Wagner the "White Pop Lloyd" (*BC*, 10). But this simple reversal is deliberately compensatory and, the narrator seems to realize, ultimately inadequate. When Jackie Robinson joins the Dodgers, Not/Bailey does not rejoice, for he perceives no real, that is, no structural and no symbolic change: "The [Branch] Rickeys of the world [are still] calling the shots because a hundred Jackie Robinsons isn't gonna really integrate baseball and baseball is *not* going to help integrate America." Like Not/Bailey's reversal, this sort of pseudo-integration, which leaves the metaphysical structuring untouched, is "nothing but a game of smoke and mirrors" (*BC*, 12).

Naylor attempts to do better than smoke and mirrors, in part by insisting on the mutual formation of discursive and ontological categories—on writing, therefore, as potential for change. For what stories we tell and how we tell them determine, in a fundamental way, the possibilities for who and what we are.[9] Naylor demonstrates that the transgression of discursive boundaries and flouting of related narrative codes make the seemingly impossible, possible. For example, the longest individual story, "Miss Maple's Blues," is on one level a familiar tale about a black man who cannot find a job suited to his qualifications because of racial discrimination. At the same time, however, this story (impossibly) manages to destabilize both gender and cultural boundaries even while it reaffirms the manhood of the systematically emasculated black male.

Stanley, whose middle names (Beckwourth Booker T. Washington Carver) read like a compendium of historically significant black men, doubts the manhood of his father, a peace-loving man of letters who ignores racial taunts and eschews confrontation. Significantly, the lack of a common language with his would-be oppressors finally forces the father to meet violence with violence. When Stanley and his wealthy, cultured father go to pick up Stanley's high school graduation present, a luxurious set of Shakespeare volumes, the resentful Gatlin brothers ridicule the black men, assault them, and lock them in a storeroom. The real insult, though, is the Gatlins' subsequent desecration of Shakespeare. Having been literally stripped naked, Stanley's incensed father dons the only clothing at hand, a "red taffeta [dress] with spaghetti straps and a huge circular skirt," to vanquish the redneck white boys (*BC*, 184). His eventual humiliation of the Gatlins is as much verbal as it is physical, however. With a woman's corset tied around his waist to protect his "balls," Stanley finally learns that the "language" one speaks—one's studied co-option of a given symbolic order—not male costumes and not macho posturing, makes the man.

Having thus inherited a manhood defined in terms of peace, compassion, and the mastery of language, Stanley finds the inner strength he needs to refuse induction during World War II, in protest against America's racial hypocrisy. He withstands his subsequent imprisonment and jailhouse rapes with his sense of self intact. Most remarkably, however, Stanley's inviolate self-definition enables him to be seen as a man despite the fact that he comes to bear a woman's name and adopts a female costume: "Miss Maple wears dresses," Not/Bailey reports (*BC*, 163). Still, he adds, "[I]t's impossible to look at the way Miss Maple walks in here and not see a rather tall, rather thin, reddish brown *man* in a light percale housedress. And that's about it" (emphasis added, *BC*, 163). Stanley's choice to wear dresses does not, as one might expect, signify his "feminization" in the face of repeated diminishment. On the contrary, his carefully considered sartorial selection declares his independence from ostensibly requisite markers of manhood. Stanley has perhaps surpassed even his father's freedom of self-definition. Although Stanley at first wears women's sundresses to avoid the oppressive discomfort of a coat and tie in hot weather, he continues to adopt female costumes and, later, some traditional female roles because of the existential flexibility such choices afford. Seeing no contradiction in working as both Eve's housekeeper and her bouncer, Stanley, a.k.a. Miss Maple, "never felt more like a man" (*BC*, 204).

Significantly, the Gatlins' defilement of Shakespeare's *The Tempest*, revered by Stanley's father as part of a "carefully chosen legacy" for his son, catalyzes Stanley's assumption of black manhood (*BC*, 174). The father finds no contradiction in his reverence for Shakespeare's art and his belief that "to accept even a single image in their language as your truth is to be led into accepting them all" (*BC*, 182). For Stanley's father, to "master" a language is not only to "co-opt" aspects of a cultural tradition he finds worthy, but also to turn language meant to be used against him—including the rhetoric of racism—into "babble" (*BC,* 182). While we have no idea how Stanley's father "reads" Shakespeare, he sees in this ostensibly inimical discourse the possibility of not only indenture but freedom. This paradox seems to underlie Naylor's own practice, a stellar example of what Houston Baker has described as the "deformation of mastery"—the transformation of an intrusive alien tongue "into a signal self/cultural expression." Such a transformation does not merely effect "a coming into being," Baker explains, "but . . . release from a BEING POSSESSED" (Baker 1986, 194).

Peter Erickson sees the Gatlins' scatological desecration of Shakespeare as a sort of declaration of independence on Naylor's part, a ritualistic "end of Naylor's artistic apprenticeship" (1993a, 34). To some extent this may be so. However, the sheer crudity of the act and the fact that it is the Gatlins—"illiterate buffoons" (*BC,* 176), the putative "real Americans" (*BC,* 172) slated to inherit Western civilization—who perform this desecration indicates not only that they are ignorant of their supposed legacy, but that it has been taken up by a more appreciative and worthy heir. Thus, Storhoff seems closer to the mark when he identifies Naylor's "declaration of independence" in *Mama Day* as "an acknowledgment of the academic canon's value, but also an assertion of her racial and gender difference (Storhoff 1995, 35). Indeed, the somewhat farcical but sincere rescue of Stanley's Shakespeare from the Gatlins would seem a literal enactment of Storhoff's contention, noted earlier, that Naylor "rescues the Shakespearean text" for an altogether different audience. In the terms of my argument, however, it would be more accurate to say that she is claiming the right to possess a literary discourse without being possessed by it, to experiment with ways around/through "Caliban's curse."

Although Naylor "deforms" Shakespearean texts throughout her oeuvre, more conspicuous in *Bailey's Cafe* is her deformation of biblical narratives, especially those traditionally used to illustrate the "nature" of woman and thereby to justify misogyny.[10] This narrative strategy entails rescripting specific characters' lives in order to expose and assault the assumptions behind the prototypes and the language out of which they are constructed. Esther and Jezebel, Eli(jah), Eve, Mary Magdalene, even God(the)father: Naylor amends the record of the Old and New Testaments by telling other sides of the stories and making visible the ideological work of narrative process and linguistic coding. In the process of adopting Judeo-Christian mythic discourse, she fundamentally changes its color and its scope, infusing it with feminist and African-American significance. Such wholesale denigration or deformation of biblical narratives leaves little doubt about their status as sacred (inviolate) texts on the one hand, or their efficacy for a poetics of (e)merging (im)possibilities on the other.

The Old Testament Book of Esther relates a story of family cohesion, the price of female disobedience, and the redemptive power of a woman's beauty. When Queen Vashti's refusal to display her beauty to the court on King Ahasuerus's command threatens to undermine the authority of men everywhere, the king first decrees that "all the wives shall give to their husbands honour" (Esther 1:20) and that "every man should bear rule in his own house" (1:22).[11] He then seeks a replacement for his willful queen among the "fair young virgins" (2:2) at his disposal. After a required twelve months of "purifications" (2:12), Esther, sent forth by her uncle, becomes the new queen by virtue of her great beauty; eventually, she saves the Jews from annihilation. Esther learns how to use her favor with the king to her advantage, drawing on his authority to turn hubris and evil against itself.

Naylor's Esther is a twelve-year-old given by her brother to his boss for the satisfaction of perverse sexual appetites that are fulfilled in the darkness of a cellar. Believing she is married, Esther at first feels lucky to have escaped the rejection "black gals" with "monkey faces" (BC, 96) had come to expect. Esther soon discovers, however, that her so-called husband's unchallenged linguistic authority not only decriminalizes his exploitation but renders her disoriented and mute. First he claims the prerogative of naming; she learns that "in the dark, words have a different meaning. Having fun. Playing games. Being a good girl" (BC, 97). Accordingly, her abuser assures her that the "leather-and-metal things" he uses are "toys." In contrast, Esther cannot "find a word for what happens between us in the cellar" (BC, 97). He cements his linguistic control by commanding, "We won't speak about this, Esther" (BC, 99). And she doesn't, even after she understands that "What we do in the cellar is to make evil" and that all along "My brother knew" (BC, 98, 99). She stays with her exploiter twelve years, one year for each year her brother took care of her ("because I am a good sister" [BC, 98]), making explicit her state of indentured servitude. Her perceived debt is paid with soul-killing degradation. The precarious position of women within the sexual economy that Naylor's story makes clear is effaced in the biblical Esther's story of a woman's sexual power. Unlike Queen Esther, whose beauty gains her permission to speak and to act, Naylor's "Tar. Coal. Ugly" Esther finds herself in a dark, silent paralysis, sealed by betrayal and complicity (BC, 95). Chattel in a sexual economy in which a woman's body is a primary means of exchange, and subjected to/by a symbolic order in which she is "unspeakable" and cannot speak, Naylor's Esther is utterly powerless against hubris and evil. With this story Naylor exposes and subverts the workings of linguistic and narrative authority.

While the outcome of "Sweet Esther" contrasts sharply with that of the Old Testament Book of Esther, other stories appear to be more analogous to their biblical counterparts. Nevertheless, Naylor always artfully "deforms" the original materials so that her story deconstructs its source. The name of Jezebel, wife of the idolatrous King Ahab, has become eponymous for wicked, depraved woman. Jesse Bell is likewise perceived as rotten to the core: a golddigger (she marries out of the working class), a duplicitous wife (she has a lesbian lover), an inadequate mother (her son turns against her), and a failed human being (she becomes a heroin addict). But Naylor's account makes it clear that Jesse Bell, whose husband's family is headed by the despotic Uncle Eli(jah), is insidiously done in by the King family's patriarchal order, internalization of white cultural values, and scorn for the working class. Her warnings and pleas ignored by her husband and son alike, Jesse knows her "words were lost, lost" (*BC*, 128). Maligned by the media, Jesse realizes that she is doomed because "it's all about who's in charge of keeping the records" (*BC*, 118) and that "nobody was interested in my side of the story" (*BC*, 131–32).

Here again Naylor revisits a familiar story, changing irrevocably the way one sees it in the process. In the Old Testament book 1 Kings, Jezebel arranges to have a man killed to uphold her husband's authority and to satisfy his avarice; she therefore shares Ahab's calumny and fate: "there was none like unto Ahab, which did sell himself to work wickedness . . . whom Jezebel his wife stirred up" (1 Kings 21:25). As punishment, "the dogs shall eat Jezebel" (1 Kings 21:23). If compared to the "original," Naylor's deformation calls attention to the fact that although the biblical Jezebel is condemned for abetting wickedness, we never hear her side of the story—only Elijah's. Highlighting this now conspicuous silence confirms that (as Hayden White has explained) history is an "emplotted narrative," the shape and moral of which depends on the teller.[12] When Jessie Bell narrates her own story, Elijah (God's spokesman and enforcer in 1 Kings) becomes Uncle Eli the transgressor, an Uncle Tom who sacrifices his cultural heritage on the altar of class privilege and white approval: "White folks . . . were Uncle Eli's [false] god" (*BC*, 125). A pretender-prophet, Eli portends complete erasure of "black expressive cultural features" (Awkward 1989, 9), emblematized here by the oxtail soup and sweet potato pie he ironically rejects as "slave food" (*BC,* 124). Thus here, as she does in "Miss Maple's Blues," Naylor uses deformations of significant cultural narratives dexterously to represent experience "simultaneously in sexual, class, and racial terms" (McDowell 1989, 53).

Moreover, as her ambiguous characterization of Eva's brownstone and its occupants suggests, in addition to telling "other sides" of the story, Naylor seeks to problematize the good/evil opposition fundamental to the Judeo-Christian creation myth and related narratives of sexual identity. As is consistent with her overall project, Naylor disrupts linearity by not beginning with Eve; more appropriately, Eve's story serves as a deconstructive center for all the stories that make up the whole. Raised by a godfather who considers himself Eve's creator, Eve is exiled for the "sins" of disobedience and knowledge. The evil that this Eve discovers is her own sexual being, an abomination in the eyes of God(the)father. During her subsequent journey, Eve re-creates herself—without divine intervention—out of the delta dust, thus earning an existential independence: "I'd lived one hundred years ten times over, so there was a lot to think about. . . . [T]he only road that lay open to me was the one ahead. . . . I had no choice but to walk into New Orleans neither male nor female—mud. But I could right then and there choose what I was going to be when I walked back out" (*BC,* 90–91). For this Eve, the wages of "sin" are not death, shame, and strictly prescribed gender roles but, rather, their nullification. Indeed, the causal sequence is reversed: shame of female sexuality is revealed as the source of "sin," not its consequence. Naylor's narrative thus belies the biblical notion of woman as the origin of sin and suffering; responsibility for this shifts to God(the)father's presumptive authority and irrational fear and loathing of female sexuality.

Down the street from Bailey's Cafe, Eve runs a whorehouse/ boardinghouse/half-way house, depending (of course) on who's describing it. In any case, transcending the borders of time, place, and prescribed myth, she provides a location free of essences and absolutes for those who have been nearly destroyed by the abuse made possible by their codified otherness. Eve—madam and mother, sinner and saint—defies definition and, ironically, becomes a new kind of savior, one that "passes no judgment" (*BC,* 92). Eve's salvation requires not forgiveness of sins but recovery of one's intrinsic worth. Her unscripted gospel thus obviates even the notion of original sin and the necessity of some extrinsic redemptive agent. Naylor's representation of Eve is but one of many examples of her effort to "reclaim language"—concepts such as "whore" and "sin" and "good girl"—from master discourses that, Naylor has complained, "have been used as weapons against women."[13]

Indeed, obsession with and/or abuse of women defined almost exclusively in terms of culpable sexuality is the salient feature of all the women's stories. The subject of "Mary (Take One)" blames herself for the "promise" of sexual gratification she sees in every man's eye, the mirror that creates her "I," a reification of the virgin/whore paradigm. Splitting into the "I" she knows as "Daddy's baby" and the "whore" she sees in the eyes of men (lust) and women (envy, fear) (*BC*, 104), "Peaches" becomes compulsively promiscuous in an attempt to save what she sees as her good self from the evil one: "I tried everything to make her go away. . . . But I could feel their eyes stripping my clothes away: they knew her promise was there. You. You. No, not me—I wasn't like that. No, never me. So I gave them *her.* Sweet, sweet relief. . . . Free, at last, *I* was free as I gave them her" (*BC*, 105). With cruel irony, she believes "[a]ny son of any man was my savior" (*BC*, 106). Unable to maintain her psychic split, she learns complete self-loathing: "I should always have hated myself. . . . I was probably always making men . . . look at me that way . . . always asking for it, asking for it. I was probably always dirt" (*BC*, 107). In order to free herself from the tacit "promise" others see inscribed on her consumable body, she intentionally disfigures her face, thus changing her prescribed role from object of desire to object of scorn or pity. To help Mary heal, to make her "whole," Eve does not purge her of "evil spirits" (Luke 8:2) but, rather, teaches her to cast out the deforming duality imposed by stories like that of Mary Magdalene, who had to be cleansed (like Esther) of evil by the son of God so she would be worthy to follow him.

While the representations of Sadie (both a 25-cent whore and a "lady") and of other characters like Mary (Peaches) problematize the virgin/whore dichotomy, the story of Mariam ("Mary [Take Two]") most strikingly insists on its dissolution. It also sets in motion the paradox that ultimately (but never finally) reconfigures the tetralogy. Mariam, an Ethiopian Jew who has undergone the cultural ritual of female circumcision/genital mutilation, apparently experiences a virgin pregnancy. Cast out of her village for her "defilement," she finds her way to Eve's and, miraculously, gives birth in the "void" behind Bailey's back door. Typically, however, this mythical promise of salvation exists side by side with the ugly "reality" of Mariam's exile. Back in Ethiopia, Mariam's mother enters the temple's inner sanctum, forbidden to women, in search of God's "pure and simple justice" for her daughter (*BC*, 156). "I am also His servant and He is my

God too," she reasons, yet her transgression against patriarchal law proves not only futile but fatal. In the eyes of her religion, her unclean presence before God is a defilement not to be borne. As if to point to the self-repro-ducing mechanism of the familiar story of women as defiled and defiling, Mariam also dies, drowning in the "endless water" she calls forth to cleanse herself after George's birth (*BC*, 228). Mariam's act thus catalyzes both George's dispossession and, with self-fulfilling irony, her eventual vili-fication. In the absence of the whole (impossible) story, the received "truth" of women's whorish nature fills the narrative void.

With Mariam's death and George's orphaning, promise is yoked to loss and frustration, the potential for change seemingly thwarted. Perhaps. But not yet. For Naylor conspicuously avoids coming to any conclusion. Not/Bailey explains, "there's nothing I'd like better than to give you a happy ending" (*BC*, 227), but the vagaries of baby George's future make for "the happiest ending I've got" (*BC*, 229). Significantly, the name George Bailey calls to mind *It's a Wonderful Life,* Frank Capra's seemingly sanguine paean to the white middle-class American dream and idealized nuclear family.[14] Christmas at Bailey's Cafe, whose patrons constitute a family of a very different sort, is a notably bad time, when suicides proliferate without angelic intercession. Life is far from wonderful for the denizens of Naylor's impossible neighborhood, and the novel mocks the film's specious opti-mism and promise of justice served. Still, the novel leaves room for hope. We remain ignorant of George's future (past). Nor do we learn what Miss Maple encounters when, a changed man, he reenters the "real" world, or whether "Peaches" ever becomes whole. The lives of the characters in this novel, like the literary traditions it invokes and partakes in, are, to borrow Not/Bailey's phrase, "in transition" (*BC*, 219).[15]

Accordingly, the conclusion of *Bailey's Cafe* is no such thing, for it makes chronology move both forward (to baby George's adult life) and backward (to *Mama Day*), creating a loop in time and understanding. Be-cause George's death in *Mama Day* is, paradoxically, followed by his birth in *Bailey's Cafe,* the latter is both an addendum to and the parent of the novel that preceded it. Appropriately, the way in which *Bailey's Cafe* rup-tures narrative and causal sequence mimics the chicken and egg dilemma inherent in the relationship between epistemological and social change, between reconceptualizing narrative acts such as Naylor's quartet and the material world. For, again paradoxically, the novel "following" George's death models the very tools George will need/needed to save his life—and change the story.

On the level of meta-narrative, *Bailey's Cafe* enacts Cocoa's lesson in the multiple "sides" of stories through its revision of Naylor's own stories— George's account in *Mama Day* that his mother was a Harlem prostitute and that his birth was the most unpromising of beginnings, for example. In *Bailey's Cafe* we learn instead that George's miraculous birth carries with it a promise of redemption that literally lit up the world for the denizens of Bailey's Cafe. Susan Meisenhelder's description of *Mama Day* as an "unfinished, dynamic story requiring constant revision" (1993, 418) is germane here, but not until *Bailey's Cafe* do we see that this is true of the quartet as a whole and, as Naylor would have it, the Western tradition itself.

While all of Naylor's novels more or less elude closure, the addition of *Bailey's Cafe* precludes it. The novel's conclusion and its network of allusions invite us to reenter all the "precursive" novels, where we can trace the textual intersections that destabilize meaning. Revisiting *Linden Hills* after a visit to *Bailey's Cafe,* for example, renders Naylor's earlier representation of the "irruption of class politics into the terrain of race politics" (Gates 1988a, 618), her inversion of the Judeo-Christian myth of good and evil, and her thwarted effort to recuperate women's lost histories more elusively ambiguous than one might have thought. In *Bailey's Cafe* we meet not only Eli(jah) King, who worships the false gods of white superiority and male dominion, but also Stanley's equally wealthy father, who eschews such idolatry. Affluence therefore does not necessarily condemn African-Americans to a Dantean hell on earth. In what seems a simple reversal, the god/ father of *Linden Hills* turns out to be Lucifer, yet *Bailey's Cafe*'s deconstruction of such dichotomies invites reconsideration of such a reading. The reburied narratives of women's sexual exploitation and existential erasure in *Linden Hills* resurface in *Bailey's Cafe,* this time imploding the historical and narrative tradition from which they were extracted.

The block on which Bailey's Cafe, Eve's brownstone, and Gabe's pawnshop sit also becomes a shadowy dimension of Brewster Place, where dreams are likewise deferred.[16] In fact, at first glance, the "final" novel of the quartet, with its separately titled stories, seems similar to the first (*The Women of Brewster Place*), which was bitterly criticized for its ostensibly single-minded (omnisciently narrated) depiction of black men as exploitative and abusive. In *Bailey's Cafe,* however, with the appointment of a male "maestro" who shares his stage with multiple female narrators and the first person narrator of "Miss Maple's Blues," Naylor achieves a polyvalent, communal narration, and balances race, class, and gender as interactive nodes of black experience. Just as Not/Bailey, an American Negro,

and Gabe, a Russian Jew, refuse to compete for victim status, Naylor refuses to privilege any type of victimization over another. If one looks
"back" on *The Women of Brewster Place* through the lens of *Bailey's Cafe*,
Naylor's portrayal, even of rapist C. C. Baker and the "young men [who]
always moved in a pack" in order to "verify their existence" (161), is more
clearly both critical and sympathetic.[17]

One could argue, perhaps, that the fantastic unrealism of *Bailey's Cafe*
disqualifies it as a meaningful interlocutor with Naylor's earlier novels. But
the indeterminate reality of Bailey's block does not undo or deny the tragedy of lived reality on mean streets of last resort; in fact, it exists only in
response to that life. Naylor's representation of black life in America, perhaps especially in *Bailey's Cafe*, belies any easy optimism her discursive
gestures might otherwise imply. *Bailey's Cafe* offers no concrete solution,
no promises fulfilled. Rather, it confirms the emancipatory potential of
discursive trespass, creating a metaphysical location—a "margin between
the edge of the world and infinite possibility"—where one prepares for the
future.[18] Before rejoining the material world, Miss Maple articulates what
could be the freed Caliban's rejoinder to Prospero: "[T]he language you
taught me is wonderful. . . . And it doesn't bother me that practically no
one in this country understands a single word I say. America is growing and
changing; we are on the brink of unimaginable possibilities. . . . Change is
hope" (*BC*, 212).

Naylor has boldly demonstrated the enormous possibility of using Caliban's curse against its perpetrators. On Brewster Place one can only dream
of tearing down the walls that separate women and men, the rich and the
poor, or Caliban's descendants and Prospero's heirs; but on Bailey's block
there are no walls. One can enter from anywhere if the need is great. And
the enormous amount of energy people of color and women have devoted
to the problem of not/speaking against oneself indicates that the need is
great indeed. In what can be construed as a literary response to that need,
with *Bailey's Cafe* Naylor has created a site of discursive emancipation—
of (e)merging (im)possibilities, if you will—where ostensibly antithetical
paradigms meet in productive co-existence.

Notes

1. Caliban complains to Prospero, "You taught me language, and my profit on't / Is, I know how to curse. The red-plague rid you / for learning me your language!" (*The Tempest* 1.2.362–64).

2. McDowell's argument builds on the earlier observations of Barbara Smith, whom she quotes here (from "Toward a Black Feminist Criticism"), and Barbara Christian, who has pointed out that one result of the black woman's struggle for complete self-expression is "the articulation of the interconnectedness of race, sex, and class as a philosophical basis for the pattern of dominance and hierarchy" (1985, 161–62).

3. In addition to the cited sources Erickson, Traub, Homans, and Goddu, see Ward and Saunders in Gates and Appiah, *Gloria Naylor: Critical Perspectives Past and Present* (1993).

4. In "'The Only Voice Is Your Own': Gloria Naylor's Revision of *The Tempest*," Gary Storhoff similarly points out that Naylor "not only rewrites . . . white canonical texts" but also "black texts": "*Mama Day* reads like a virtual encyclopedia of African-American expressive culture. In a multitude of literary allusions and narrative echoes, Naylor pays homage to (among others) Charles Chestnutt, Toni Morrison, Alice Walker, Ralph Ellison, Jean Toomer, Ernest J. Gaines, Ishmael Reed, and (of course) Zora Neale Hurston." For Storhoff, the crucial difference in her approach to the two sets of texts is that "while she is occasionally critical of earlier black texts, she more often supplements the insights expressed in their works" (Storhoff 1995, 36).

5. In "Significant Others," Henry Louis Gates, Jr., responds to Homans's essay, in particular her use of Irigaray. Although he recognizes that Irigaray is centrally concerned with "the apparent absence of any Archimedean point outside the discursive practices of patriarchy" (607), he finds her solution "politically inert" because of "her conception of the patriarchal order as wall-to-wall, all-pervasive" (1988a, 621–22).

6. In a National Public Radio interview, Naylor explained that the story of Sadie and Ice Man Jones is her attempt to "transliterate Duke Ellington's 'Mood Indigo'," a composition that leaves her "feeling every sort of lack, every sort of 'might have been' imaginable" (Naylor 1992). In a later interview with Charles Rowell, Naylor explains that the entire novel began with an image of Sadie and Ice Man conjured by Ellington's tune. When she began *Bailey's Cafe*, Naylor explains, "the only thing I knew . . . about this novel [was] that it was going to be shaped by jazz" (Rowell 1997, 182).

7. Kubitschek finds that Cocoa and George embody a series of "dichotomies," including female and male, "rural and urban, Western and African American," connected and disconnected (1994, 87). Although Kubitschek adds that Naylor does not reduce Cocoa and George to mere stereotypes, I would like to emphasize that, as my discussion of their symbolic significance indicates, George and Cocoa are individually more paradoxical than the notion of "dichotomies" allows.

8. In contrast, Mama Day (like Naylor) is empowered by her ability to do just that. See Storhoff for a Jungian reading of George's failure to meet Miranda's challenge to become whole by symbolically "set[ting] aside his own masculine will . . . and choos[ing] another totem that expresses a[n] . . . aspect of his repressed character"—the hens' eggs that, tragically, he "cannot even perceive" (Storhoff 1995, 41).

9. Naylor attests to the truth of this observation in her own experience. In the Rowell interview, she speaks of "something [having] clicked" when she read Poe and Dickens. "[W]hat was clicking," she explains, "was . . . my own birthing," paradoxically adding, "I was waiting to deliver. That would not have been possible if I had not gone on to discover . . . writers who reflected me and my own life" (1997, 180). Apropos of the narrative project I discuss here, then, Naylor carries the genetic coding of two different culturally expressive traditions, to which she in turn gives new and different life.

10. In the NPR interview, Naylor remarked that "you have to go to the Judeo-Christian ethic to understand where we root in perceptions about female sexuality."

11. All biblical quotations are from the King James Version.

12. See, for example, White, "The Historical Text as Literary Artifact" (1978).

13. Naylor identifies "whore" and "lesbian" as the two words most often used in this way (NPR interview).

14. A closer look at Capra's film reveals that its happy ending belies its subversive suggestion that George Bailey is a defeated man, trapped in a reluctant and coerced allegiance to the American dream and the bourgeois patriarchal family. The only way he can avoid despair is to repress his resentment and embrace that which entraps him.

15. About the novel's "melancholy tone" and indeterminate outcomes, Naylor comments—echoing her phrasing in the text—that "[W]e could wrap it all up with a lot of happy endings to leave you feeling real good that you took the time to listen. But I don't believe that life is supposed to make you feel good or to make you feel miserable either. Life is just supposed to make you feel" (NPR interview).

16. For a useful discussion of The Women of Brewster Place as a response to Hughes' "A Dream Deferred," see Matus, who argues that "Naylor inscribes an ideology that affirms deferral; the capacity to defer and to dream is endorsed as life-availing" (1993, 138). This reading constructs the novel's conclusion as more similar to that of Bailey's Cafe than mine does.

17. An excerpt from Naylor's novel The Men of Brewster Place indicates that it is an explicit (and perhaps apologetic) revision of Naylor's first novel—a (re)vision made possible by the transformative power effected by Bailey's Cafe. In "Dusk," the male narrator reminds us, "this street gave birth to more than its girl children ya know," but denies a hierarchy of suffering: "I ain't seen no favoritism, one way or another, all had a hard way to go" (769). The excerpt ends with an image of physical, spiritual, and narrative mutuality: "she was the other half; the other arm, the other eye—stepping right up on his shoulders to reach for a dream. . . . I don't know

fancy words, but I do know men. . . . and with each of 'em—no matter who he was—there was always a Her in his story" (Naylor 1996, 791).

18. This is Naylor's own description of the location of *Bailey's Cafe* (NPR interview). Appropriately, Montgomery finds that this "unusual location . . . represents the unexplored boundaries of a creative consciousness" (1995, 31).

Works Cited

Awkward, Michael. *Inspiriting Influences: Tradition, Revision, and Afro-American Women's Novels*. New York: Columbia University Press, 1989.

Baker, Houston A., Jr. *Blues, Ideology, and Afro-American Literature: A Vernacular Theory*. Chicago: University of Chicago Press, 1984.

———. "Caliban's Triple Play." *Critical Inquiry* 13 (Autumn 1986): 182–96.

Carroll, Rebecca. *I Know What the Red Clay Looks Like: The Voice and Vision of Black Women Writers*. New York: Carol Southern Books, 1994.

Christian, Barbara. "Creating a Universal Literature: Afro-American Women Writers." In *Black Feminist Criticism: Perspectives on Black Women Writers*. New York: Pergamon Press, 1985. 159–64.

Erickson, Peter. "Review of *Bailey's Cafe*." In *Gloria Naylor: Critical Perspectives Past and Present*. Eds. Henry Louis Gates, Jr., and K. A. Appiah. New York: Amistad, 1993a. 32–34.

———. "'Shakespeare's Black?': The Role of Shakespeare in Naylor's Novels." In *Gloria Naylor: Critical Perspectives Past and Present*. Eds. Henry Louis Gates, Jr., and K. A. Appiah. New York: Amistad, 1993b. 231–48.

Gates, Henry Louis, Jr. "Canon Formation, Literary History, and the Afro-American Tradition." In *Afro-American Literary Study in the 1990s*. Eds. Houston A. Baker and Patricia Redmond. Chicago: University of Chicago Press, 1989. 14–39.

———. "Significant Others." *Contemporary Literature* 29 no. 4 (1988a): 606–23.

———. *The Signifying Monkey: A Theory of African-American Literary Criticism*. New York: Oxford University Press, 1988b.

Goddu, Teresa. "Reconstructing History in *Linden Hills*." In *Gloria Naylor: Critical Perspectives Past and Present*. Eds. Henry Louis Gates, Jr., and K. A. Appiah. New York: Amistad, 1993. 215–30.

Homans, Margaret. "The Woman in the Cave." In *Gloria Naylor: Critical Perspectives Past and Present*. Eds. Henry Louis Gates, Jr., and K. A. Appiah. New York: Amistad, 1993. 152–79.

Kubitschek, Missy Dehn. "Toward a New World Order: Shakespeare, Morrison and Gloria Naylor's *Mama Day*." *MELUS* 19 no. 3 (1994): 75–90.

Matus, Jill. "Dream, Deferral, and Closure in *The Women of Brewster Place*." In *Gloria Naylor: Critical Perspectives Past and Present*. Eds. Henry Louis Gates, Jr., and K. A. Appiah. New York: Amistad, 1993. 126–39.

McDowell, Deborah E. "Boundaries: Or Distant Relations and Close Kin." In *Afro-American Literary Study in the 1990s*. Eds. Houston A. Baker and Patricia Redmond. Chicago: University of Chicago Press, 1989. 51–70.

Meisenhelder, Susan. "'The Whole Picture' in Gloria Naylor's *Mama Day*." *African American Review* 27, no. 3 (1993): 405–19.

Montgomery, Maxine Lavon. "Authority, Multivocality, and the New World Order in Gloria Naylor's *Bailey's Cafe*." *African American Review* 29 (Spring 1995): 27–33.

Naylor, Gloria. *Bailey's Cafe*. New York: Vintage, 1993a.

——. "Dusk." Excerpt from *The Men of Brewster Place*. *Callaloo* 19 (1996): 789–91.

——. Interview with Tom Vitale. "Morning Edition." National Public Radio. New York. Sept. 22, 1992.

——. *Linden Hills*. New York: Viking Penguin, 1985.

——. *Mama Day*. New York: Vintage, 1993b.

——. *The Women of Brewster Place*. New York: Viking Penguin, 1982.

Naylor, Gloria, and Toni Morrison. "A Conversation." *The Southern Review* 21 no. 3 (1985): 567–93.

Neal, Larry. "Some Reflections on the Black Aesthetic." In *The Black Aesthetic*. Ed. Addison Gayle, Jr. Garden City, N.Y.: Doubleday (Anchor Books), 1972. 257–74.

Rowell, Charles H. "An Interview with Gloria Naylor." *Callaloo* 20 (1997): 179–92.

Saunders, James Robert. "The Ornamentation of Old Ideas: Naylor's First Three Novels." In *Gloria Naylor: Critical Perspectives Past and Present*. Eds. Henry Louis Gates, Jr., and K. A. Appiah. New York: Amistad, 1993. 263–84.

Storhoff, Gary. "'The Only Voice Is Your Own': Gloria Naylor's Revision of *The Tempest*." *African American Review* 29 (1995): 35–45.

Traub, Valerie. "Rainbows of Darkness: Deconstructing Shakespeare in the Work of Gloria Naylor and Zora Neale Hurston." In *Cross-Cultural Performances: Differences in Women's Re-Visions of Shakespeare*. Ed. Marianne Novy. Urbana: University of Illinois Press, 1993. 150–64.

Ward, Catherine C. "*Linden Hills*: A Modern *Inferno*." In *Gloria Naylor: Critical Perspectives Past and Present*. Eds. Henry Louis Gates, Jr., and K. A. Appiah. New York: Amistad, 1993. 182–94.

White, Hayden. "The Historical Text as Literary Artifact." In *Tropics of Discourse: Essays in Cultural Criticism*. Baltimore: Johns Hopkins University Press, 1978. 81–100.

Women's Screams and Women's Laughter

Connections and Creations in Gloria Naylor's Novels

Jenny Brantley

From the screams of Ciel, as Mattie removes the splinter of her grief in *The Women of Brewster Place,* to the screams of Mariam, her vagina sewn nearly shut, giving virgin birth to George in *Bailey's Cafe,* Gloria Naylor's first four novels are unified, in part, by the sounds of screams and laughter. Patterns of screams and laughter are essential to each novel separately, where these human sounds often signal a narrative turn; at the same time, they serve as an important connecting device among the novels. As both Katie Cannon and Mae Henderson maintain, "The Black Woman's body *is* the text" (Cannon 1995, 74), and if the body is the text, then the physical sounds, the sounds without words, become the sounds of the story.

In Naylor's novels, these sounds without words help to connect the narratives. For example, the virgin birth of George and his accompanying "first thin cry" (*BC* 1992, 225) tie us to the same George who saves Baby Girl, his final act accomplished with both screams and laughter in *Mama Day.* As the sounds of pain and joy build in the novels, Gloria Naylor achieves the epitome of human grace. Human differences become human salvation — women and men, African-Americans and Jews, poor and rich — we become essential for each other. As Naylor writes in *Bailey's Cafe:* "It is a white-hot world of pain. A world filled with high-pitched screams, with the singing of women, with the gentle moans of her mother and grandmothers, with the press of soft breasts and soft arms against her heaving body. It is a world that will not end" (151). In imagining a world that will not end, Naylor uses screams to signal narrative changes—be they births, deaths, moves, or losses—which emphasize that pain can lead both characters and readers to a new, higher level of existence. As Julia Kristeva writes in *Powers of Horror,* a narrative is "the recounting of suffering: fear, disgust, and abjection crying out, they quiet down, concatenated into a story"; thus, presenting pain becomes part of making a narrative, of making something that is "commonplace and public at the same time, communicable, shareable" (1982, 144–45).

So with the screams, we have the creation of narrative, of a story to be shared. Laughter, usually seen in opposition to screams, opens a place to begin the healing, and the healing leads to salvation. In *Revolution in Poetic Language,* Kristeva writes that laughter may come from the pleasure of lifting prohibitions. The pleasure obtained from this lifting "is immediately invested in the production of the new. Every practice which produces something new . . . is a practice of laughter: it obeys laughter's logic and provides the subject with laughter's advantages. When practice is not laughter, there is nothing new: where there is nothing new, practice cannot be provoking; it is at best a repeated, empty act" (1984, 225). Thus, while Naylor's narratives may at first seem to be primarily the recounting of suffering and screams, the presence of the laughter within the scream-induced narratives enables them to become also a place for the creation of something new, something beyond "a repeated, empty act." The creation of the new is the creation of human grace and salvation. Screams and laughter, their intermingling and the products they give birth to, story and grace, are essential elements to understanding the depth and importance of Naylor's novels.

Part of this particular creation of the new involves a joining of the verbal and preverbal, of the male and female. This joining is also part of the salvation I explore in my discussion of each novel. Specifically, I contend that Gloria Naylor has done the seemingly impossible in many ways; she has articulated—in a written text—what Kristeva would identify as preverbal sounds by introducing screams and laughter into verbal texts. Thus, she incorporates the preverbal without utilizing meta-language. Naylor never tries to explain or deconstruct these preverbal sounds; she allows them to function as narrative techniques. She also allows them to function as evidence of the body. These preverbal sounds in Naylor's novels actually help her to resolve a tension Kristeva explored, that of the "hysteric split between non-verbal substance (defined as the body, the drives, the *jouissance*) on the one hand, and the Law [of the Father] on the other" (Moi 1986, 10). The way in which Naylor is able to mend this split as she uses the preverbal sounds of screams and laughter in a verbal text—without deconstructing these sounds or seeing them as any less useful techniques than actual words—brings about a kind of healing of the split Kristeva has suggested is necessary for true, revolutionary change.

To clarify this point, I cite Kristeva's essay "The System and the Speaking Subject." Here, she discusses "a shortcoming of linguistics itself: established as a science inasmuch as it focuses on language as a social *code,* the science of linguistics has no way of apprehending anything in language which belongs not with the social contract but with play, pleasure, desire" (1986, 26). She sees this limitation of language as also a limitation that will hinder individuals in their efforts to rediscover the importance of bodily drives. The preverbal sounds of screams and laughter are (and indeed must be) that which escape, that which rise above the social code. *The Women of Brewster Place, Linden Hills, Mama Day,* and *Bailey's Cafe* are all novels that explore social codes, yet the backbones of the narratives—the sounds of screams and laughter—work outside the social codes, and do so in order that Naylor can deepen our understanding and create the conditions for our potential salvation.

Naylor's first novel, *The Women of Brewster Place,* begins the cycle of women screaming and laughing, a cycle both painful and redemptive. In six segments, framed by "Dawn" and "Dusk," the lives of seven women are explored. Here, however, I will limit the discussion to three of the sections, concentrating on five of the women. One is Mattie Michael, a mother who has created a self-centered lout of a son, but who, paradoxically, becomes the healing matriarch of the novel. The second, Etta Mae, has lived a wild, sexually active life before coming "home," finally, to Brewster Place. The pivotal character, however, to the analysis of *The Women of Brewster Place,* is Ciel, a young woman desperate to keep a worthless man; in the process of seeing his true side, she loses a child. Finally, "The Two" serve as balance for the two beginning characters of Mattie and Etta Mae. The "two" women are Theresa and Lorraine, lesbians who have fled the homophobia of the world, only to have their lives destroyed by rumor and, finally, rape and murder at the end of Brewster Place.

Much of Mattie Michael's adult life is riddled with emotional traumas punctuated by screams. Her section of the novel resounds with her screams, the screams of her father, and the screams of her son. Mattie is not healed from the effects of these screams until Ciel's section of the novel, when

Mattie is able to rock into freedom the grief-strangled screaming moan of Ciel. Ciel's screams seem to heal Mattie, to lead her to salvation from the sounds that have destroyed her life.

Mattie had been isolated and pampered by her father, who felt no man was good enough for his daughter. One summer day, Mattie discovers Butch and sex. From this encounter, Mattie becomes pregnant, and her father is furious. It is not, however, Mattie's pregnancy that so enrages him, but her refusal to tell him the name of the father. In refusing to name the baby's father to her own father, Mattie seems to metaphorically reject all that Kristeva says is embodied in the linguistic Law of the Father. In this first instance of screaming in the novel, Mattie feels she "wanted to choke. She felt as if the entire universe had been formed into a ball and jammed into her throat . . . [she] sent it hurling out of her mouth and into a whirl-wind that crumbled her father's face and exploded both of their hearts into uncountable pieces. She saw them both being spun around the room and sucked out of the windows along with everything that had ever passed between them. She felt the baby being drawn by the winds, but she held on tightly, trembling violently, because she realized that now this was all she would ever have" (*WBP,* 22). This passage adumbrates the hurricane in *Mama Day,* whose screams are figured as the ultimate in female power. It also portends the pregnancy in *Bailey's Cafe* that will bring salvation. Here in *The Women of Brewster Place,* Naylor sets the preverbal against the ver-bal, semiotic against symbolic. At this point, the preverbal loses, is beaten down; later this will not be the case. At this point in the narrative of *The Women of Brewster Place,* Naylor gives us a "whirlwind" and winds pow-erful enough to "suck" things out the window—a foretaste of the hurri-cane. But the female power is silenced, choked, brutally beaten. Mattie's father hits her with a broomstick, as "he tried to stamp out what had hurt him the most and was now brazenly taunting him—her disobedience"; his anger wears him out until he is "sweating and breathing . . . pound[ing] the whimpering girl on the floor" (23). This beating, made more horrific by the father's "love" that fuels it, is stopped by Mattie's mother's screams and her shotgun blast through the ceiling.

This explosion of sound is paralleled by two more in Mattie's section. After expulsion from her home, Mattie flees north where, living in poverty, her world is shattered by the screams of Basil, her son, when he is bitten on the cheek by a rat. After Basil has grown into a very self-absorbed man, Mattie's ears again endure the roar of screams. This time it begins in a dream involving Butch and sugar cane: "He grabbed her by the throat to keep the saliva from being swallowed, and she opened her mouth and screamed and screamed—shrill notes that vibrated in her ears and sent terrible pains shooting into her head" (*WBP,* 44). These dream-screams become the sound of the phone ringing, Basil's voice on the other end informing her of his arrest for the murder of a man in a bar fight and an assault on a police officer.

Each of these three episodes of screams signals a change in Mattie's life. The first scream, involving the beating by her father, signals her move northward and the loss of her mother and father. The second scream, precipitated by the rat bites, involves another physical move; she finds the house and open arms of Miss Eva, Ciel's grandmother. The third scream, that of the dream and the phone, signals the loss of Mattie's house, the loss of her son, and her move to Brewster Place. With each scream/event, Mattie is both corporeally and psychically dislocated. Yet as Mattie is stripped of her ties to home, she comes closer to a new community of women; the screams in the narrative contribute to the creation of the conditions for establishing the "new." With each preverbal episode, Mattie moves closer to Brewster Place, where the preverbal, the *jouissance,* merges with the verbal, and women heal themselves. All three episodes of screams are triggered by horrid events, but the final outcome is the salvation of women on Brewster Place.

A prime example of female bonding that is central to this new community is the love between Etta Mae and Mattie. Etta Mae's section begins with the origin of her love of music: *"It wasn't the music or the words or the woman that took that room by its throat until it gasped for air—it was the pain"* (*WBP,* 55). It is the *sound* of the pain, of the preverbal, that so captures Etta Mae, not the music nor the words. Oddly, Naylor's writing style in Etta Mae's section is not loud, not boisterous, despite the character's boisterous life. In order to balance the triad of screams in Mattie's section, Etta Mae's section is bookended by the lovely sounds of laughter. The laughter emphasizes the "newness" of the created community in ways that recall Kristeva's point that without "the practice of laughter there is nothing new . . . at best [there is] an empty repeated act" (1984, 225). In this story, Naylor presents a newly created community, a place where, for Etta Mae, the music of the blues, the sound of the pain, the preverbal captures her. It heals her, brings her salvation.

When Etta Mae arrives on Brewster Place she brings laughter. Driving up in a stolen green Cadillac, she has the pink and red shorts of the married owner in her possession to ensure his silence. In spite of herself, Mattie has to laugh with Etta Mae: "Each time the laughter would try to lie still, the two women would look at each other and send it hurling between them, once again" (*WBP,* 59). Naylor's choice of the word "hurl" produces a healing connection to Mattie's beating when she "hurled" the words that destroyed her life with her family. This "hurling" laughter with Etta Mae creates a new family. The initial narrative of screams is modulated by the laughter. The creation of the new *is* the salvation.

Etta Mae's section ends with more laughter, healing Etta Mae and bonding her and Mattie; but this final laughter is preceded by a heartbreaking episode when Etta Mae has sex with a preacher. She sees this as a fast trip to respectability. After the preacher's final pelvic thrusts into her "like a dying walrus" (*WBP*, 72), she returns to reality and sees the tawdriness of the motel room, like so many motel rooms she has known. The preacher returns her to Brewster Place, a defeated "middle-aged woman in the wrinkled dress and wilted straw hat" (*WBP*, 74). She is rescued by the sound of music from Mattie's window as Mattie plays Etta Mae's "loose-life music" (*WBP*, 74). Etta Mae stops, "trying to decipher the broken air waves into intelligible sound, but she couldn't make out the words. She stopped straining when it suddenly came to her that it wasn't important what song it was" (74). Knowing that Mattie is there waiting for her is all that matters and "Etta laughed softly to herself as she climbed the steps toward the light and the love and the comfort that awaited her" (74). The preverbal sounds, not the meanings of the words, tie the woman's body as text to the text itself. Etta Mae's body has been used, and she is almost defeated. But she is saved by the sounds, as she had been before by laughter. She then steps back into the female community that Mattie here represents.

As in the beginning of Etta Mae's section, when the reader is told that it is not the music or the words but the sound of the pain that matters, now at the end of the section the importance is in the sound of love and comfort. The laughter in Etta Mae's section works in healing opposition to the sounds of screams in Mattie's section. Again, when the noise is quieted down into text, we have the creation of the new—a woman's community that will bring salvation to both Mattie's and Etta Mae's tattered lives.

In Ciel's section, Naylor intermixes the association of screams with pain and screams with healing in what Virginia Fowler calls "not only the emotional origin of the novel but its emotional center as well" (1996, 42). In this episode, the cycle of pain and healing begins as Serena, Ciel's baby, sticks a fork into an electrical outlet, curiously searching for a roach. The child's death-scream interrupts an argument between Ciel and her boyfriend, Eugene. Ciel's response to the death is silent, dry-eyed withdrawal. She refuses to bathe, refuses to eat. The baby's death, with the scream as synecdoche for that death, has sapped her ability and desire to live and feel. Ciel has chosen a slow death.

When Ciel's grief is just on the verge of killing her, and Mattie Michael sees Ciel's eyes, she responds immediately with her whole being: "'Merciful Father, no!' she bellowed. There was no prayer, no bended knee or sackcloth supplication in those words, but a blasphemous fireball that shot forth and went smashing against the gates of heaven, raging and kicking, demanding to be heard" (*WBP*, 102). This "blasphemous fireball" that shoots forth once again returns us to the scene of Mattie's beating. During that scene, her father beat her because of her silence regarding the father of her child; the female voice is silent. Here Mattie's voice returns so strongly that it "smash[es] against the gates of heaven, raging and kicking, demanding to be heard." Mattie here screams (figuratively) against a male trinity: God—the father, Sam Michael—her father, and Basil—her son. Yet, no longer begging for her own life, Mattie, in her angry salvation of Ciel, is also saving herself.

Mattie rushes in and begins to rock Ciel, and Ciel begins to moan, a screaming, high-pitched moan, an answering sound to her baby's scream. The rocking and the answering moan, the preverbal sounds, work in unison to take Mattie and Ciel beyond the room, connecting them to a painful history. Naylor writes: "Propelled by the sound, Mattie rocked her out of that bed, out of that room, into a blue vastness just underneath the sun and above time. She rocked her over Aegean seas so clean they shone like crystal, so clear the fresh blood of sacrificed babies torn from their mother's arms and given to Neptune could be seen like pink froth on the water. She rocked her on and on, past Dachau, where soul-gutted Jewish mothers swept their children's entrails off laboratory floors. They flew past the spilled brains of Senegalese infants whose mothers had dashed them on the wooden sides of slave ships. And she rocked on" (*WBP*, 103). In essence, Mattie is taking Ciel to the place of the female collective scream, the place beyond words, a place of pure pain, and once Ciel sees and knows this place, she can be healed. The scream becomes a source of salvation.

This rocking back into history recalls Helene Cixous's words in "The Laugh of the Medusa": "As subject for history, woman always occurs simultaneously in several places. Woman un-thinks the unifying, regulating history that homogenizes and channels forces, herding contradictions into a single battlefield. In woman, personal history blends together with the history of all women, as well as national and world history" (1981, 252–53). In order to "un-think" male-recorded history, women must (at least initially) work with the preverbal—the sounds of moans and screams and laughter. Once the sounds have created the "new"—the new narrative, the new women's community—then this history can merge with or perhaps replace the verbal text. Thus, a new history can be told. With the scream, Ciel has given birth to herself, healing herself and Mattie, as well as, perhaps, the reader. Another "new" is created. Another salvation is given to the woman's body, which is the text.

In the penultimate story, "The Two," Theresa and Lorraine are left without healing; they are (in fact) sacrificed to offer healing to the reader. Theresa and Lorraine, two lesbians, are never encircled into the circle of saving grace of the women of Brewster Place because of their sexuality. Lorraine's rape by C. C. Baker and his gang is a horrifying episode, and, unlike Ciel or Mattie or Etta Mae, Lorraine is never healed. Yet through her suffering, the reader is given new insight and thus given the possibility of salvation. Laura E. Tanner, in *Intimate Violence,* claims that "the reader of *The Women of Brewster Place* is gendered female and victim," that the rape scene "strips the reader of [the freedom of moving freely throughout text], pinning him or her to the victim's body and communicating an experience of rape that genders the reader—whatever sex he or she may be—female" (1994, 32). Tanner argues that traditional literary convention often seems to "authorize" an "imagised and eroticized" response to rape (Tanner 1994, 28). Gloria Naylor challenges this convention; the reader is made to understand rape as she/he views the rapist through Lorraine's eyes, and Lorraine is sacrificed for the reader's understanding. Another salvation, this one for the reader, is being created outside the text. It is signaled by and created through a silenced scream.

Lorraine's rape is graphically described, yet she is unable to scream. In fact, "The screams tried to break through her corneas out into the air, but the tough rubbery flesh sent them vibrating back into her brain, first shaking lifeless the cells that nurtured her memory" (*WBP*, 170). The rape is "all one continuous hacksawing of torment that kept her eyes screaming the only word she was fated to utter again and again for the rest of her life. Please" (*WBP*, 171). Lorraine's inability to scream may make the reader want to scream, for she remains pinned, according to Tanner, to Lorraine's body.

Lorraine's screams are finally brought forth by the screams of Mattie when Mattie sees Lorraine bashing in Ben's skull: "Mattie's screams went ricocheting in Lorraine's head and she joined them with her own" (*WBP*, 173). Lorraine has turned her anger toward Ben, the old janitor, the only person who has shown her kindness in the novel. Blinded by the screams trapped behind her corneas, Lorraine cannot see Ben's individuality but views him instead as every man.

Through the preverbal, then, Naylor has moved the reader into the text, "pinning him or her to the victim's body" as Tanner described it. Through this grim identification, though, Naylor saves the reader from being constrained by the literary conventions of rape portrayals, and thus creates alternative ways for the reader to engage the representations and the discourse. Because of the intensity of this situation, and the requirement that the reader locate him- or herself in a female consciousness, she prepares the reader to regard Willie, in *Linden Hills,* as a male character who is gendered female. Moreover, she alerts readers to see his quest to reach the source of the screams in that novel as a central part of the text.

Linden Hills, a novel about the loss of African-American values in the search for the "American Dream," is set in an upscale African-American neighborhood managed and manipulated by the demonic Luther Nedeed. Nedeed, hating the whiteness of his son's skin, has put both his wife, Willa, and his son in the basement with very little food and water. Missy Dehn Kubitschek in *Claiming the Heritage* states that Naylor explores "the cost of conformity to the ideals of the isolated self" (1991, 93). She further states that the women of *Linden Hills* "must try and endure that contradiction in African-American culture, the isolate self" (Kubitschek 1991, 117). Unlike the women in *The Women of Brewster Place,* Willa Nedeed isolates herself by choosing to marry for material wealth. She is further isolated by her imprisonment. Her screams, the preverbal sounds, are an attempt to rejoin community. Again, Naylor sets up the screams as signaling the creation of the new, a narrative, but this time one without community. Unlike Ciel's screams, Willa's are sounds of resistance.

Her howls are heard throughout the novel, binding Willie to her, and binding her to the women in *The Women of Brewster Place* who have also lost children. Ciel's healing moan for the loss of her child becomes conflated with Willa's eerie wail for her dying son. Lorraine's unvocalized screams of rape horror become the horror of a woman locked (thus mostly unheard) in her husband's basement. She is symbolically locked into the "Master discourse" and must rely on the screams, the preverbal, to save her by reconnecting her to the outside world.

The first mention of a scream in *Linden Hills* occurs in the kitchen of Norman and Ruth Anderson, two of Willie's and Lester's friends. Ruth brings the men's attention to it, saying, "That wasn't an animal. I don't know what it was, but God, it wasn't an animal." The sound is blown into the kitchen by the winter air, and "they didn't know if it was the freezing air or the long, thin howl it carried with it into the kitchen that made the hair stand up on their arms" (*LH,* 42).

Willie and Lester hear it again, later in Lester's bedroom as a "cold burst of wind" that brings with it "a long thin wail." As Willie and Lester listen, "they each sat alone in the dark, trying to link some sort of human emotion to that sound because an ancient instinct told them it wasn't an animal sending out that cry into the world. They knew it didn't sound like someone in pain or danger. And it didn't echo the heightened edges of despair. Lester and Willie were totally confused, since there was really nothing that had touched their twenty years to help them locate its cause—they had not lived long enough to recognize a plea for lost time" (*LH,* 60).

Lester and Willie are unable to recognize this scream because they are young and male. But by the apocalyptic end of the novel, Willie, in just a few days, will grow into an understanding that is both aged and female. In this way, Naylor links the preverbal to the verbal at the same time that she joins the female and the male. Willie transforms the preverbal screams of Willa into verbal text, for they enable him to begin a new poem.

At the climax of the narrative, Willie has come to the source of the screams; he has finally reached the bottom of Linden Hills, Luther Nedeed's house. He and Lester are helping Luther put up his Christmas tree. Just as Willie has reached the bottom, Willa reaches the top, escaping from the basement, carrying the body of her son. Willie sees the woman, "her hair tangled and matted, her sunken cheeks streaked with dirt" (*LH,* 298). This sight makes him want to "scream so he could breathe again." Willie is "frozen in a space of time without a formula that lost innocence or future wisdom could have given [him]" (*LH,* 299). He has joined the group of women who mourn for lost children; Willie has taken on the screams that previously belonged to women, yet he cannot make the sounds vocal. His pain remains unheard, as Lorraine's screams were unheard. Through his silence and loss of voice, Willie is gendered female and holds the traditional female role of silence. Yet perhaps the knowledge that he brings back to the world is the saving grace of this novel—a story that ends as the neighbors, refusing to offer aid, watch the Nedeed house burn.

The male adoption of female pain and screams is a pattern repeated in *Mama Day,* Naylor's third novel. *Mama Day* focuses on three primary characters: Miranda Day, the magic conjure woman of Willow Springs, an island not on the map (not even part of a state, it is somewhere off the coast of South Carolina and Georgia); Cocoa, Mama Day's grandniece who has moved to New York City and comes home to Willow Springs once a year; and George, Cocoa's husband, who is completely of the New York world, a man with a head for engineering, football, and rationality. Part of the novel takes place in New York and is alternately told by George, then Cocoa, remembering their lives together, many years after George's death.

The remainder of the novel takes place on the island of Willow Springs, a place spiritually far removed from New York. This section of the novel is told by the collective voice of the island folk as well as by George and Cocoa. When Cocoa brings George to Willow Springs, they are faced with some destructive powers even Mama Day has difficulty resolving.

In this novel of power, belief, destruction, and salvation, screams *and* laughter are essential to recovering from the devastation that marked the end of *Linden Hills*. In fact, early in the novel, Mama Day thinks about the fire that destroyed Willa Nedeed, her grandniece. Even though Mama Day believes that Willa had "not a whit of courage," she also believes that she did not deserve her fiery end (*MD,* 39). The reader knows, however, that Willa Nedeed developed a special kind of courage in the basement. The difference here in perspective between the reader and Mama Day is important. Despite Mama Day's sage, spiritual wisdom, she has yet to learn the full importance of screams and laughter; she does not yet know that a man's laughter will create the new world on Willow Springs. But because the reader has lived in Linden Hills with Willa, she/he knows the importance of Willa's vocalization of the screams, knows the strength she displayed in the face of the isolation that characterizes Linden Hills. Therefore, the reader is alert to the sounds of the third novel as signals that even Mama Day does not yet know how to interpret.

At the beginning of *Mama Day,* Mama Day compares Willa to Cocoa, who "came into the world kicking and screaming" (*MD,* 39). Willa exited the world kicking and screaming. It will take the courage and belief of George, Mama Day, and Cocoa to heal the pain symbolized by the screams of Willa. Cocoa, whose real name is Ophelia, was named for her great-grandmother, the mother of Mama Day and Abigail (Cocoa's grandmother). The first Ophelia contributed to a cycle of screams that the second Ophelia, Cocoa, must heal. Peace (Mama Day and Abigail's sister) fell to her death at the bottom of a well when she was only a child. Mama Day remembers, *"Her mama's wail and the angry thud of her daddy's hobnail boots"* (*MD,* 36). The mother, Ophelia, never recovers from this loss, unlike Ciel in *The Women of Brewster Place.* But as was true for Ciel, the memory of the loss of Peace, both child and thing, can be healed though a series of screams.

After the death of Peace, the mother sits on the porch, rocking and twisting pieces of thread. Mama Day, a child herself at the time, must become an adult and never has the time to be young. Mama Day, now an old woman, still hears "[t]he cry [that] won't die after all these years, just echoes from a place lower and lower with the passing of time" (*MD,* 88). The cry of Peace falling in the well and the scream of the mother over her loss continue to reverberate in Willow Springs. Like Willa's screams in *Linden Hills*, these screams also originate from a dark place, from a trapped place. Moreover, the initial sounds of these cries, as in *The Women of Brewster Place*, signal loss—the loss of sister, mother, wife, daughter. Mama Day lost a lover and a chance to have her own babies because she could not leave her family. She remembers wondering, "How could she have gone, with Abigail terrified to go near that rocker, trembling and choking for air when the woman rises up to scream, Peace, Peace? . . . A voice dancing on the fading night wind. Mama and child. Mama and sister. Too heavy a load to take away" (*MD*, 89). The mother of Peace becomes so disturbed that she adds another scream to the little island; she jumps to her death from the bluff, "screaming Peace" (117).

The recovery from these losses, signaled by the screams, can only occur through the generation of still more screams, from the merging of the pre-verbal with the verbal text. Cocoa and George, with their own horrible screams, will finally still the cries of mothers and children—thereby enabling Cocoa's eventual understanding. As Bonnie Winsbro writes, "Cocoa's new world becomes possible . . . because she learns that physical separation does not preclude spiritual connection; she learns, that is, as her ancestors never did, how to let a loved one 'go with peace'. . . . [she] discovers . . . 'the meaning of peace'" (1993, 128).

The screams and final stillness that end the novel are counterpointed by laughter when George first arrives on the island. His laughter instigates the creation of the new text, the one that merges verbal and preverbal. The laughter guides him into this place where he will save Cocoa, dying in the process, but finally finding the home he has always needed. As George first meets Mama Day and Abigail, he notes: "Their laughter had been waiting for me, and as it circled around us, I could finally tell that they were sisters. The heads thrown back in similar angles to let out a matching pitch of flowing sound. Miss Abigail put her hands up on each side of my face— Well, bless your heart, child—and a lump formed in my throat at their gentle pressure. Up until that moment, no woman had ever called me her child" (*MD*, 176). This laughter flows and circles much as do the screams for Peace that George cannot hear.

This initial instance of laughter is paralleled by the laughter when George, who usually does not drink, gets roaringly drunk while playing poker with some of the men of Willow Springs. He is deposited at the front stoop, and he "concentrated carefully to avoid slurring my words, but after a moment of stillness, soft laughter encircled me before three pairs of even softer arms were guiding me up the steps" (*MD*, 215). Once again, George is encircled in soft laughter, saved by the women who wait for him. This episode can be compared to the moment in *The Women of Brewster Place* when Etta Mae returns from her devastating one-night stand with the preacher, hears Mattie playing her records, and laughs "softly to herself," climbing "the steps toward the light and the love and the comfort that awaited her" (*WBP*, 74). Even though George is to die later, his essence, his soul, is saved on the island because of the healing circle of laughter. Through laughter, George helps to create—and in doing so also joins—a new community.

But first the new healing series of screams must happen, and they are initiated by the hurricane. Mama Day tells the citizens of the island to listen to the crows instead of the news bulletins—"When it gets so they start screaming, the wind's gonna come in screaming too" (*MD*, 236). And indeed the wind does come screaming. Mama Day and Abigail listen to "the heaving, screaming winds." They know the source, know the power. Naylor writes:

> [I]t ain't a matter of calling them winds by a first name, like you'd do a pet dog or cat, so what they're capable of won't be so frightening— a prank or something that nature, having nothing better to do, just decided to play: one time a female, one time a male. But Abigail and Miranda is sitting side by side, listening to the very first cries from the heaving and moaning outside. . . . Feeling the very earth split open as the waters come gushing down—all to the end of birthing a void. Naw, them winds will come, rest and leave screaming . . . while prayers go up in Willow Springs to be spared from what could only be the workings of Woman. And She has no name. (*MD*, 250–51)

The screaming power of the hurricane is not to be pacified or tamed by naming her Camille or Hazel or Danny. She is not to be patronized or claimed; the hurricane is beyond what our language is capable of giving us. As Elaine Scarry writes in *The Body in Pain*, "physical pain does not simply resist language but actively destroys it . . . [reducing it] to the sounds and cries a human being makes before language is learned" (1985, 4). The hurricane is the sound of pain made vocal, a scream. It is, metaphorically, the preverbal writ large, for the hurricane is also female, Woman with a capital W, analogous to the collective female voicing of pain, to the screams of Ciel, Mattie, Lorraine, Willa, Ophelia, and Peace, to the sounds of sorrow for lost children and because of rape. In fact, the hurricane is described as splitting open, waters breaking, birthing a void.

At this point, readers might expect the devastation of the hurricane to complete the cycle of screams, yet Naylor does not settle for such an easy solution. The hurricane only initiates the horrible screams of Cocoa, which lead into the final screams of George, which resolve the novel in stillness. In fact, in the narrative, the screams of the hurricane literally turn into the screams of Cocoa's dream, a dream she does not initially understand.

Cocoa is hexed by Ruby, a mountain of a woman who lives in Willow Springs. Ruby is incredibly jealous of her husband, Junior Lee, who has roving hands and eyes. Ruby catches Junior Lee grabbing Cocoa. For a woman like Ruby, only the woman is to be blamed. She offers to braid Cocoa's hair, ostensibly as an apology for Junior's behavior. Cocoa sits between Ruby's legs, remembering her past, thinking Ruby's legs "were a fortress I could hide between and her voice was soothing" (MD, 245). The mother and birth images occur again, but Ruby has no comfort in mind for Cocoa. She is planting the seed of screams in Cocoa's head as she plaits her hair, twisting it up in threads of twine, an image that jolts the reader back to the image of Ophelia, going mad, grieving for Peace, rocking on the porch and twisting threads. Ruby has placed the "mother" of all hexes on Cocoa, and even Mama Day needs some help from the rational George to heal her.

In her mirror, Cocoa begins to see her flesh smeared and hanging, and "I couldn't help myself—I screamed" (MD, 276). At this point, she and George tell themselves Cocoa's illness is nothing more than a virus. Cocoa begins to realize something more is going on when she feels worms eating her insides; feeling them gnawing at her and again, "I opened my mouth to scream" (MD, 290). When the worms begin to pour over her from the shower head, wriggling into her body, she tries not to scream, because screaming "only allowed more of them to slide down [her] throat" (MD, 297). At first, when George hears the water running in the shower, he decides to "join her. How long since we'd done something normal like bathing together—or even laughing together. It seemed an eternity. And that's how long your screaming seemed to echo" (MD, 297). Indeed, Cocoa is making vocal a long history of screams.

Mama Day must go to the source of the original screams before she can heal Cocoa. In order to save her, Mama Day journeys to the well where Peace died, trying to find the answer to ensure Cocoa's salvation. She must go to the well, here a symbol of entrapment and of the preverbal. When the answer to how to achieve Cocoa's salvation comes, "it comes with a force that almost knocks her on her knees. She wants to run from all that screaming. Echoing shrill and high, piercing her ears." Looking into the well, Mama Day hears "Circles and circles of screaming. . . . How was she ever gonna look past this kind of pain?" (*MD*, 284). At this point, Mama Day begins to more fully understand the power of laughter and of screams.

Mama Day realizes that she can only heal Cocoa by joining hands with the motherless child, George. Although George is the epitome of rationality, a disbeliever in spirituality, he is willing to make the trip to the hen house as Mama Day instructs if it will enable him to help save Cocoa. He is willing to bring back what he finds under the setting hen and to endure brutal attacks by the hen. But when he finds the nest empty, he is unable to believe that she wants "nothing but my hands" (*MD*, 300). In a rage, he destroys the chickens and the coop, amid the shrieks and screams of the chickens. Oddly, George begins to laugh "and kept laughing until it started to hurt" (*MD*, 301). George laughs as he destroys the screaming chickens; in that moment, he and Mama Day have destroyed the screams. Their powers have merged—the power of self and rationality, which is conjoined with the verbal, post-Oedipal world of discourse, is being combined with the power of the spiritual and irrational, consistently linked to the pre-Oedipal, preverbal. This merging saves Cocoa. The episode in the chicken house has caused George's death as his faulty heart bursts, but he wants Cocoa to know "something about my real death that day. . . . As my bleeding hand slid gently down your arm, there was total peace" (*MD*, 302). George has learned to go "with peace," and Cocoa will later learn to let him go "with peace" (Winsbro 1993, 128). The screams of women on the island joined with Cocoa's screams have resulted in George's death amid laughter, thereby giving birth to the creation of something new.

The novel ends with both Mama Day and Cocoa listening, and "both can hear clearly that on the east side of the island and on the west side, the waters were still" (*MD*, 312). The screams have ceased, and the novel ends in water to quench the apocalyptic fires of *Linden Hills*. George has sacrificed himself to heal the women. In order to understand how George is able to accomplish this, a reader must do as Mama Day has done in her journey to the beginning of screams, confronting the source in the well. A reader must journey to the beginning of George, to the moment of his birth signaled by screams at the end of Naylor's fourth novel, *Bailey's Cafe*.

The novel is framed by the voice of Bailey, a man haunted by the sights and sounds of World War II. Although he does act as a governing voice, most of the other characters tell some or all of their own stories. Remarkable characters pass through the triad of places in the novel—Gabe's Pawn Shop, Bailey's Cafe, and Eve's Boarding House, where men are "entertained." Sweet Esther, a sexually abused woman who lives in Eve's basement, tells the reader her story. Peaches arrives at Bailey's Cafe with her story and a long scar down her face, evidence that, in self-loathing, she cut her beautiful face with a bottle opener. Jesse Bell tells her story of heroin addiction and the love of another woman, both of which contributed to the ruin of her former life. Miss Maple, a man with a Ph.D., dresses as a woman, writes soap ditties, and works as a bouncer at Eve's. The final character of the novel is Mariam, an Ethiopian Jew, a virgin mother who bears George and brings salvation and hope to the lost souls on "the edge of the world" at Bailey's Cafe (*BC*, 28).

The screams of mother and son at the end of the novel are balanced by the lovely laughter of Sadie, the first woman whose story we hear. Like the story of Mariam, Sadie's story is one of two not told in first person. Although Sadie is a wino and 25-cent whore who plies her trade on the street, she is also a true lady. Nadine, Bailey's wife, brings Sadie a cup of tea in a thick mug with "cracks and stains," but by the time it reaches Sadie's table, it has the quality of china surrounded by "monogrammed silver and linen" instead of the "bent tin spoon and paper napkin" (*BC*, 40). Despite her life of poverty and despair, selling herself for exactly the amount of money needed for the wine, Sadie can still laugh. Bailey says, "Her laughter was like music. And the whole cafe stood still. In the presence of something that beautiful and rare, you're afraid to move, afraid to even breathe" (*BC*, 73). Sadie's laughter brings pleasure to the customers of Bailey's, but even more than pleasure, it brings ineffable beauty.

This beautiful laughter is countered by the screams of Mariam, the last woman's story to be told in the novel. Nadine and Eve narrate her piece. Both Eve and Nadine believe Mariam's claim that she is a virgin yet pregnant. Eve says, "There was no way for the girl to be lying, or the whole village would have heard her screams" (*BC*, 146). Mariam has had her vagina almost entirely sewn shut to increase her value as a woman, and Eve explains that "if it had been rape, the whole village would have heard her screams. Even on the wedding night, the ensaslaye, with a willing bride and a cautious husband, the village will hear the screaming" (*BC*, 152). And no one has heard Mariam's screams, not yet.

As Eve prepares a place for Mariam to give birth, Bailey claims that he is "dreading the thought of having to hear Mariam screaming." Eve, however, has created a way "to alter the pain" (*BC*, 224). And because every person who lives on the street comes to the cafe to be present for the birth, all are able to witness the magical display of colors meant to quell the pain: "Pearls. Iridescent pinks. . . . Glowing copper. Gilded orange. And all kinds of gold. . . . Emerald. Turquoise. Sapphire. It went on for hours." Finally the baby is born. Bailey says, "Then we heard the baby's first thin cry—and the place went wild" (*BC*, 225). George and Mariam's screams have begun a healing process that will end with the stillness of *Mama Day*. The sounds of his thin cry bring a smile to Esther's haunted face, and Gabe, the Jew, hugs Bailey, the black man. As one critic has said, "The miracle of George's birth at the end of the novel and the community it creates together evoke an underlying optimism, a belief in the ultimate resistance of the human spirit to attempts to destroy it" (Fowler 1996, 139).

George's thin baby screams at the end of *Bailey's Cafe* thrust the reader backward into the other Naylor novels, yet forward in time. George's cries here and in *Mama Day* are signals of the coming together into, and saving capacity of, a community. The importance of what Naylor has done through these sounds and through her more general fusing of the preverbal and the verbal is constructing a way to blend the male and the female, the symbolic order and the semiotic, without privileging one over the other. In allowing her characters to "speak" the unconscious through these sounds, she makes these sounds part of the way that she connects the novels into a cycle. Without recognizing the important role that the preverbal sounds play, we cannot easily see the ways that the verbal texts work together. Without the verbal, though, the preverbal would—of course—remain outside our understanding.

And so we are back at the beginning, but these four novels by Naylor have no beginning; instead, they establish a seamless journey back and forth through a world of pain and hope, punctuated by laughter and screams. These preverbal sounds are instrumental to the narratives, to the creation of the new—to the creation of a community that carries in it the potential for salvation. As Bailey tells us at the end of *Bailey's Cafe,* "And that's how we wrap it folks. It's the happiest ending I've got. Personally, I'm not really too down about it. Life will go on" (*BC*, 229).

Works Cited

Cannon, Katie Geneva. *Katie's Canon: Womanism and the Soul of the Black Community.* New York: Continuum, 1995.

Cixous, Helene. "The Laugh of the Medusa." In *New French Feminisms*. Eds. Elaine Marks and Isabelle de Courtivron. New York: Schocken Books, 1981. 245–64.

Fowler, Virginia. *Gloria Naylor: In Search of Sanctuary.* Twayne's United States Authors Series. New York: Twayne, 1996.

Kristeva, Julia. *Polylogue.* Paris: Seuil, 1977.

———. *Powers of Horror: An Essay in Abjection.* Trans. Leon S. Roudiez. New York: Columbia University Press, 1982.

————. *Revolution in Poetic Language.* Trans. Margaret Waller. New York: Columbia University Press, 1984.

————. "The System and the Speaking Subject." In *The Kristeva Reader.* Ed. Toril Moi. New York: Columbia University Press, 1986. 24–33.

Kubitschek, Missy Dehn. *Claiming the Heritage: African-American Women Novelists and History.* Jackson: University Press of Mississippi, 1991.

Moi, Toril. "Introduction." *The Kristeva Reader.* New York: Columbia University Press, 1986. 1–22.

Naylor, Gloria. *Bailey's Cafe.* New York: Harcourt Brace Jovanovich, 1992.

————. *Linden Hills.* New York: Penguin, 1985.

————. *Mama Day.* New York: Vintage, 1988.

————. *The Women of Brewster Place.* New York: Penguin, 1982.

Scarry, Elaine. *The Body in Pain: The Making and Unmaking of the World.* New York: Oxford University Press, 1985.

Tanner, Laura. *Intimate Violence: Reading Rape and Torture in Twentieth-Century Fiction.* Bloomington: Indiana University Press, 1994.

Winsbro, Bonnie. *Supernatural Forces: Belief, Difference, and Power in Contemporary Works by Ethnic Women.* Amherst: University of Massachusetts Press, 1993.

"Weapons Against Women"

Compulsory Heterosexuality and Capitalism in *Linden Hills*

Kimberly A. Costino

According to Michel Foucault, the term "homosexual" did not emerge into Western discourse until about 1870. Speaking about the category homosexual in a narrower context, John D'Emilio, in "Capitalism and Gay Identity," argues that the emergence of this category in colonial New England is directly related to the "historical development of capitalism" (1993, 468). He says that prior to the rise of capitalism, "[t]here was, quite simply, no 'social space' in the colonial system of production that allowed men and women to be gay . . . family was so pervasive that colonial society lacked even the category of homosexual or lesbian to describe a person" (D'Emilio 1993, 470). That is, before the emergence of the free labor system, men and women were unable to claim a homosexual identity because the family was an independent and interdependent unit of production. The survival of every man and woman required the cooperation and contribution of each family member, which meant that producing offspring was necessary for survival, and hence that the necessity of procreation determined one's sexual identity as heterosexual. However, as the capitalist system of free labor developed, the categories of gay and lesbian became possible. Once individuals began working independently for wages, rather than working as part of an interdependent unit, they were economically able, if they so desired, to separate from their family unit and claim a homosexual identity.

Once this category came into being, once we had a word for people who were attracted to other people of the same sex, a strict binarism between homosexuality and heterosexuality developed. As Eve Kosofsky Sedgwick notes in "Axiomatic," the introduction to *Epistemology of the Closet,* what happened as a result of the emergence of the term *homosexual* was that "the world-mapping by which every given person . . . was necessarily assignable to a male or female gender, was now considered necessarily assignable as well to a homo- or heterosexuality, a binarized identity" (1993, 245). While the number of individuals assigned a female gender and the number assigned a male gender are relatively equal, the number of individuals who are assigned a heterosexual identity far outweighs the number of those assigned a homosexual identity. According to D'Emilio, this discrepancy is due, in large part, to a capitalist ideology that drives people to claim a heterosexual identity and to live a heteronormative lifestyle regardless of their sexual desires (1993, 473).

Thus, while D'Emilio argues that capitalism is one of the primary contributors to the emergence of homosexual identity, he complicates the relationship between the two by further arguing that this economic system is equally complicit in the power structures that keep homosexual identity in a marginal position. Although capitalism enables a homosexual identity by providing individuals with the opportunity for economic independence, it simultaneously discourages individuals from embracing this identity by enshrining the family. As D'Emilio explains, "on the one hand, . . . capitalism has gradually undermined the material basis of the nuclear family by taking away the economic functions that cemented the ties between family members. . . . On the other hand, the ideology of capitalist society has enshrined the family as the source of love, affection, and emotional security, the place where our need for stable, intimate human relationships is satisfied" (1993, 473). These needs could, of course, be satisfied within structures other than that of the nuclear family. But D'Emilio notes that this particular familial structure coincides rather well with capitalist relations of production: "ideologically, capitalism drives people into heterosexual families: each generation comes of age having internalized a heterosexist model of intimacy and personal relationships" (D'Emilio 1993, 473). In outlining these contradictory threads connecting capitalism and sexual identity, D'Emilio indicates that the relationship between the two is both complicated and problematic. In his words, "[i]n the most profound sense, capitalism is the problem" (1993, 474).

By examining the link between capitalism and sexual identity, D'Emilio exposes the social and economic pressures that drive people to claim a heterosexual lifestyle regardless of their sexual preferences. In so doing, he implicitly calls into question heterosexuality's privileged status. This sort of questioning is one response to Adrienne Rich's call, in "Compulsory Heterosexuality and Lesbian Existence," for an examination of compulsory heterosexuality as a political institution. In this article, Rich argued that little, if any, feminist scholarship asked "whether, in a different context, or other things being equal, women would *choose* heterosexual coupling and marriage." She said that acknowledging that "heterosexuality may not be a 'preference' at all but something that has had to be imposed, managed, organized, propagandized, and maintained by force is an immense step to take if you consider yourself freely and 'innately' heterosexual" (1993, 229, 238–39). She further argued that the strict binarism between heterosexual and homosexual should be eradicated, that we should "consider the possibility that all women . . . exist on a lesbian continuum [and] see ourselves as moving in and out of this continuum whether we identify ourselves as lesbian or not" (Rich 1993, 240), because she believed that the elaboration of this sort of spectrum would create more tolerance and a sense of solidarity between heterosexual feminists and lesbians.

Gloria Naylor's novel quartet suggests that she, too, believes that examining compulsory heterosexuality as a political institution and developing a spectrum of sexuality rather than a strict binarism is both useful and important. Like D'Emilio, Naylor notes the complicated and intricate relationship between capitalism and sexual identity. Her novels—the first two in particular—acknowledge the fact that the free labor system enables people to claim a homosexual identity and expose the ways in which this same economic structure establishes conditions in which social and economic pressures force people into a heterosexual or heteronormative lifestyle. Thus, the first two novels in Naylor's quartet suggest that she also views capitalism as "the problem" (or at least a part of the problem). As Rich advocates, Naylor begins to tackle this problem by interrogating the strict binarism between hetero- and homosexuality and elaborating more of a continuum: in three novels in her tetralogy, she creates characters who fall in the liminal spaces between the two extremes of gay and straight. Important to note, however, is that while Rich calls for a lesbian continuum, Naylor presents a spectrum of sexual identities for both women and men. This choice suggests that despite the fact that she is most often credited with exploring the intersections of race and class with gender for females, she is, in fact, also interested in the ways that these identity matrices—and the matrix of sexuality itself—can (and should) be differentially understood for both women and men. Doing so, moreover, enables Naylor to unsettle the category of "gender" itself, although she does so less fully than she does the categories of sexuality. But in unsettling gender at all, particularly given that she interrogates sexuality in a variety of ways, she is able to disentangle these two often conflated attributes.[1]

Examining compulsory heterosexuality as a political institution and interrogating the strict binarism between hetero- and homosexuality is useful in fighting heterosexism and homophobia in the sense that it exposes the socially constructed nature of heterosexuality's privileged position. This sort of exposure, however, does little in terms of severing the connection between economic privilege and compulsory heterosexuality. In other words, it does little to solve the "problem" of capitalism. This exposure is a necessary precursor, though, to severing or at least loosening the connection between heterosexual performance and capital success. And in the last of her novel quartet, *Bailey's Cafe,* Naylor presents liminal characters who subvert the capitalist/compulsory heterosexuality matrix. Locating this inquiry in the fourth book, the text that locks the novels into a cycle, both suggests the lengthy effort it will take to achieve this destabilization and encourages us to reevaluate the interplay between sexuality and capitalism in each of the preceding books.

Naylor's first novel, *The Women of Brewster Place,* is the only work in the quartet that contains openly homosexual characters (that is, characters whom others in the novel know are homosexual). In this work, Naylor explicitly links the ability to claim a homosexual identity and the ability to participate in a homosexual lifestyle with the capitalist economic structure. We see this link most clearly when Lorraine explains her relationship with her father to Ben. She tells him "My father . . . kicked me out of the house when I was seventeen years old. He found a letter one of my girlfriends had written to me, and when I wouldn't lie about what it meant, he told me to get out and leave behind everything that he had ever bought me. . . . So I walked out of his home with only the clothes on my back. I moved in with one of my cousins, and I worked at night in a bakery to put myself through college" (*WBP,* 148).[2] Because Lorraine chooses to claim a lesbian identity, she is forced to sever all connections to her natal family. However, if the economic system were not one in which Lorraine could work to earn enough wages to survive independently of that unit, her decision to "refuse to lie about what [those letters] meant" would not have been a viable option. Instead, she would have been forced either to deny her feelings and live within prescribed heterosexual norms or to act on those feelings and live in secrecy and in fear. In either case, she would have been unable to claim a homosexual identity. However, because the free labor system provided Lorraine with the opportunity for economic independence, she was able to make the decision to act on her homosexual desires and to claim a lesbian identity.

Although capitalism makes this decision possible, it does not necessarily make it profitable. In other words, although Naylor makes it clear that the free labor system played a significant role in enabling the emergence of homosexual identity (or at least for the emergence of Lorraine as an individual asserting a homosexual identity), she complicates this relationship by making it equally clear, in this first novel, that choosing such an identity often means giving up complete access to economic privilege. For example, although Lorraine is able to "work[] at night in a bakery to put [her]self through college" (*WBP,* 148) and thereby earn her teaching certificate, her lesbian identity subsequently causes her to lose her teaching position. Not only does Lorraine lose her job because of homophobia. She and her partner Theresa are also limited in where they can reside; they are effectively forced to live on Brewster Place. When Lorraine starts to sense that even the women of Brewster Place exclude them, that even "they" regard Lorraine and Theresa as freaks, Theresa reminds her that there is no place left for them to go:

> "They, they, they!" Theresa exploded. "You know, I'm not starting up with this again, Lorraine. Who in the hell are they? And where in the hell are we? Living in some dump of a building in this God-forsaken part of town around a bunch of ignorant niggers with the cotton still under their fingernails because of you and your theys. They knew something in Linden Hills so I gave up an apartment for you that I'd been in for the last four years. And then they knew in Park Heights, and you made me so miserable there we had to leave. Now these mysterious theys are on Brewster Place. Well, look out that window, kid. There's a big wall down that block, and this is the end of the line for me." (*WBP,* 134–35)

Clearly Theresa and Lorraine do not reside on Brewster Place because they cannot afford to live elsewhere; they live on Brewster Place because communities like Linden Hills and Park Heights refuse to accept them because of their homosexual identity. In other words, because Theresa and Lorraine refuse to conform to traditional notions of the nuclear family, no "respectable" neighborhood will accept them.

While Naylor makes this connection between economic privilege and heteronormativity clear in her first novel, she exposes the social and economic pressures to claim a heterosexual identity even more emphatically in *Linden Hills,* the second novel in her quartet. Unlike a residence on

Brewster Place, which indicates having nowhere left to go and being unable to afford anything "better," a Linden Hills address signifies ultimate achievement: "practically every black in Wayne County wanted to be a part of Linden Hills. . . . making it into Linden Hills meant making it" (*LH,* 15).

Significantly, the social status and economic privilege that Linden Hills residents enjoy is utterly dependent upon their willingness to conform to heterosexual norms. Naylor makes it clear at the outset of this novel that in order for the Nedeeds to cultivate their dream of creating and maintaining an "ebony jewel," what they think of as "a beautiful black wad of spit right in the white eye of America" (*LH,* 9), each Luther Nedeed must marry a woman and produce a "squat carbon copy" of himself.[3] Thus, each generation of Luthers goes away from Linden Hills, brings back a light-skinned bride, and produces a son who has "the father's complexion, protruding eyes, and first name" (*LH,* 7). These men engage in heterosexual sex for the sole purpose of (re)producing a male heir. They keep charts and journals that trace "the dates and times of penetrations, conceptions, and births for every Nedeed in Linden Hills" (*LH,* 18) so that each generation will be able to reproduce a sole male heir. Once this son is born, the wives are no longer necessary and are therefore erased from both the father's and the son's lives. Thus, for the Nedeeds, a heterosexual identity and lifestyle is claimed solely for the purpose of producing an heir to perpetuate the Nedeed capitalist reign in Linden Hills.

Not only do the Nedeeds hold this standard for themselves, but they also hold a version of it for all those who reside or ever hope to reside in Linden Hills. One place this standard is evident is in the leases that the Nedeeds extend to the original residents of Linden Hills. When Luther Nedeed "sold the land practically for air to the blacks who were shacking there, [he] gave them a thousand-year-and-a-day lease — provided only that they passed their property on to their children. And if they wanted to sell it, they had to sell it to another black family or the rights would revert back to the Nedeeds" (*LH,* 7). This proviso makes the link between economic privilege and heteronormativity practically inextricable for the residents of Linden Hills.

At first glance, this lease seems relatively kind. The Nedeeds' requirement that the land be sold to another black family if no heirs exist suggests that their primary concern is not with ensuring heterosexuality but rather with providing for other black families. However, as Luther well knows, "Linden Hills wasn't black, it was successful" (*LH,* 17). So, when Luther enforces the terms of the leases, he is not securing the future for fellow blacks. He is securing the connection between economic privilege and heteronormativity.

A counterinstance in the novel makes this point apparent. When Laurel and Howard Dumont decide to divorce, Laurel assumes that she will be able to remain in their Linden Hills estate because she is "more than able to buy [Howard] out of whatever rights he feels are his." Luther quickly explains to her that "this land was only leased to the Dumonts in 1903, and subsequently the Tupelo Realty Corporation underwrote the mortgage for the house that was built on it. Now, that gave them the right to live here for a thousand years and a day, which in effect is a small eternity, but it's still a lease. And under our stipulations, if the Dumonts no longer wish to reside here and there are no children to inherit the lease, the property reverts back to the original owners: my family—the Nedeeds" (*LH,* 244). Of utmost importance in this scene is the fact that if Laurel Dumont had had children, the product of heterosexual coupling, to inherit the lease, she would not have lost her home to the Nedeeds; however, because this couple did not completely conform to heterosexual norms by producing heirs, Laurel suffers.

The pressure to conform to the traditional notions of the nuclear family may be clearest in Winston's decision to forsake David for Tupelo Drive. Unlike Theresa and Lorraine, who are willing to give up full participation in the economic order to claim a homosexual identity, Winston Alcott is not. Relatively early in the novel we learn that Winston and David shared a happy, healthy, loving relationship for eight years. However, because society, especially the society of Linden Hills, does not "cherish" (*LH,* 80) what these two men share, Winston is forced to choose between David, on the one hand, and his career and life in Linden Hills, on the other. As Luther tells the ushers for Winston's wedding, a married life is "the only way [of life] if a man wants to get somewhere in Linden Hills." When David challenges Luther by telling him that he knows "plenty of single men who've done just that," Luther says, "[b]ut where are they living David? In those small apartments on Second Crescent Drive. And who would want to spend the rest of their lives there? No one's been able to make it down to Tupelo Drive without a stable life and a family. Besides, Winston didn't want to stay single, did you son? You didn't want to go it alone" (*LH,* 75)As Winston, David, and Luther all well know, Winston would not have had to "go it alone"; he could have had a "stable life and a family" with David. However, because this option is not even acknowledged, let alone valued, Winston does not recognize it as a choice. When David reminds Winston that he offered him another life, Winston says, "If you really understood, you wouldn't be standing there trying to make me choose when there's really no choice about it. . . . I have to do this" (*LH*, 79). In other words, Winston is so steeped in the capitalist ideology that says he must "make it" financially and do so within the traditional family structures that he is unable to see that he could live happily, but differently, with David.

Luther ensures that this cycle will continue by rewarding Winston for making the "right" choice. During the wedding toast, Luther makes the announcement that:

> Winston Alcott has been an outstanding member of this community, doing it great pride and showering it with his talents and vitality. And now today, he has taken the step which will insure the stability and growth of Linden Hills. . . . So it does me great pleasure to announce that after your return from your nuptial retreat, you will not be bringing the new Mrs. Alcott back to Second Crescent Drive. You have proven your dedication to Linden Hills and now Linden Hills will open its arms to you. . . . The Tupelo Realty Corporation has decided to give you a mortgage on Tupelo Drive. (*LH*, 86–7)

By rewarding Winston for fulfilling the expectations that capitalist ideology has established, Luther maintains and reinforces the connection between economic privilege and heterosexuality and is therefore complicitous in the cycle of oppression that allows heterosexuality to maintain its privileged position.

Exposing the link between the category heterosexuality and economic privilege in these first two novels, Naylor indicates that the category heterosexuality is, itself, far less stable than many people assume. By examining the social and economic pressures that drive people to conform to heterosexual norms, Naylor suggests that heterosexual performance is a strategy, a means to an end. In revealing heterosexuality as a strategy, she thereby suggests that sexuality is not innate or inevitable. We can carry her explorations a step further and say that if sexuality is not innate or inevitable, then it is not necessarily fixed and stable. Furthermore, such instability at the individual level indicates the possibility of categorical instability. And, indeed, in her first two novels, Naylor examines and exposes such categorical instability by quietly interrogating the rigid binary of hetero-/ homosexuality. In so doing, Naylor begins to elaborate a spectrum or continuum that defies the strict binarism of homo-/heterosexuality, by presenting two pairs of characters whose juxtaposition forces us to rethink this binarism. Etta Mae's and Mattie's intimacy, when seen beside that of

Theresa and Lorraine, allows us to rethink the lesbian versus heterosexual binarism, while Willie's and Lester's friendship is tacitly counterpointed to David's and Winston's relationship. The latter has been recuperated into the binarized framework by being labeled "homoerotic." However, I would argue that in terms of the other relationships, we see that such a designation risks flattening out some of the far-reaching implications of Naylor's overall critique.

In *The Women of Brewster Place*, Etta Mae and Mattie share an intensely emotional and supportive relationship; however, as Helen Fiddyment Levy notes in "Lead on with Light," a "paternalistic social practice offers no publicly validated form for the celebration of that friendship and love" (1993, 266). So although their relationship may provide them both with emotional support, it does little in the way of offering financial support and social respect. Instead, Etta Mae seeks financial security and respectability through a string of men—all of whom fail her in the end. Realizing that she is not as young as she once was, Etta Mae makes one last effort to find security with Reverend Woods. She tells Mattie: "[E]ach year there's a new line to cover. I lay down with this body and get up with it every morning, and each morning it cries for just a little more rest than it did the day before. Well, I'm finally gonna get that rest and it's going to be with a man like Reverend Woods" (*WBP*, 69–70). However, like the many before him, Reverend Woods deserts Etta Mae after their sexual encounter. Afterward, when Etta Mae returns to Mattie's, we see that although Mattie is unable to provide the kind of financial security and social respect Etta Mae so desires, she is able to provide her with unconditional love and support: "When Etta got to the stoop, she noticed there was a light under the shade at Mattie's window. . . . Someone was waiting up for her. Someone who would deny fiercely that there had been any concern—just a little indigestion from them fried onions that kept me from sleeping. . . . Etta laughed softly to herself as she climbed the steps toward the light and the love and the comfort that awaited her" (*WBP*, 74). Although society does not appreciate or valorize the love between two women, Etta Mae and Mattie certainly do.

The presence of Theresa and Lorraine on Brewster Place leads Etta Mae and Mattie to examine and discuss the two women's love for each other. In the middle of Theresa and Lorraine's story, Etta Mae and Mattie begin to question the difference in friendships between heterosexual women and relationships between women who identify as lesbian:

> "Etta, I'd never mention it in front of Sophie . . . but I can't help feelin' that what [Theresa and Lorraine] are doing ain't quite right. How do you get that way? Is it from birth?"

"I couldn't tell you, Mattie. But I seen a lot of it in my time and the places I've been. They say they just love each other—who knows?"

Mattie was thinking deeply. "Well, I've loved women, too. There was Miss Eva and Ciel, and even as ornery as you can get, I've loved you practically all my life."

"Yeah, but it's different with them."

"Different how?"

"Well . . ." Etta was beginning to feel uncomfortable. "They love each other like you'd love a man or a man would love you—I guess."

"But I've loved some women deeper than I ever loved any man," Mattie was pondering. "And there been some women who loved me more and did more for me than any man ever did."

"Yeah." Etta though for a moment. "I can second that, but it's still different, Mattie. I can't exactly put my finger on it, but . . ."

"Maybe it's not so different," Mattie said, almost to herself. "Maybe that's why some women get so riled up about it, 'cause they know deep down it's not so different after all." She looked at Etta. "It kinda gives you a funny feeling when you think about it that way, though."

"Yeah, it does," Etta said, unable to meet Mattie's eyes. (*WBP,* 140–41)

I have quoted this passage at length because I believe it is important to note the confusion and embarrassment these women experience as they work through this issue. As uneasy as it makes them, by the end of the conversation Etta Mae and Mattie are not far from formulating a notion akin to Rich's idea of a "lesbian continuum." According to Rich, this term refers to "a range—through each woman's life and throughout history—of women-identified experience, not simply the fact that a woman has had or consciously desired genital sexual experience with another woman." Rich expands the term *lesbian* to include many more forms of primary female-female relationships such as "the sharing of a rich inner life, the bonding against male tyranny, and the giving and receiving of practical and political support" (1993, 239). And we learn that Etta Mae and Mattie share precisely this kind of intimacy when Etta Mae arrives on Mattie's doorstep: Etta "breathed deeply of the freedom she found in Mattie's presence. Here she had no choice but to be herself. The carefully erected decoys she was constantly shuffling and changing to fit the situation were of no use here. Etta and Mattie went way back, a singular term that claimed co-knowledge of all the important events in their lives and almost all of the unimportant ones. And by rights of this possession, it tolerated no secrets" (*WBP*, 58). Although these two women feel little physical attraction for each other, the intensity of their feelings for each other and the trust that they share work to open a space that seems to exist in between the two poles labeled "heterosexual" and "lesbian."

Whereas Rich calls for a specifically lesbian continuum, Naylor's spectrum is more inclusive. Not only does she juxtapose Etta Mae and Mattie's relationship with Theresa and Lorraine's in *The Women of Brewster Place*; she also juxtaposes Willie and Lester's friendship with the story of Winston and David in *Linden Hills*. Though both Willie and Lester have had what Henry Louis Gates labels a "homoerotic fantasy" (Gates 1988, 609)— Lester thinks uncomfortably about a poem he wrote about how "it felt looking at the strong, muscular body of Hank Aaron twist around when he swung a bat" (*LH*, 26), and Willie "once . . . had gotten the same crazy feelings from staring at the thighs of a Knicks center that he got from touching pretty Janie Benson" (*LH*, 28)—each man identifies himself as heterosexual. These two men, however, do share an intense and loving relationship. In fact, according to Levy, "Willie and Lester share the most intense and sensitive relationship in the book. They bring to each other their dreams and their fears, together they seek a definition of manhood that will defeat the sterility and calculations of the personal relationships they see on Tupelo Drive" (Levy 1993, 271). Indeed, the two poets are led to compare their relationship with that of Winston and David on the morning of Winston's wedding:

> "Now here's something for you." Lester turned to Willie. "I coulda sworn that guy was gay and now he's getting married today."
> "Who?"
> "Winston Alcott from Second Crescent Drive . . ."
> "Well, looks like he's not if he's getting married."
> "Yeah." Lester frowned slightly. "But I wondered for a while. He was always hanging around with this tall, dark-skinned dude—"
> "And you hang around with a short, dark-skinned dude. That don't mean that you're a fruit." (*LH*, 72–73)

Later, Willie says to Lester, "God, we might as well have been married as much time as we've spent together," and Lester responds, "That's no lie. The only thing we didn't do is sleep together." At this point, "Willie cringed and Lester noticed it" (*LH*, 282). Gates points out, however, that "Lester misstates the facts; the two boys spend the night before the wedding sleeping in the same bed, and Lester complains to his friend in the morning, 'You hugging me worse than a woman'" (Gates 1988, 609). Gates then goes on to argue that "'White' Willie Mason functions as a sexual cynosure in the novel . . . an object of erotic cathexis" (1988, 610). While there is certainly erotic tension between the two boys, I believe Naylor explores this sort of tension for reasons other than allowing Willie to "function as a sexual cynosure." On the contrary, I believe that, as she does with Etta Mae and Mattie's relationship, Naylor highlights the intensity of Willie and Lester's friendship in order to call into question the huge gap that exists between being heterosexual and being "a fruit." In other words, I feel that such an exploration helps Naylor to elaborate and revise Rich's notion of a continuum.

Counterpointing Etta Mae and Mattie's relationship with Theresa and Lorraine's and Willie and Lester's relationship with that of Winston and David forces us to call the strict binarism between hetero- and homosexuality into question because it implies that sexual categories are more fluid than the binarism suggests. By beginning to elaborate this sort of continuum in the first two novels, Naylor generates for herself a space she can then use in the later novels to explore the role played by other sexually liminal characters. Thus, in *Bailey's Cafe* we meet Jesse Bell, a bisexual woman; Eve, a woman who is effectively asexual; and Stanley/Miss Maple, a man who wears women's clothing but is not a homosexual. However, unlike the sexually liminal characters in the first two novels, the characters in this last novel defy the seemingly inextricable link between economic success and compulsory heterosexuality.

Jesse Bell is a bisexual woman "from the docks" (*BC*, 118) who "marrie[s] into the Kings and [goes] to Sugar Hill" (*BC*, 121). However, unlike Winston, who benefits both socially and economically from a heterosexual marriage and from conforming to heterosexual norms, Jesse's heterosexual marriage precipitates her ultimate downfall. Jesse knew from the beginning that marrying "up there" was dangerous for a woman:

> [T]hose women got treated any old way and took it . . . cause this son of a bitch is a doctor somebody or a lawyer somebody—or maybe just a man somebody that she feels she's nobody without. Women up there look at other women as nothing unless they're attached to some man's name. And attached they stay, no matter what he does. And personally, I knew a few of them who actually got their butts beaten worse than some women down on the docks. But they got beaten by stone sober men behind stained-glassed doors. And with all their money, they couldn't afford to cry. (*BC*, 121–22)

Jesse was willing to take this risk and marry "up there" because she believed her "husband was different. Way different. He loved everything about women" and also because "from the very beginning he understood about her" (*BC*, 123). Unfortunately, Uncle Eli wasn't different. Because Jesse was "from the docks," he refused to accept her as one of the King family; even after her marriage, he refused to refer to her as Mrs. King, as he did the other wives. And when Jesse gave birth to her son, he worked relentlessly to destroy the child's connection to the Bell family. While Jesse's class made her unable to achieve social acceptance from Uncle Eli, her heterosexual marriage temporarily allowed her economic privileges, privileges she could not have enjoyed had she not gone to great lengths to hide her relationship with "her." These privileges do, indeed, cease once Uncle Eli uncovers and discloses Jesse's bisexuality:

> [W]hen that dyke club got raided and Uncle Eli used every bit of influence he had to make sure my name hit the newspapers and stayed in the papers, throwing dirt on everything about my life, just digging, digging, until they dug up my special friend and my husband had to say, *had* to say he didn't know, cause, after all, he was a man and a King and there was his son to consider, so I'm out there by myself, on display like a painted dummy in a window as the name Jesse Bell came to mean that no-good slut from the docks and the nineteen years I'd put into my marriage didn't amount to dog shit; the care I'd given my son—dog shit; the clothes I wore, the music I liked, the school I went to, the family I came from, everything that made me *me*—dog shit. (*BC*, 131)

With Jesse Bell, Naylor provides a case where conforming to heterosexual norms, or performing heterosexuality, is not enough to stave off economic, emotional, and spiritual ruin. Jesse hides her lover, publicly performs a heterosexual role, and still suffers. In depicting this denigration, Naylor not only begins to sever the link between heteronormativity and economic privilege. She simultaneously exposes the inherent danger that such a link, if left unchallenged, can hold for women.

One place that women can find a haven from such danger is at Eve's brownstone. Eve is yet another one of Naylor's sexually liminal characters. But unlike Jesse, who enjoys both men and women as sexual partners, Eve is unpartnered and effectively asexual. And whereas "no man has ever touched" Little Mariam, practically *no one* has ever touched Eve. When trying to remember how the "game" with Billy Boy started, Eve rules out "tag because that would have meant touching" and for Eve, "there is no touching" (BC, 86). Consequently, the closest Eve comes to any kind of sexual contact is this "game" she plays with Billy Boy. However, once Godfather discovers "Billy Boy parading up and down his back walkway [and Eve] spread-eagled on [her] stomach," he tells her she is "going to leave him the same way he'd found [her], naked and hungry" (BC, 88). Eve leaves Godfather's house "buck naked" (BC, 89) and after walking a thousand years, she "finally reached Arabi . . . [t]en miles outside of New Orleans" (BC, 90). She says that "by then I'd lived a hundred years ten times over, so there was a lot to think about. . . . The only road that lay open to me was the one ahead, and the only way I could walk it was the way I was. I had no choice but to walk into New Orleans neither male nor female— mud. But I could right then and there choose what I was going to be when I walked back out" (BC, 90–91). Eve does, in fact, walk back out "ten years later with three steamer trunks of imported silk suits, not one of them brown; fifty-seven thousand, six hundred and forty-one dollars, not one of them earned on my back; and a love of well-kept gardens" (BC, 91). Again, Naylor begins to sever the connection between heteronormativity and capital success by allowing the unpartnered Eve, who defies both conventional sexual and gender binarisms—she is neither heterosexual nor homosexual, "neither man nor woman"—to achieve astonishing economic success.

Like Eve, Stanley/Miss Maple is able to achieve financial success despite his defiance of strict gender and sexual binarisms, for he, too, earns more than fifty thousand dollars by writing winning product jingles. And like Eve, he does not participate in any heterosexual relationships either during the course of the novel or in the recounted experiences. Moreover, although Stanley never identifies himself as heterosexual, he also insists that despite his homosexual experience he "is not a homosexual." He says, "I was never raped because I never resisted. And I bet you're thinking, so that explains it. Well, you're as wrong as Jesse. I'm not a homosexual, but I'm not stupid either. He was six-feet-two, as broad as he was tall, as ugly as he was mean, a repeat offender serving for three counts of murder with nothing left to lose. And he wasn't a homosexual either . . . for weeks I had to hear each night after the lights were out, I'm gonna fuck you or kill you" (BC, 193). Clearly, Stanley's homosexual experience arises out of necessity rather than desire. Such necessity could be likened to the pressures that drive people to perform heterosexuality; in other words, we could identify Stanley's experience as "compulsory homosexuality." Stanley, however, refuses such an identification because his homosexual performance is not ongoing; he does not participate in the homosexual lifestyle or claim a homosexual identity. Instead, he leaves his sexual identity utterly ambiguous. Thus, we can argue that through this foregrounding of sexual ambiguity Naylor again subverts the close link between capital success and compulsory heterosexuality.

Further, not only is Stanley similar to Eve in that he frustrates our conventional notions of sexuality, but he is also like Eve in that he frustrates conventional notions about gender by wearing women's clothing. Stanley dresses like a woman because the combination of the heat and his flannel suit caused him incredible discomfort at job interviews, and women's clothing seemed much cooler and more comfortable. Despite his attire, "there is no doubt—nor will there ever be—that [Stanley is] a man" (*BC*, 212). As Bailey explains, "[I]t's impossible to look at the way Miss Maple walks in here and not see a rather tall, rather thin, reddish brown man in a light percale housedress" (*BC*, 163). Through Stanley/Miss Maple, Naylor seems to be suggesting that not only is it important to disrupt the binarizing of sexual identities, but that it is equally valuable to disrupt the gender binarism. In fact, of the three characters in Naylor's quartet who subvert the capitalist/compulsory heterosexuality conjunction, only Stanley and Eve—the two who also defy strict gender categories—are able to achieve economic success.

When we review Naylor's oeuvre, we see that in the first two novels of her quartet she examines heterosexuality as a political institution and exposes the seemingly inextricable link between economic success and compulsory heterosexuality. In doing so, she shows the difficulties one has in performing a homosexual identity in a capitalist economy. In her last novel, Naylor further illustrates the problems raised by this conflation by showing some of the ways in which women are hurt even when they conform to heterosexual norms. In showing women who have been destroyed by heterosexuality and the capitalist system, Naylor points out another set of limitations of the system that prevails in *Linden Hills*. Through illuminating these various, tangled problems, Naylor is not offering simple answers; on the contrary, her novels, when taken as a whole, suggest that capitalism and sexuality are intertwined in ways that render their relationship even more complicated than it is usually recognized to be. Although she does present characters who succeed economically (Stanley and Eve), they do so within the limbo of *Bailey's Cafe*. Therefore, overall, Naylor manages to complicate the relationships between sexual identity and capitalism, and, to a lesser degree, between body and gender identity by elaborating a spectrum of sexuality that defies the strict binarism of hetero-/homosexuality and highlights the instability of such categories. This effort creates a crack in the link conjoining capital success with heterosexual performance, a crack that may well be widened through further interrogation.

Notes

1. Moreover, by including gay men, who defy and therefore challenge the notion of traditional or conventional masculinity, she is working to destabilize the hegemonic position of straight males.

2. Lorraine's father's words resonate with those spoken by Eve's Godfather after he discovers "the game" she plays with Billy Boy. I address this issue later.

3. The Nedeeds' dependence on repetition in order to maintain their power is quite similar to Judith Butler's notions in "Imitation and Gender Insubordination" about the ways in which heterosexuality's privileged position is perpetuated; however, such an analysis is beyond the scope of this argument.

Works Cited

Butler, Judith. "Imitation and Gender Insubordination." In *The Lesbian and Gay Studies Reader*. Eds. Henry Abelove, Michele Aina Barale, and David M. Halperin. New York: Routledge, 1993. 307–20.

D'Emilio, John. "Capitalism and Gay Identity." In *The Lesbian and Gay Studies Reader*. Eds. Henry Abelove, Michele Aina Barale, and David M. Halperin. New York: Routledge, 1993.

Gates, Henry Louis, Jr. "Significant Others." *Contemporary Literature* 29, no. 4(1988): 606–23.

Levy, Helen Fiddyment. "Lead on with Light." In *Gloria Naylor: Critical Perspectives Past and Present*. Eds. Henry Louis Gates, Jr., and K. A. Appiah. New York: Amistad, 1993. 263–84.

Naylor, Gloria. *Bailey's Cafe*. New York: Harcourt, Brace, Jovanovich, 1992.

———. *Linden Hills*. New York: Penguin, 1985.

———. *The Women of Brewster Place*. New York: Penguin, 1983.

Rich, Adrienne. "Compulsory Heterosexuality and Lesbian Existence." In *The Lesbian and Gay Studies Reader*. Eds. Henry Abelove, Michele Aina Barale, and David M. Halperin. New York: Routledge, 1993. 227–54.

Sedgwick, Eve Kosofsky. "Axiomatic." In *The Cultural Studies Reader*. Ed. Simon During. New York: Routledge, 1993. 243–68.

Good Housekeeping

Domestic Ritual in Gloria Naylor's Fiction

Maxine Lavon Montgomery

The days it wasn't laundry between the 5:15, 7:20, 11:55, and 3:12, it was sewing. And the days it wasn't sewing, it was firing and scraping the cast-iron pots. And the days it wasn't that, it was working on her garden. But each day all activity stopped when Daniel came home.

—Gloria Naylor, *Bailey's Cafe*

Bailey's Cafe, the fourth in a series of novels by Gloria Naylor, culminates with a utopian portrait of a home place constructed around Mariam, an Ethiopian Jew, and her newborn son, George. What makes this portrait of a radically transformed domestic space so compelling is not only the eclectic mix of individuals present (there is an international group of individuals representing various races, religions, and cultures), but the inclusion of men and women, many of whom defy gender-specific labels. Indeed, when one pauses to consider the journey to *Bailey's Cafe*, in terms of both Naylor's development as a creative artist and the trek her characters make while en route to this elusive site,[1] one realizes that the journey is filled with representations of the housewife, beleaguered by an endless round of cooking, cleaning, and mothering. Whether it is Lucielia Louise Turner, who must work outside the home and then find time to do housework and mother her daughter Serena; or Evelyn Creton-Nedeed, who is confined to the kitchen; or the feisty working-class woman Jesse Bell, whose culinary skills, as much as her sexuality, are directed toward pleasing her man, Naylor's female characters often find themselves mired in domesticity. A consummate literary craftsperson whose canon reveals her keen awareness of the plight of women of color worldwide, Naylor foregrounds the domestic plot as have other women writers, but she does so in a way that directs attention to the cultured and gendered context out of which her novels evolve.

Far from being a replica of domestic novels by white women writers, Naylor's texts mirror the unique realities of black women. Black feminist theorists have argued persuasively for a reading of black women's texts that takes into account the interlocking influences of race and gender,[2] and as far as black women's domestic novels are concerned, those novels reveal black women's domesticity as being bound within a distinct history traceable to slavery. In a manner unlike their white counterparts, black women have inhabited two spheres of work: a paid labor force (or slave economy) and a private home, either theirs or those of whites (Jones 1985, 4–7). Black women, in other words, because of larger social, economic, and political conditions, have not only had to participate in the workforce, they have had to be good housekeepers as well. The ex-slave Nanny in Zora Neale Hurston's classic text *Their Eyes Were Watching God* lends dramatic emphasis to this reality when she tells her naive granddaughter Janie of being both a "work ox" and a "brood sow" (1978, 31). Nanny is doubly marginalized within a hierarchical plantation system. She had to work from sunup to sundown in the fields along with black men, and in her own home she was not afforded the security or material comforts free white women enjoyed. Nanny was subject to the white slave master's sexual advances and the reproaches of a jealous mistress. Emancipation liberated Nanny from slavery, but not from the burdens of domesticity, as she became a maid for the Washburn family. Her broom and cook pot are domestic staples allowing Nanny to provide for herself and her daughter, Leafy.

Like Hurston's text, Naylor's first novel, *The Women of Brewster Place*, fictionalizes these two worlds of work, along with the psychological tensions accompanying the attempt on the part of marginalized women to establish and maintain domestic order. The women in the community find their lives circumscribed by, in the words of Stephen Henderson (1969), "survival motion." Theirs is an attempt to negotiate a way through the strictures of a bureaucracy that is white and patriarchal. With the exception of community activist Kiswana Browne, the women in the text reside on Brewster because there is no other place for them to go. Brewster is, in a very real sense, the end of the road. The lesbians Theresa and Lorraine entertain the possibility of living elsewhere, but the truth underlying their situation is that there is no other place to which they could go. Society's persistent homophobia will always limit the women's ability to find acceptance.

Naylor's focus on the lives of the urban poor results in the creation of a community where women must work outside of the home or, like Cora Lee, depend upon public assistance. Mattie Michael is a single mother whose arrival in the city brings her a heightened awareness of the need for economic security, so she joins countless others in the frustrating search for employment and affordable housing. As her son, Basil, grows older, Mattie's desire for a home prompts her to assume two jobs in order to carry the mortgage. Lucielia Louise Turner offers to take a second job when she learns that she is again pregnant. For the women in the community, participation in the paid labor force is a necessity stemming from the desire for stability.

It is this same desire that motivates the women in their attention to domestic tasks. While their work outside the home fails to rescue the community from the mandates of the political system responsible for Brewster's creation, the women's performance of so-called women's work within the confines of their own home becomes a way of redefining traditional notions of "home." Nowhere is this more apparent than in Cora Lee's narrative, in which Naylor explores the potentially subversive dimensions of black women's domesticity. Cora Lee, like many of the women in the text, is socialized to embrace the roles of wife and mother. Her parents gave her a doll each Christmas while she was a child, preparing Cora Lee for a specifically gendered place within the domestic sphere. As an adult, Cora Lee is little more than a breeder, bearing seven children by six different men. Her relationships with these men are only temporary ones based upon sex, and the men are quick to resort to violence whenever she fails to attend to her housekeeping chores. A visit from Kiswana Browne, along with the excitement of attending Abshu Ben-Jamal's production of *A Midsummer Night's Dream,* prompt an awakening on Cora Lee's part. For the first time Cora Lee realizes the connection between her attention to domestic tasks and her children's futures. Naylor's focus on Cora Lee's evolving consciousness reveals the young woman's musings on her childhood love for school and on her brother and sister residing in Linden Hills. That evening Cora Lee, who had neglected her home and her children, devotes her time to washing, pressing, and mending her children's worn clothing. She even intends to make certain she attends PTA meetings and checks her children's homework assignments. At the play she envisions her daughter Maybelline saying fine things onstage. On the way home, her son Sammy asks her if Shakespeare was black, and she responds optimistically, "Not yet," feeling guilty that she had beaten him for writing rhymes on her bathroom walls (*WBP*, 127).

The ending of Cora Lee's narrative, with its account of the return of a male visitor who lets himself in with his own key, is disappointing in light of the awakening the woman undergoes. When the reader next sees Cora Lee, it is during Mattie Michael's dream-nightmare of the block party, and Cora Lee is pregnant again. Nevertheless, her narrative directs attention to the revolutionary potential associated with the performance of domestic tasks, especially when politically conscious women carry out the tasks necessary to the maintenance of the home, and thereby explores the close relationship between the home place and the creation of a utopian society where there is freedom from socially imposed restraint. The kind of housekeeping the women of Brewster Place carry out in the privacy of their own living spaces represents the women's insistence on maintaining the kind of home place that bell hooks refers to as "a site of resistance and liberation struggle" (1990, 45). Such a revisioning of the idea of "home," as hooks points out, is not only political but distinctly womanist in nature, for it reflects the historical tendency on the part of black women to use the home as a site from which to effect positive change within an oppressed black community. Attention to domestic tasks among marginalized women becomes a means of withstanding the imposition of an indifferent and, at times, hostile bureaucracy.

Major hindrances to the creation of a utopian society that consists mainly of marginalized women arise from both a white, patriarchal system and black women themselves. Because of their social conditioning, these women often carry the burden of guilt when their relationships with men are unstable. Rather than assert themselves in challenging the men in their lives, the women sometimes insist on remaining in a subservient posture. This is Lucielia Louise Turner's dilemma. It is Eugene's inability to find suitable employment that is the catalyst for many of the couple's arguments, and when he loses yet another job, he directs his anger toward Ciel. She, in turn, blames herself for their problems. Naylor offers insight into Ciel's psychology while the young woman carries out her daily housekeeping tasks. Instead of voicing her anger over Eugene's protestations when he learns that she is pregnant with their second child, she folds their towels with greater intensity. Ciel is in a state of denial even after Eugene tells her that he is leaving again. She remains quiet during his tirade as he blames her for their economic situation, but while Ciel rinses rice in preparation for dinner, her thoughts reveal her silent frustration: "The second change of the water was slightly clearer, but the starch-speckled bubbles were still there, and this time there was no way to pretend deafness to their message. She had stood at that sink countless times before, washing rice, and she knew the water was never going to be totally clear. She couldn't stand there forever—her fingers were getting cold, and the rest of the dinner had to be fixed, and Serena would be waking up soon and wanting attention. Feverishly she poured the water off and tried again" (*WBP*, 94). Just as Ciel is unsuccessful at ridding the water of starch, she is unable to suppress the truth concerning her marriage to Eugene. Ciel then places the pot of rice on the stove and continues cooking.

Ciel's persistent attention to the daily routine associated with housekeeping and mothering, even in a socioeconomic context that suggests the women's efforts at maintaining an orderly home are futile, takes on ritual dimensions in narrative action (Romines 1992, 10–14). Collectively, through a repetition of the chores such as cooking and cleaning, Ciel engages in the completion of tasks, which suggests the possibility of transcending the difficult reality she faces. It is Ciel who, with Mattie's careful maternal guidance, reverses the psychologically destructive effects of temporality and enters a realm peopled by bereaved mothers across time and space. In the most moving scene in the text, Mattie bathes Ciel, and the ritual act allows the two women to share in a global community of women, one centered around the mother-child relationship.

Mattie, everybody's mother and the first in a long line of larger-than-life maternal figures in Naylor's canon, is the medium through whom the community's hopes for a radically transformed future are channeled. Given her prominence among the women in the community, it is only fitting that Mattie dreams the women's collective dream. Jill Matus is correct in her reading of Mattie's dream of the block party in terms of that dream's thematic, linguistic, and sociopolitical relevance to the evolution of the novel (1990, 133–38). What is especially important to an understanding of Naylor's concern with domesticity is the dream's reflection of history. The women's hopes for freedom, given fullest expression in Mattie's dream, along with their collective efforts at tearing down the brick wall, mirror the revolutionary spirit present during the Black Power Movement, which has inspired Kiswana and Abshu. Naylor leaves no question that tearing down the wall is women's work, stressing the important role women have played in furthering the goal of black freedom. While the men of Brewster Place are noticeably absent during the event, the women assume center stage in challenging the white male power structure that has attempted to define the community's reality.

Thus, at the close of the novel, because of the women's devotion to good housekeeping, the community's final end is indefinitely forestalled. The home place is destroyed, but not the women's communal bond (Levy 1992, 204). In "Dusk," the omniscient narrator mentions the ritual tasks that have consumed much of the women's time and energy: "But the colored daughters of Brewster, spread over the canvas of time, still wake up with their dreams misted on the edge of a yawn. They get up and pin those dreams to wet laundry hung out to dry, they're mixed with a pinch of salt and thrown into pots of soup, and they're diapered around babies. They ebb and flow, ebb and flow, but never disappear. So Brewster Place still waits to die" (*WBP*, 192). The performance of domestic rituals therefore suggests a violation of the temporality that the novel's strict dawn-to-dusk structure implies, as the novel concludes with Brewster Place poised both in and out of time and space, either en route to or defying its promised end.

Whereas the home place in *The Women of Brewster Place* is a potentially revolutionary site revealing urban black women's survivalist tendencies, in *Linden Hills* the home place is an arena under patriarchal domination divorced from the political struggle of contemporary black America. The Nedeed wives are guardians of notions of women's place and duty that bourgeois ideology perpetuates; and as a result, they become unwitting co-conspirators with their male counterparts in female subjugation. In this context, the Nedeed home, a large, white clapboard structure built during the antebellum era, is a locale where the hierarchical sociopolitical structure responsible for the marginalization of black women is replicated. The Nedeed wives are little more than their husbands' servants, and the Sisyphean housekeeping tasks the women carry out place them in a hell-like state that is even more debilitating than that which the residents of Brewster Place experience.

Naylor levels a stinging indictment of marriage as a social institution in this second novel. Because of societal conditioning, the women who marry into the Nedeed family do so primarily in hopes of finding an identity within a staunchly middle-class setting. What they discover is that marriage to an upwardly mobile, propertied businessman such as Luther Nedeed not only fails to occasion any personal fulfillment, it furthers the women's sense of "otherness." As Angela Davis puts it, "the housewife, according to bourgeois ideology, is, quite simply, her husband's lifelong servant" (1981, 225). The central dilemma that the Nedeed wives face is that they have no self apart from the social role each assumes in her pursuit of marriage and middle-class respectability. Luwana Packerville-Nedeed sums up the irony surrounding the women's plight: "Was she so busy being needed that it never dawned on her she wasn't being married?" (*LH,* 118). Unlike the women of Brewster Place, the Nedeed wives do not have to participate in a paid labor force, so their work all takes place in the confines of their own home. Here, isolated from the larger community, the women fashion tenuous selves that depend on establishing domestic order and harmony.

The Nedeed wives, like the other residents of Linden Hills, fail to look inward at the mirror, which, according to Grandma Tilson, can allow an individual to form an identity apart from the institutions, conventions, and ideals of bourgeois society. "So you keep that mirror," Lester relays his grandmother's timely advice, "and when it's crazy *outside,* you look inside and you'll always know exactly where you are and what you are" (*LH,* 59). While confined to the basement of the Nedeed home, Willa reads herself through a perusal of the documents revealing the "shared domestic tragedies of the Nedeed wives" (Levy 1992, 213). Those documents—cookbooks, diaries, and photographs—reflect who Willa is, or more accurately, who she is not. Only as Willa acknowledges her true self—an act figured by the discovery of her name—does she acquire the self-confidence necessary to ascend the stairs leading to the Nedeed kitchen. In the fictional world Naylor constructs, then, knowledge is liberating, for like slaves whose introduction to literacy brought about a desire for freedom, Willa's newfound knowledge motivates her to rise from her subjugated state, and she does so in the midst of housecleaning.

Narrative emphasis on the daily tasks the women perform, along with a focus on different sites within the home, reveals the imposed limits of female domesticity. The bedroom, for instance, is the place where the Nedeed wives are subjected to male desire and privilege. Once the women help to fulfill their husbands' patriarchal goal of fathering a son, the husbands lose interest in them. Willa tries to put the spark back into her marriage by visiting New York and trying various beauty products designed to enhance her sex appeal, in addition to consulting *Cosmopolitan* and *Ladies Home Journal.* She rejects the shame-weed her great-aunt Mama Day recommends as a way to regain Luther's affection. For all of Willa's efforts at restoring her marriage, though, Luther remains cold and distant. Luther's punishment of Willa and young Luther—confining mother and son to the basement for her alleged infidelity—is his way of ensuring his control in a situation where female sexuality is a potential threat to Luther's hegemonic rule.

Just as the Nedeed men view female sexuality as a threat, so, too, do they consider women's culinary art a possibly subversive medium. The kitchen thus becomes a battleground in the war between the sexes. After learning of a woman in Tennessee who was hanged for poisoning her master's soup, Luwana Packerville-Nedeed's husband feels compelled to hire a housekeeper to cook and wash (*LH,* 119). Evelyn Creton-Nedeed devotes so much time and energy to cooking that the kitchen is her entire reality: "The woman cooked as if she were possessed. What drove her to make that kitchen her whole world?" (*LH,* 141). Willa recognizes in Evelyn's meticulous handwriting evidence of the woman's fanatical dedication to good housekeeping: "This woman never had a curl out of place, a ribbon knotted loosely, a stick of furniture not glowing with lemon oil. She gave the right parties at the right time for the right people. There were two sets of china and silverplate, a suit for each occasion, a set of boots for each season—and a porcelain exterior that accented whatever room it was placed in. There were probably a dozen words that the friends and enemies of the Nedeeds used to describe her, but one of them just had to be 'perfect'" (*LH,* 187). When Evelyn's marriage begins to deteriorate further despite her efforts, her attention to cooking becomes compulsive. She spends countless hours at grocery stores purchasing food and then recording the buying of the ingredients she hopes will allow her to restore her marriage. Gradually, as if to indicate the discord that is the ironic end result of Evelyn's fanatical devotion to cooking, her attention to food gives way to overeating and purging, with her recipe books chronicling her retreat into insanity.

The documents that the Nedeed wives author attest to the home as a place of bondage and subjugation. In fact, Willa's awakening to self, which occurs in terms of a rebirth, is occasioned by a knowledge of what Barbara Christian refers to as "herstory," a history both by and about women (1993, 116). In discovering "herstory," Willa discovers herself. This discovery renders Willa's decision to reenter the Nedeed home at the novel's end highly ambiguous. On the one hand, she appears to challenge the place to which bourgeois society would consign housewives; on the other hand, Naylor's rendering of the woman's psychology during the cleaning of the Nedeed home suggests that Willa is still operating within a socially prescribed context. As Naylor points out in an interview with Toni Morrison, Willa enjoys being a housewife, much to the author's dismay (Naylor and Morrison 1985, 587). Willa is either unable or unwilling to abandon externally imposed definitions of domesticity; indeed, the narrator describes Willa's ascent to the home, saying "each step was bringing her closer to the kitchen and the disorder whose oblivion was now inextricably tied to her continuing existence" (*LH,* 297). Consequently, her ascent to the home constitutes only a partial triumph over Luther's hegemonic rule.

Linden Hills thus offers a powerful commentary on the dangers of a domesticity divorced from community empowerment. Rather than being liberating, either for themselves or the larger community, the tasks that the Nedeed wives perform lead to madness, solitude, and despair. The women in the novel affirm the vital sisterhood that Larry Andrews (1993) sees as central to the text, but they fail to enact positive sociopolitical change. In this sense, Willa's housekeeping at the novel's end is both destructive and self-destructive. The entire Nedeed family falls victim to the disorder Willa, alone, tries futilely to contain.

The destruction of the Nedeed home, a patriarchal construct relegating women to the position of subservient "other," is an apocalyptic prelude to the creation—in *Mama Day*—of Willow Springs, a post-catastrophic Eden peopled by semi-divine women. George, an urbanite from New York, and his wife, Cocoa, journey to this female pastoral site where the tasks associated with maintaining the home closely approximate what Kathryn Rabuzzi describes as "housework as ritual enactment" (1982, 96). Women's work, such as the cooking the female characters complete in preparation for Candle Walk (the community's alternative to Christmas), or the midwifery that Mama Day performs in her attempts to assist Bernice, suggests the women's reconnection with the sacred time of Willow Springs' beginnings. In *Mama Day*'s fictional world, women are guardians of indigenous culture, and their efforts at maintaining the home place allow them to reaffirm a vital spiritual oneness with island matriarch Sapphira Wade.

The legend of Sapphira Wade, an ex-slave whose radical redefinition of black female domesticity is figured by the bill of sale announcing Bascombe Wade's purchase of her, is central to narrative action, and her stormy marriage to Wade reveals the complex gender and race issues George and Cocoa must work through. Sapphira subverts the patriarchal ownership claims Bascombe Wade would assert and establishes an autonomous self free of externally imposed definitions. As the bill of sale reads, Sapphira is "inflicted with sullenness and entertains a bilious nature, having resisted under reasonable chastisement the performance of field or domestic labour. Has served on occasion in the capacity of midwife and nurse, not without extreme mischief and suspicions of delving in witchcraft" (*MD*, 1). Sapphira refuses to allow whites or men to proscribe her actions. That the women in the text ascribe divine status to her is a telling commentary on their attempts to continue the legacy Sapphira bequeaths.

More than in her previous texts, Naylor here explores the subject of black female spirituality in the creation of a radically transformed home place constructed around the mother-daughter relationship. The novel's genealogy suggests the exalted role of women as creators and bearers of cultural tradition. Mama Day, born to the seventh son of a seventh son, is a conjure woman whose contact with the supernatural allows her to transcend externally imposed notions of female place. Her knowledge of various herbs allows this elder wise woman to establish a reputation that rivals that of Dr. Smithfield. When Cocoa is ill, Mama Day offers George cryptic advice that, ironically enough, results in Cocoa's recovery and George's untimely death. Nevertheless, Mama Day's influence is a positive one ensuring a continuation of a matrilineal past.

The women's involvement in what Houston Baker labels "spirit work" allows them to transcend the gender-specific roles that those beyond the bridge would prescribe. It also enables them to link their private tasks to the welfare of the island community (1993, 282). The women's use of magic can be destructive, as Ruby's jealousy indicates, but the supernatural is an important medium in redefining the home place. Weeks of cooking in preparation for Candle Walk unify the women. Similarly, quilting, a repetitive task that Mama Day and Abigail carry out, is an art form suggesting the women's reconstruction of their family history, a history that Cocoa and George are to maintain. The rift between Cocoa and George concerning the placement of the finished quilt points to the ideological differences between the two and recalls the central conflict in Alice Walker's "Everyday Use." Cocoa wishes to place the quilt on the couple's bed while George wishes to hang the quilt up in their living room.

This rift is important, for even George's journey to Willow Springs fails to occasion his acceptance of a woman-centered world. His is a fear of the female principle, symbolized largely by the hens on Mama Day's property (Meisenhelder 1993). His visit to the chicken coop near the novel's end suggests Naylor's ambivalence concerning George's role in narrative action. It is as if the masculine principle with which George is closely associated must be sacrificed if Willow Springs' matrilineal society is to continue.

In *Mama Day*, then, the home place exists without boundaries and offers the possibility for rebirth and renewal. Far from being mundane or burdensome, women's work takes on spiritual dimensions, allowing black women to transcend imposed notions of female place. The novel is a key text revealing women's expanding sphere of influence, even as it signals Naylor's artistic focus on women's spirituality.

The portrait of a radically transformed home place constructed around Mariam and George in *Bailey's Cafe* represents a culmination of Naylor's artistic focus on domesticity. The seven narrators whose stories comprise the novel are united by, among other things, the tasks they perform relative to the home—either theirs or someone else's. Naylor suggests that house-work is one of few jobs available to black women, especially those in the city, and while such work is not profitable in an economic sense, the perfor-mance of domestic tasks can help to liberate women worldwide from the tyranny of patriarchy.

What distinguishes domestic ritual in Naylor's fourth novel from its manifestation in her earlier novels is not so much the kind of tasks the women carry out in maintaining the home; rather, it is the geographical scope of Naylor's focus. More than in her previous novels, Naylor directs attention to the plight of women in a global community whose devotion to the routine tasks associated with housekeeping and mothering results in a loss of self. Not surprisingly, then, the new world order emerging in the novel's climactic scene—involving the birth of George—arises outside the home, the space within which the oppression of women has been situated. Susan Willis's observation—that the utopian future black women writers inscribe is to be developed out of the old, familiar places that circumscribe women's lives—is thus relevant here (1987, 218). Narrative emphasis on magic, or the power of conjure, makes the kind of transformation resulting in a reconfigured home place entirely believable, for in the changing, post-apocalyptic society giving birth to *Bailey's Cafe,* anything is possible.

Naylor's inclusion of Miss Maple, the housekeeper and bouncer whose performance of domestic ritual is both efficient and economically profit-able, is preceded by her focus on the housewife beset by a daily routine filled with cooking, cleaning, sewing, and mothering. Sadie, who feels she must turn to prostitution when her work as a maid fails to provide her with economic security, is a woman whose situation typifies the dilemma the women face. Sadie is socialized to believe that her self-worth is predicated upon her success as a homemaker, so she tries to become the ideal house-keeper, first, in order to win her mother's approval and, later, that of her elderly husband, Daniel. In an effort to support herself after her mother's death, Sadie becomes a maid at a house of prostitution, and her daily rou-tine is characterized by nearly constant cooking, washing, and ironing. Moreover, her employer, a white female prostitute, is quick to remind Sadie of the realities of race: "It's a shame you're a nigger, Sadie, the blonde confided one slow evening, or you could make out really well here" (*BC,* 48).

Instead of releasing Sadie from her enslavement to domestic tasks, her marriage to Daniel heightens her feelings of bondage. The couple resides in a squalid, three-room shanty near the railroad tracks on Chicago's south side. That Naylor chooses to associate Sadie's repetitive performance of the daily chores necessary for maintaining domestic order with the rhythmic pace of nearby trains suggests the inescapable and burdensome monotony of women's work. Despite her fanatical devotion to good housekeeping, Sadie will never be able to transform their shanty into the space she has dreamed of inhabiting. Daniel's declaration that "Woman, this is my damn house" (BC, 55) directs attention to what Sandra Gilbert and Susan Gubar refer to as the architecture of patriarchy and thus to the imprisonment Sadie experiences (1979, 85). Daniel's death frees Sadie from an unfulfilling marriage, but not from her enslavement to domesticity. Sadie, an aging widow, turns to prostitution when she fails to make a living from day cleaning. Her move to a women's shelter marks the end of her futile search for a home, and her displacement underscores the plight of aging women of color in the city.

If Sadie's narrative indicates the burdensome nature of housework in the lives of marginalized women, it reveals as well the possibility of transforming the home into a place where women, in particular, experience a measure of freedom, dignity, and creativity. Sadie envisions a romantic dinner with Iceman Jones. After dinner, the two share cleanup responsibilities, and Jones offers to polish Sadie's crystal. Unlike with Sadie's marriage to Daniel, then, Sadie's imagined relationship with Jones is one where gender roles are as fluid as the space out of which Bailey's Cafe emerges. Existing everywhere and nowhere, the cafe is situated "on the margin between the edge of the world and infinite possibility" (BC, 76). This liminality is also significant to Eve, the novel's central mother-figure, who encourages a reconceptualization of the patriarchal ideology that has restricted the women's achievement. Her garden is a liminal space where she is free to express her creativity; and having defined herself on her own terms on her trek to that garden, she can assist other women in their journeys toward wholeness.

Miss Maple's arrival at Bailey's Cafe marks the end of his search for a place in modern America. At Eve's, he is someone who encourages a reconceptualization of so-called women's work. Naylor intends Miss Maple to be the alternative to the burdened housewife, for unlike the women in the text, he not only works only half a day but is free to write award-winning jingles. Not surprisingly, the jingle that brings him the most satisfaction is one generated as a result of his research into the new attitudes of American housewives desirous of a dishwashing detergent "that would leave them feeling both married and sexy" (BC, 215).

Finally, in a womanist revision of the classic Christmas story, the text culminates with a portrait of a radically transformed global society where all externally imposed labels are blurred.[3] Prefigured in *The Women of Brewster Place* by the women's communal efforts at dismantling the restrictive brick wall, the utopian post-war new world order that emerges in *Bailey's Cafe* is constructed around Mariam, a type of madonna who gives birth to the future, figured by young George. Mariam, the outcast mother, is a bridge between the past and future in terms similar to those Daryl Dance sets forth. "She is unquestionably a Madonna," Dance writes regarding the African-American mother, "both in the context of being a savior and in terms of giving birth and sustenance to positive growth and advancement among her people" (1979, 131). Eve, whose act of scoring the plum is a ritual reversal of the genital mutilation that Mariam endures, assumes the role of midwife in George's birth.[4] Consistent with the woman-centered cosmology that Naylor re-creates, a new social order appears with a family of choice replacing the traditional nuclear family. Naylor elevates the women in the text to a position of honor with a revisioning of the once restrictive home place. It is Peaches who, at first, intones the gospel song inscribing the sacred identities of Mariam and George: "Anybody asks you who you are? / Who you are? / Who you are? / Anybody asks you who you are? / Tell him—you're the child of God" (*BC,* 225). As the other members of the group join in with the singing of the popular Christmas carol, now a cultural code among an international community of marginalized people, their voices re-create a call-and-response pattern expressing the hope for world peace: "Peace on earth, Mary rocked the cradle./Mary rocked the cradle and Mary rocked the cradle./Peace on earth, Mary rocked the cradle./Tell him—was the child of God" (*BC,* 226).

In the fiction of Gloria Naylor, then, the home is not a neutral space but is relevant to the struggle for freedom from oppression. Ordinary tasks associated with maintaining domestic order assume political dimensions, liberating women from patriarchal domination and uniting them with a community of women across time and space. The liberation Naylor fictionalizes is to be global in scope and will include men and women worldwide. Naylor's texts imply that routine tasks such as cooking, cleaning, and mothering can be means of furthering the cause of freedom, and her novels chronicle an expansion of her artistic and political vision as women move—without moving—from margin to center.

Notes

1. Tananarive Due (1992) mentions Naylor's envisioning her first four novels as a series and *Bailey's Cafe* as the text which, in Naylor's opinion, establishes her as a serious writer.

2. I refer to critics such as Deborah McDowell, Barbara Christian, Barbara Smith, and others whose writings reveal a black feminist or womanist approach to the tradition of black women's literature.

3. Naylor employs a rhetorical strategy reminiscent of that which Reverend Jesse Jackson uses in pointing out the hypocrisy of the republican presidential administration, whose social policies reveal an insensitivity to the particular needs of historically disenfranchised groups. In Reverend Jackson's carefully aimed broadsides, the biblical Mary is a symbol for the economically disadvantaged single mother and King Herod a figure for an indifferent and at times hostile political system.

4. Naylor's treatment of genital mutilation or female circumcision recalls that involving Tashi in Alice Walker's *Possessing the Secret of Joy* (1992).

Works Cited

Andrews, Larry R. "Black Sisterhood in Naylor's Novels." In *Gloria Naylor: Critical Perspectives Past and Present*. Eds. Henry L. Gates, Jr., and K. A. Appiah. New York: Amistad, 1993. 285–301.

Baker, Houston. "Workings of the Spirit: Conjure and the Space of Black Women's Creativity." In *Zora Neale Hurston: Critical Perspectives Past and Present*. Eds. Henry L. Gates, Jr., and K. A. Appiah. New York: Amistad, 1993. 280–308.

Christian, Barbara. "Naylor's Geography: Community, Class and Patriarchy in *The Women of Brewster Place* and *Linden Hills*." In *Gloria Naylor: Critical Perspectives Past and Present*. Eds. Henry L. Gates, Jr., and K. A. Appiah. New York: Amistad, 1993. 106–25.

Dance, Daryl C. "Black Eve or Madonna?: A Study of the Antithetical Views of the Mother in Black American Literature." In *Sturdy Black Bridges: Visions of Black Women in Literature*. Eds. Roseann P. Bell, Bettye J. Parker, and Beverly Guy-Sheftall. New York: Anchor Press, 1979. 123–31.

Davis, Angela. *Women, Race, and Class*. New York: Random House, 1981.

Due, Tananarive. "Naylor's Specialty: Bruised Characters in Soul-Searing Tales." *Miami Herald* 8 (Nov. 1992): F2.

Gilbert, Sandra, and Susan Gubar. *The Madwoman in the Attic: The Woman Writer and the Nineteenth Century Literary Imagination*. New Haven: Yale University Press, 1979.

Henderson, Stephen. "Survival Motion: A Study of the Black Writer and the Black Revolution in America." In *The Militant Black Writer in Africa and the United States*. Eds. Mercer Cook and Stephen Henderson. Madison: University of Wisconsin Press, 1969. 65–129.

hooks, bell. *Yearning: race, gender, and cultural politics*. Boston: South End Press, 1990.

Hurston, Zora Neale. *Their Eyes Were Watching God*. Urbana: University of Illinois Press, 1978.

Jones, Jacqueline. *Labor of Love, Labor of Sorrow: Black Women, Work and the Family, from Slavery to the Present*. New York: Random House, 1985.

Levy, Helen Fiddyment. *Fiction of the Home Place: Jewett, Cather, Glasgow, Porter, Welty, and Naylor*. Jackson: University Press of Mississippi, 1992.

Matus, Jill. "Dream, Deferral, and Closure in *The Women of Brewster Place*." *Black American Literature Forum* 24 (1990): 49–63.

Meisenhelder, Susan. "The Whole Picture in Gloria Naylor's *Mama Day*." *African American Review* 27, no. 3 (1993): 405–419.

Naylor, Gloria, and Toni Morrison. "A Conversation." *Southern Review* 21. 3 (1985): 567–93.

Naylor, Gloria. *Bailey's Cafe*. New York: Harcourt Brace Jovanovich, 1992.

———. *Linden Hills*. New York: Ticknor and Fields, 1985.

———. *Mama Day*. New York: Vintage, 1993.

———. *The Women of Brewster Place*. New York: Penguin, 1982.

Rabuzzi, Kathryn Allen. *The Sacred and the Feminine: Toward a Theology of Housework*. New York: Seabury Press, 1982.

Romines, Ann. *The Home Plot: Women, Writing, and Domestic Ritual*. Amherst: University of Massachusetts Press, 1992.

Willis, Susan. *Specifying: Black Women Writing the American Experience*. Madison: University of Wisconsin Press, 1987.

Metaphor and Maternity in *Mama Day*

Amy K. Levin

The title of Gloria Naylor's third book, *Mama Day,* suggests that the novel will concern maternity. Yet Miranda Day, the title character, is *not* a biological mother. She has never married or borne a child. Instead, as the ruling matriarch of the Day family and the island community of Willow Springs, as healer, advisor, midwife and conjurer par excellence, the old woman offers a model of mothering based not on biological kinship or the Freudian reading of the nuclear family, but on female solidarity and a vision of women's leadership that can be traced to West African women's traditions.

Recent critical discussions on mothers and motherhood in novels by African-American women writers have, for the most part, participated in the feminist dialogue concerning mothers and daughters. For instance, Marianne Hirsch's *The Mother/Daughter Plot* analyzes works by Alice Walker and Toni Morrison in light of the myth of Oedipus. Instead of following a Freudian reading and concentrating on Oedipus, Hirsch focuses on Jocasta. Although this perspective gives a new dimension to Hirsch's interpretations of literature, her reading remains dominated by the Greek myth and a Eurocentric theoretical framework that obscures African influences in Walker's and Morrison's writing.

Other discussions of maternity in African-American women's fiction have departed from European archetypes, comparing fictional characters to mothers in actual African-American families and attributing their strength to economic, political, and cultural circumstances. Such critics as Celeste Fraser have taken this perspective on Gloria Naylor's first novel, *The Women of Brewster Place,* as well as on works by other authors, such as Paule Marshall. Similarly, in "Trajectories of Self-Definition: Placing Contemporary Afro-American Women's Fiction," Barbara Christian describes Silla Boyce in Marshall's *Brown Girl, Brownstones* sympathetically: "the role of *mother* for this black woman is in conflict with her role as *wife,* because of the racism that embattles her and her community. Marshall's novel . . . was certainly affected by society's attitude that black women were matriarchs, domineering mothers who distorted their children who in turn disrupted society—a vortex of attitudes that culminated in the Moynihan Report" (1985b, 239).

In *Being & Race,* Charles Johnson takes this mimetic assumption one step further, suggesting that "It is against this depressing, perhaps even disastrous background of the black family's internal contradictions and near collapse that we must understand the angrier work of some black women authors" (1988, 96). Yet in their more magical moments, many novels by African-American women reject both sociological mimeticism and reductive psychoanalytic theories. In Morrison's *Beloved,* Sethe, a silent woman, must resolve her relationship with the ghost of a daughter. And in *Mama Day,* the title character renders a woman fertile and saves her great-niece from a hideous curse.

Indeed, a review of novels by African-American women in the last half of this century reveals a multitude of texts that diverge from the "realistic" mode, with its negative depictions of maternity and its emphasis on the "black family's internal contradictions." The portraits of mothers in urban poverty are balanced by those of women in rural communities and small towns. The latter novels often combine two elements: a positive model of maternity (or female leadership) and a trace of magic or the supernatural.

This touch of the supernatural indicates that the authors' aesthetic interests are not limited to depicting the "depressing" nature of urban life for many African-Americans. Instead, surreal elements in novels may be read as signs of an African presence, while the mother figures may be viewed as expressions of a conception of female authority derived from West African women's traditions. Such a reading privileges what is distinctively female and African. In doing so, it complements much contemporary criticism of literature by African-American women, which focuses on feminist and/or

African-American aspects of texts, but rarely on the African part of the African-American appellation. Increasingly, critical works, such as *The Signifying Monkey,* by Henry Louis Gates, Jr., do trace African influences, but these do not consistently distinguish between male and female traditions. For instance, Lindsey Tucker suggests that Mama Day is a trickster in the tradition of the Yoruban Esu-Elegbara (1994, 182), described by Gates in *The Signifying Monkey.* Yet despite Gates's claim that Esu is "genderless, or of dual gender," "his remarkable penis feats" render this claim paradoxical, and the comparison of Mama Day to Esu is questionable as well (Gates 1988, 29). It is the argument of this essay instead that *Mama Day* harkens back to distinctly female African traditions.

The necessity for such novels has been indicated by Patricia Hill Collins in *Black Feminist Thought,* as well as by other Afrocentric feminist scholars. Collins's book is built on the premise that Africans in America gained some authority by "retaining significant elements of West African culture" and that "the knowledge produced in Black communities was hidden from and suppressed by the dominant group" (Collins 1991, 10). Throughout the book, Collins traces black American women's West African heritage, considering the importance of "othermothers" and strong maternal leaders (Collins 1991, 115–23). She asserts that female bonding is further evident in an "ethic of caring" (Collins 1991, 215) derived from African traditions. Yet these qualities of African-American women's lives are often absent from cultural products; in particular, Collins decries the effects of "controlling images," such as "the mammy" and Jezebel, which "form a nexus of elite white male interpretations . . . meshing smoothly with systems of race, class, and gender oppression" (Collins 1991, 70–8). Collins argues that these "controlling images" should be replaced by an "Afrocentric feminist aesthetic for beauty" (1991, 88) and, indeed, by developing her story around strong women who are influenced by African traditions, Gloria Naylor succeeds in presenting an alternative to the dominant culture's representations of black women.

Barbara Christian's "An Angle of Seeing: Motherhood in Buchi Emecheta's *The Joys of Motherhood* and Alice Walker's *Meridian* (1984)" also provides a conceptual framework for reading *Mama Day.* Christian traces the relationships between traditions of motherhood in West Africa, and especially in Nigeria, and the behavior of characters in two contemporary novels. Christian effectively summarizes the varied and often contrasting views of motherhood in West Africa, noting sources of women's subordination as well as of their power. She shows how conventions that devalue women, such as the bride price, oppress mothers. At the same time, she explains, women's organizations and other traditional structures empower women, giving them support and some measure of control over their lives (Christian 1985a, 214–15).

Christian describes these exclusively female organizations, or secret societies, as sisterhoods that "buttress" women, providing friendship and the aid of peers (1985a, 215). Yet these closed societies are also strongly hierarchical in their structure, which repeats the ranking of women within families, from senior wives down to junior wives. The societies fulfill many maternal functions, and their leaders act as surrogate mothers, educating adolescent girls. If we expand our discussion of African traditions in contemporary women's novels beyond biological motherhood, we can include these leaders, thereby gaining useful insights into the magic of such novels as *Mama Day,* as well as into Naylor's other novels—most notably *The Women of Brewster Place,* in which Mattie Michael provides a moral center for the women on her street, and *Bailey's Cafe,* in which Eve offers a refuge for outcast women. Naylor's most recent book, *The Men of Brewster Place,* is less magical, but deals with similar issues as they apply to men by focusing on definitions of manhood and male leadership in an environment detached from traditions and such rituals as initiation ceremonies.

West African women's secret societies with their female forms of leadership have existed for hundreds of years, and it is hard to imagine that every trace of their traditions was erased with the slave trade. More likely, secret society beliefs and practices were transmitted directly and indirectly in a variety of forms, including folk medicine, superstitions, and tales about conjurers or tricksters. Some of the most obvious vestiges of secret society rituals are found in voodoo, as Margaret Creel has shown in *"A Peculiar People": Slave Religion and Community-Culture Among the Gullahs.* Other remnants of African traditions are apparent in practices in Gullah communities, which are similar to Willow Springs in *Mama Day.* The sources of such inherited rituals and beliefs have been largely forgotten by those who still practice them, and secret society traditions have gradually been woven into the fabric of African-American life. These traditions surface in novels and other forms of art, rendering a multicultural angle of interpretation appropriate and illuminating.

A close reading of *Mama Day* in the context of these women's secret societies suggests ways of understanding the novel that go beyond surface allusions to canonical works, such as *The Tempest, Hamlet,* and *Clarissa.* The superiors of West African women's secret societies offer a version of

maternity that is not based exclusively on biological kinship or a cata-
strophic view of the family. This model emphasizes earned respect as well
as a conception of the female community itself as family.

The Sande society of Sierra Leone, the Ivory Coast, and contiguous regions seems particularly pertinent to discussions of *Mama Day* because
Sande is widespread and strong. As Margaret Creel has shown, many of the
Gola slaves brought to the coastal areas of South Carolina belonged to
Sande or its male counterpart, Poro (Creel 1988, 45–52). These societies
were also common to the Mende people, who were actively involved in the
slave trade (Creel 1988, 41). Moreover, although information on all of the
secret societies is difficult to obtain, the practices and rituals of Sande are
relatively well documented, largely due to Sylvia Ardyn Boone's excellent
book-length study of the organization, *Radiance from the Waters: Ideals of
Beauty in Mende Art*. Boone's descriptions of Sande iconography are fundamental to understanding how the society's leadership may be used as a
model for understanding maternity in *Mama Day*.

As Boone indicates, Sande is a society of women who have reached the
age of puberty. Young women are admitted following an initiation ceremony and an induction period, during which they are taught the essentials
of Sande medicine, etiquette, and law. Only after their initiation are Sande
women permitted to marry; thus, initiation is ordinarily a prerequisite for
motherhood. Moreover, while biological mothers play an important role in
their children's upbringing, Sande controls mothering by training pregnant
women in the necessary skills and by joining biological mothers in teaching
their daughters. Ultimately then, Sande offers a model of maternity that is
based not solely on biological kinship (or even the duties Western society
associates with mothering), but on seniority and earned respect.

A critical structural feature of Sande is that it parallels the hierarchy of
women in the family, where a senior wife trains and supervises junior
wives. The head wife, like the local Sande leader or *Sowei,* is referred to as
"a mother and a mistress and [a junior wife] will call her *yie,* 'mother,' or
ma, 'lady'" (Boone 1986, 6). Encoded in Mama Day's very name is this
metaphorical concept of maternity, which involves female leadership as
well as the responsibilities associated with biological motherhood in European and American societies. Miranda Day is not called mama because she
is a biological mother, or because she has acted as a mother toward others
around her, but because she is the "lady" or leader of the women in Willow
Springs. While Europeans and Americans also use words for "mother" as
names for older women (such as Old Mother Hubbard of nursery rhyme
lore), the application of this term to such characters as Mama Day is differ-

ent because, like Sande leaders, they command enormous respect and authority.

A summary of the duties of the Sande Sowei, or leader, reveals deeper similarities between her position and Mama Day's role in her community. The Sowei is a powerful woman who is elected to office. Much of her power is directly attributable to her knowledge of society secrets from which other members are excluded. Another distinguishing feature is the Sowei's mastery of society practices. She knows its techniques of healing, she dances in its rituals, and she wears the black *sowo* mask, which is the embodiment and articulation of the society's ideals. As Boone indicates, sowo means expert (1986, 28), and, as such, the leader is responsible for supervising the education of initiates, perpetuating society traditions, and adjudicating in marital disputes. The Sowei oversees women's regular retreats to a special enclosure, where they gain further training and often fatten themselves to become more fertile. Finally, the Sowei is powerful because she is a liminal being. Monni Adams interprets the blackness of the Sowei's wooden mask as a symbol of the mystery of the woods and the spirits that inhabit them; worn into town by the leader of the society, the mask represents the taming and control of anarchic forest spirits. Thus, the Sowei is one who links forest and village, the spirit realm and the human world, order and chaos (Adams 1982, 62).

Several other features of the female leaders of secret societies, and especially Sande, are important to our discussion. In many societies, the leaders carry intricately carved staffs of office. The societies have their own private words or languages and give their members special names that may indicate their rank (Butt-Thompson 1969, 30–32, 33). Furthermore, many societies appoint an anti-leader who plays a complex but crucial role in the life of the community. In Sande, this figure is called *Gonde*. If the Sowei is expert in all the female arts, her mask an expression of the beauty of her soul, her tiny, slit eyes a sign of her mystery, then Gonde is, in contrast, a vision of failure. Her clothing is torn and disreputable, her gait unsteady, her behavior frequently ridiculous. She "coaches" the initiates, but she is also "a funny, lovable character who lightens the gloom and reminds everyone that Sande is not always so deadly serious" (Boone 1986, 30).

According to Boone, Gonde is essential to the structure of Sande society: there are "two masks because it takes *both* to *express fully* the realities of the social milieu"; Gonde is compared to one of the "rival chiefs who always struggle against each other publicly" even though they are "united in their basic aims and ideology." The two are "complementary" (Boone 1986, 39). While the Sowei represents and exercises control (Adams 1982,

62), Gonde resembles the woman who has "let herself go" (Boone 1986, 40). The ridicule heaped on Gonde minimizes the threat such a woman poses to the order and stability of the community, and especially to male power.

Other aspects of Sande offer explanations for important parts of *Mama Day* and are inextricable from Naylor's portrayal of maternity. First, hair-braiding is an important art form in Sande, where it is considered an expression of woman's beauty. Female hair, in its abundance, is seen as a sign of fertility, and is thus not to be handled casually. In fact, hair is so important that one should only allow a trusted associate to braid it, for "Offering to plait another woman's hair is a way of asking her to become your friend. A beautiful, distinctive style is considered a gift of love" (Boone 1986, 189).

Another expression of Sande is the chicken, woman's confidant and protector. The bird alerts women of approaching danger. But more than that, the chicken, which may accompany a woman in her daily tasks, is a sign of domesticity, of community: "The Mende word for chickens, *te,* and the word for town, *ta,* are the same in the definite, *tei*" (Boone 1986, 210). The chicken is associated with Sande in another way, too. Like the Sowei, the chicken is a liminal creature, capable of traveling on the ground or in the air, of perceiving internal and external realities. Frequently carved on the crown of the sowo mask, a chicken signifies "clairvoyance"; in addition, "Chickens [are] able to see into the human heart" (Boone 1986, 208, 210). The sowo mask is also often topped with carvings of snakes, which represent goodness; when they are combined with chickens or birds "the theme seems to be the certainty and inevitability of struggle, and the probability of a stalemate at best" (Boone 1986, 214–15).

These and other elements of Sande iconography are prominent in *Mama Day*. The connections between Sande and the novel permeate the very structure and texture of the narrative, deepening the portrayal of maternity therein. Mama Day functions as a Sowei in Willow Springs, controlling communication and the women in the community. Her arch-rival Ruby fulfills the role of Gonde and is integral to the working of the plot. The chicken Clarissa, like her counterparts in Sande, is an extension of the Sowei. And, just as much Sande activity revolves around the search for worthy successors to transmit the society's values, the conflict in Naylor's plot may be derived from Miranda Day's hope that her great-niece (called Ophelia, Cocoa, or Baby Girl, depending on the context) will continue her traditions.

The importance of finding a female to succeed Mama Day as matriarch of Willow Springs is in part due to the weakness of the men in the community. The male inhabitants of Willow Springs are shadowy and passive, at best powerless and at worst ridiculous. Doctor Buzzard, who might be considered Mama Day's male conjurer counterpart, is a gambler who cheats at cards. His only medicine is the liquor he distills in the woods outside of town. Instead of confronting or controlling spirits, he is terrified by Mama Day's joking imitations of ghosts in the woods. Another man, the son of Reema, the hairdresser, is an anthropologist so obsessed with jargon that he has forgotten the language of the people around him. Ambush Duvall, despite his powerful name, is dominated by his mother, Pearl. And Junior Lee is a ridiculous figure, ruled by his wife, Ruby.

To all intents and purposes, then, Willow Springs is a matriarchal society, its roots going back to the slave girl Sapphira who murdered her master, Bascombe Wade, after he deeded her his land. Sapphira later walked over a cliff into the ocean, away from her seven sons. Yet Sapphira has lived on in the minds of her descendants, her death the subject of whispers. Her name comes to Mama Day in a dream after she has prayed to the "Father and Son as she'd been taught" (*MD*, 280), suggesting that Sapphira inhabits a powerful realm beyond the level of consciousness. She has become a mythical figure because of her strength and ruthlessness—after all, a man died because he loved her, and she abandoned seven sons. In fact, Sapphira is viewed as the "Great Mother" of Willow Springs, the first in a line of strong mother figures, of whom Mama Day is the latest. Sapphira herself is never named publicly (*MD*, 4), as if to name her were to invoke powers too awesome to face. Sapphira's death is commemorated in a local ritual called Candle Walk or "18 & 23 night," in which the inhabitants of Willow Springs march through the town carrying candles, singing and chanting "Lead on with light, Great Mother" (*MD*, 111). Gifts are exchanged on the occasion; in particular, the villagers bring tokens of their respect to the current matriarch, thanking her for her beneficent offices during the year and paying homage to her magical abilities.

Significantly, Sapphira's sons and their descendants do not bear Wade's name, but one she chose—Day. Although the Day family has produced seven sons of seven sons, the line has run to women. The story of Sapphira who "could break a man's heart" (*MD*, 151) and leave her children has been repeated several times over the centuries as other women have drowned deliberately or accidentally, leaving their men to die for them and their children to grieve.

Despite the dwindling size of the family, the Days have remained influential in Willow Springs. In fact, the community, much like Sande, revolves around Mama Day's authority. Her slight stature belies her strength. Within her family, she has taken her mother's place since the latter's death, helping to raise her siblings and their children and grandchildren. Within the community, she has occupied a position of leadership. Her authority, like that of the Sowei, has various sources. First, she is associated with birth and fertility in a number of ways. As midwife, she has assisted at the births of most of the children on the island, having "Caught babies till it was too late to have my own" (*MD*, 89). Mama Day also possesses the secrets to enable other women to become fertile; when young Bernice Duvall fails to conceive, Mama Day works with her until she becomes pregnant.

Mama Day is the healer on the island, too. She cures Bernice Duvall's cysts and is an expert at herbal remedies. As in Sande, Mama Day's remedies are as much spiritual as physical; she can remove a curse, and part of her remedy for Bernice's infertility involves planting seeds. Even though Mama Day lacks formal medical training, she has gained the respect of Dr. Smithfield from the mainland as well as of the other townspeople.

But the greatest source of Miranda Day's power is her knowledge of family mysteries. Mama Day alone regularly traverses the graveyard to the "other place," the old family homestead, repository of its secrets. She goes there to work her magic with Bernice; the remedy for Ophelia's curse must be found after a journey to the "other place" as well. In fact, even though the "other place" was originally the plantation of Bascombe Wade, it has become equivalent to a female enclosure, visited by women on errands with Mama Day. Significantly, the only male who is allowed to enter the "other place" is doomed to die, because, like male visitors to the enclosures of West African women's societies, he presents a challenge to female authority.

In addition to ruling over the mysteries of the "other place," Mama Day also possesses the power of divination, which goes beyond intuition. She knows when the weather is about to turn. She can see into her great-niece's heart and discover that Cocoa is in love. And most important, she senses the approach of evil and death. Finally, Mama Day has linguistic power. She knows just how to phrase a letter to Cocoa to achieve a desired response. She knows how to persuade Bernice to trust her. She has used language as well as medical knowledge to gain the respect of the mainland doctor.

Mama Day's powers are accompanied by several of the marks of the Sowei's authority. The matriarch carries an intricately carved walking stick that she has inherited from her father. This stick becomes associated with its bearer; it functions as a staff of office. Although the snakes carved on the sides of the stick (*MD*, 88) may be read as symbols of Satan, a reading that centers the "otherness" of African women's societies emphasizes their beneficent aspects, and is more consistent with Mama Day's personality. Finally, Mama Day spends a great deal of time tending to her chickens, which are ultimately extensions of her will and protectors of the order on Willow Springs.

Just as the Sowei in Sande must preoccupy herself with the transmission of society's values, Mama Day must find a worthy successor. Cocoa is the last remaining Day, and she has the requisite strong will. As Mama Day indicates, "If I had known then what I was knowing all along, I woulda named her something else. Sapphira" (*MD*, 151). Cocoa has inherited the blackness of the sowo mask, the darkness that indicates mystery and power over nature and people: "*the* Baby Girl brings back the great, grand Mother. We ain't seen 18 & 23 black from then till now. The black that can soak up all the light in the universe, can even swallow the sun" (*MD*, 48).

Yet Ophelia poses a problem in this respect. Cocoa has left Willow Springs for another island, Manhattan, where she has been quick to acquire a false polish, an odd dialect, and a disregard for family traditions. What really draws Ophelia away from Mama Day's influence, though, is her marriage to George Andrews, a strong, independent businessman. George's background is the antithesis of Willow Springs; an orphan, he knows little about his kin. His last name, inherited from the benefactor of the orphanage where he grew up, indicates no blood ties. As George himself comments to Cocoa, "You had more than a family, you had a history. And I didn't even have a real last name" (*MD*, 129).

Within the structure of Naylor's novel, George represents an African-American culture that has been torn from African traditions; he is ignorant of the identity of his mother, Mariam, an Ethiopian refugee (which is revealed in *Bailey's Cafe*). Thus, even though he is only a second-generation American, he is more deracinated than are the inhabitants of Willow Springs. His scientific, rationalistic bias has failed to prepare him for the mystical nature of knowledge in Willow Springs, and his congenital heart defect is an expression of his emotional rigidity. Because of his personality, he draws Cocoa further away from her roots, making it unlikely that she will succeed Mama Day. In fact, George refuses to accompany Cocoa to Willow Springs for her annual vacations, and he only yields under (real or feigned) duress the year most of the events in the novel occur.

George's much postponed visit to Willow Springs precipitates the climax of the narrative. The intrusion of a strong male in the matriarchal community of the coastal island immediately disrupts its order; the fact that this male is an engineer who scoffs at magic and folk medicine heightens the disruption. George underestimates Mama Day, believing he "was reasonable in expecting wrinkles, sagging skin, some trembling of the limbs" (MD, 175), and thus offends her pride. After Miranda leads him on an exhausting walk through the woods, though, he begins to respect her strength. She in turn is convinced of his limitations, which she treats somewhat humorously. But George threatens the matriarchy in another way as well. During the first half of the novel, Naylor stresses that George and Cocoa's relationship is based on a struggle for power, and by the time the two reach Willow Springs, this battle is being played out in George's desire to have a child. If George and Cocoa do conceive a baby, it will be even more unlikely that Cocoa will return to the women's community of Willow Springs. Therefore, much as she desires her niece's happiness, Mama Day has cause for wanting the relationship to fail. Although Lindsey Tucker suggests that George becomes an "initiate" (1994, 182), he must be removed from the island for the order of Willow Springs to be perpetuated. This creates a dilemma—as beneficent matriarch and loving great-aunt, Mama Day is not prepared to initiate the process.

Another woman on the island, Ruby, ultimately takes care of the problem for her. Ruby is presented as Mama Day's rival. She is a heavy, slattern woman, her eyes "pressed into tiny slits" (MD, 134) resembling those on a Sande mask. For the most part, Ruby is a grotesque figure of fun and ridicule. Yet Ruby is extremely protective of her husband, Junior Lee, and will use magic to eliminate any rival. In fact, she has led Junior Lee's previous lover to her death. When Cocoa catches Junior Lee's eye, Ruby casts a spell to eradicate her new rival, a spell that ultimately has the effect of killing George. Thus, although Ruby initially appears to be Mama Day's rival and opposite, an Afrocentric perspective enables us to see that Ruby functions as an extension of Mama Day, just as Gonde works in concert with the Sowei.

Together with Abigail, Mama Day and Ruby form a complete image of maternal leadership. Abigail, who bears the name of the second president's wife, offers an Americanized vision of womanhood. Although she assists Mama Day in nurturing and educating, she shows no desire for leadership. Her assimilation into the dominant culture is most evident in her exclusion from the secrets of Mama Day's medicine and her absence from the other place. She complements Mama Day and Ruby, who transcends ridiculous qualities to represent the sexual, angry aspects of womanhood. Ruby's energy is reflected in the disorder with which she is associated, while her power is apparent in the fact that Mama Day herself fears Ruby's spells.

Ruby's manner of placing a curse on Cocoa seems drawn directly from West African traditions, for she offers a false gesture of friendship, braiding Cocoa's hair into an elaborate style. As she does so, she rubs Cocoa's scalp with a poisoned pomade. Cocoa, who has been away from the island and is not initiated into its secrets, cannot "read" Ruby's intentions, and this ignorance leads to disaster. Had she been living on the island, Cocoa would have known that Ruby has "rubbed out" other rivals in the past in a similar manner; she would have respected Ruby's power.

Instead, Cocoa is doomed to suffer a hideous illness that causes her physical and mental agony. For a time, her life is in danger. George finds himself frustrated and helpless. A storm seems to conspire with the women to cut the island off from the mainland, preventing George from rushing his wife to a "real" doctor. He is thrown back on Mama Day's resources, provoking a confrontation between their opposing worldviews. It will take nothing less than recourse to magic to rescue Cocoa, recourse to magic that involves cutting off her braids and destroying Ruby's house. The remedies of the mainland doctor favored by George will not suffice.

If George is frustrated because he cannot rely on science to cure his wife, Mama Day is distressed because "'It's gonna take a man to bring her [Cocoa] peace'—and all they had was that boy" (*MD*, 263). The two characters are so far apart that they do not speak the same language; as Mama Day says, "We ain't even got his kind of words to tell him what's going on" (*MD*, 267). Even the characters' definitions of the problem are different. George acknowledges a conflict between his rationalistic view of the world and Mama Day's intuitive, mystical knowledge. Mama Day has a broader perspective, which includes George's assessment of the conflict as well as the problem of finding a worthy successor. She knows that the real battle is over possession of Cocoa.

The resolution must weave together these different strands. It must preserve Cocoa; it must reduce Ruby's power; and it must eliminate George before he draws Cocoa away from Mama Day's influence permanently. Mama Day's design ultimately fulfills all of these objectives. She acts at once as judge, doctor, and guide.

Mama Day sends George to the old chicken coop with the family walking stick and ledger, ordering him to bring back whatever he finds under the nest of the old red hen, Clarissa. These are odd instructions, indeed, and they invoke the West African dimensions of mothering in the novel. In the walking stick, George is taking a reminder of Mama Day's rank and power. Bearing the family ledger, he carries its history by his side. And, as he enters the chicken coop, an enclosure at once rural and female, he is completely removed from all that is familiar to him. George is puzzled to find nothing under the hen's nest—and this discovery elicits a moment of insight: "But there was nothing to bring her. *Bring me straight back whatever you find.* Could it be that she wanted nothing but my hands?" (*MD*, 300). Still, George remains unsure about Miranda's purpose: "There was nothing that old woman could do with a pair of empty hands. . . . All of this wasted effort when these were *my* hands, and there was no way I was going to let you [Cocoa] go" (*MD*, 301). Unwittingly, George stumbles on the truth—that Mama Day wants him to offer all he has, to relinquish Cocoa.

The hen, Clarissa, valiantly pecks away at this intruder in her realm, defending Mama Day's territory by attacking George. Her behavior is consistent with Sande iconography in several ways. Most obviously, she protects her owner and the community. In addition, both Ruby (because of her name) and the rust-colored hen are associated with the color red. The chicken also shares Ruby's massive proportions, her thick neck, and her jealousy (*MD*, 300); in fact, the two are metaphorically related. Clarissa, like Ruby, ultimately functions as an agent or extension of Mama Day. Her pecking forces George to lash out with such fear and frustration that his fragile heart gives out, and he dies.

George's death reconfirms Mama Day's power over Ophelia, who admits that "one of my worlds" had ended (*MD*, 302). Miranda visits the "other place" a final time on the next Candle Walk night, knowing she will not return again because "the other place holds no more secrets that's left for her to find. The rest will lay in the hands of the Baby Girl—once she learns how to listen" (*MD*, 307). Like Bascombe Wade and some of his descendants, George has died because he has attempted to possess what man cannot own; he is "another one who broke his heart 'cause he couldn't let her go" (*MD*, 308). His death opens the path for Cocoa's initiation, for her learning to listen and to understand her heritage, to reach back to "the beginning of the Days" (*MD*, 308).

Mama Day's victory is tempered by her understanding that Cocoa must "go away to come back to that kind of knowledge [about the Days]" (*MD*, 308) as well as about the reasons for her husband's death. Just as the bird and snake together on the sowo mask suggest the inevitability of conflict, the story that links the chicken and the snake-carved walking stick is repeated over and over in a man's struggle to control one of the strong Day women. The succession of the Days assured for the time being, Cocoa moves to Charleston. But Naylor makes clear that Charleston is not completely beyond the family's influence, for Cocoa walks "in the midst of familiar ground" there (*MD*, 308–9). Her new husband is "second-best" and does not try to wield as much power over her as George did (*MD*, 309). Cocoa eventually bears two sons, thus perpetuating the family and preparing for the struggle to be renewed in future generations. The closing scene of the novel shows Mama Day at peace on Willow Springs.

Mama Day may rest at the end of the novel because she has succeeded in finding someone to "listen" and carry on her traditions. She has fulfilled her role as leader on the island, removing obstacles to her power, curing the spiritually and physically infirm, and working in concert with her protector, the hen Clarissa, and her complement, Ruby.

Our reading of the novel is deepened and complicated by attending to the various references to West African women's closed societies, which allow us to understand the workings of magic in the text as well as the role of such characters as Ruby, who appear to be enemies of Mama Day, yet ultimately work her will. This angle of reading also allows us to understand how Mama Day can initially approve of George's influence over the recalcitrant Cocoa but later turn against him when he poses a threat to her own authority over Cocoa. Finally, this perspective helps us to accept Cocoa's second marriage, which we are encouraged to approve of, even though in many ways it represents a diminishment of the love and passion Cocoa experienced with George.

Moreover, though the connections to African traditions are most evident in *Mama Day*, similar visions of maternity and female leadership are evident in Naylor's other works as well. In *The Women of Brewster Place*, Mattie Michael (like Eva before her) leads the community of women, providing continuity with the past (*WBP*, 103). She rocks Ciel through her grief after she loses her baby, and she dreams of unity at the end of the book. To some extent, her friend Etta Mae Johnson functions as a Gonde figure. Etta Mae Johnson is the picture of vibrant sexuality: "She stood out like a bright red bird among the drab morality that dried up the breasts and formed rolls around the stomachs of the other church sisters. This woman was still dripping with the juices of a full-fleshed life" (*WBP*, 67). This physical appearance is only one manifestation of her rebelliousness, for she is "a black woman who was not only unwilling to play by the rules, but whose spirit challenged the very right of the game to exist" (*WBP*, 59). Her complementarity to Mattie is most evident when Mattie offers to bake a cake for Ciel's wedding and Etta Mae volunteers to dance at the event (*WBP*, 178). Nevertheless, in the world of Brewster Place, Etta Mae is largely powerless, as is apparent when she comes home to Mattie after failing to marry the reverend. Finally, while the pairing of Mattie and Etta Mae exemplifies Naylor's use of dual leaders, *The Women of Brewster*

Place also offers a successor in Kiswana Browne, who adopts an African name, treasures the statue of an Yoruban god, and strives to unite the community in a tenants' association. Although Kiswana previously inhabited the community of Linden Hills, which assimilated the norms of mainstream white society, she is attempting to reconstruct or revive her heritage.

In *Bailey's Cafe,* Eve's house serves a function similar to a Sande enclosure, as Eve takes in women of all ages who have suffered as a result of their relations with men. This suffering acts as their initiation, a symbolic excision (and while many of them carry physical scars, one of them has actually been circumcised). Like Sande enclosures, Eve's home functions as a retreat; Mariam gives birth while living there, Jesse Bell goes through drug withdrawal, and the flowers surrounding the house are evidence that it rests on fertile soil. Although male visitors are allowed into the house, they are required to follow Eve's regulations, or "they can stay away" (*BC,* 92). The only male member of the community is named Miss Maple, and he wears female garments for a considerable portion of the year (not only does he find dresses cooler, but they come to represent his marginality in the white working-class world). Moreover, Eve's house is surrounded by a certain mystery. Bailey, the narrator, cannot explain what makes a woman "ready" for Eve's or how Eve decides what to charge for rent (*BC,* 80). Others in the community gossip curiously about Eve's, wondering whether it could be a "whorehouse," because they have no other way of categorizing the female household (*BC,* 81). Significantly, although Eve's is central to the book and most of the intertwined narratives focus on women, the novel's title refers to a male-owned space, a circumstance that indicates the liminal nature of the female society.

Naylor's fifth book, *The Men of Brewster Place,* also refers to a male space. While the book focuses on men, Naylor indicates that "there was always a Her in his story" (Naylor 1998, 8), frequently delineating the role of a man. Like Naylor's first book about the same locale and many of the same characters, *The Men of Brewster Place* is generally in a realistic mode, though Naylor performs some authorial magic by reviving the character Ben, who died in *The Women of Brewster Place.* Part of Ben's story takes place on a plantation whose geographical location is as elusive as that of Willow Springs: "No point in looking for it on the map 'cause Richland only existed in the map of our minds" (Naylor 1998, 11). And significantly, Ben, who traces the stories of the last generation of Brewster Place men, is named after the youngest of Jacob's sons.

An important scene in *The Men of Brewster Place* is reminiscent of Mama Day frightening Dr. Buzzard in the forest by howling like a ghost; in this case, the Reverend Moreland Woods (whose very name recalls the setting of the scene in *Mama Day*) is ridiculed at a church board meeting for his pretentious claims to have heard the voice of God. Seymour, a young actor, hides, making sounds and calling the minister's name, thus mocking the call from God and exposing its falsity. Like Dr. Buzzard, Reverend Woods is revealed to be a sham, using false magic to take advantage of others. And appropriately in this case, the tormentor is an actor, whose name indicates that he can "see more" than what is on the surface.

Beyond these allusions to "other" kinds of knowledge, *The Men of Brewster Place* explores what happens to men who are separated from their roots, while suggesting that initiations into racism, humiliation, and violence have replaced more traditional rituals for entering and acknowledging manhood. Ben presents the dilemmas in his initial account of his grandfather's childhood. The grandfather's sister dies after being raped by a white man, and when he objects to a minister's false piety at the funeral, his mother slaps him, saying "Shut your mouth. Be a man" (Naylor 1998, 16). From the beginning then, silence and manhood are equated.

Throughout *The Men of Brewster Place,* Naylor's characters variously pose the question "What does it mean to be a man?" (Naylor 1998, 28), struggling with the way manhood is defined for them because of their race and class. Ben, for instance, comments that "We called ourselves boys even though in my late twenties I was the youngest one there" (Naylor 1998, 19). Eugene's erratic behavior toward his wife is explained when readers learn that he is gay; his struggle comes out of the gap between "everything I [Eugene] believed a black man should be" and his homosexuality (Naylor 1998, 71). C. C. Baker, an antagonist in *The Women of Brewster Place,* kills his brother on orders from a drug lord known as the Man and thanks "God for giving him the courage to . . . be a man" (Naylor 1998, 129). In contrast, Brother Jerome, named after the biblical scholar, is apparently developmentally impaired but is nevertheless able to make his "piano tell any story that he wanted. And it was *your* story if you listened real hard" (Naylor 1998, 32). Where males are oppressed by definitions of manhood, Jerome offers a hope and an irony—suggesting that the truth comes not from God, as father, or his representatives (Moreland Woods and the minister at the funeral), but from a perpetual child, one who communicates nonverbally.

The final episode of the text occurs in the male enclosure of a barbershop, recalling the barbershop George visits in *Mama Day:* "If those chairs could talk, they would be at it day and night with sadder and sadder stories" (Naylor 1998, 161). Greasy, another character who is mentally impaired, keeps repeating "I am a Man" (Naylor 1998, 165). One day, he holds a razor to the barber's throat. When the men try to stop Greasy, he slits his own throat. Realizing that they have scapegoated him, made him "the garbage can to hold all our fears" (Naylor 1998, 167), the men feel unsettled both by the life and death of Greasy. Significantly, his death signals the demise of Brewster Place as well: "Max's place [the barbershop] will be the last holdout. . . . This is the only place for us men to get together, to look into each others' eyes and see what we need to see—that we do more than just exist—we thrive and are alive" (Naylor 1998, 167). Thus, the men's story ends in a pessimistic vein, in contrast to the tempered optimism offered through the possibility of the transmission of traditions at the end of *Mama Day*. Ironically, the bleakness reinforces the importance of those traditions, memorializing their passing.

Naylor's other largely male-narrated novel, *Linden Hills*, is even more problematic in an Afrocentric context. Mama Day herself surfaces to visit her relatives, and she brings recipes to make wayward men attend to their wives. A type of conjure is also evident in the formulas that Willa Nedeed discovers in the basement. These recipes, tested by one of her predecessors, point to a central theme of the novel—the disastrous consequences of the fragmentation and suppression of the female community with their assimilation into the middle class. Generations of Nedeed women have been obliterated by their husbands, so thoroughly that one is actually seen fading out of her own photographs. Other women in Linden Hills find themselves alone or unhappy, devoid of any female support. Lester Tilson's sister Roxanne affects an Afro, but refuses to assist in the liberation of Zimbabwe (*LH*, 57). Her prospective husband, Xavier, is deeply troubled about her dark color and sees it as deleterious to his career. When Lycentia Parker dies, her husband has every trace of her removed from the house even before her funeral is over; and when Laurel Dumont divorces, she is evicted from the community. Such alienation, which radically contrasts the strong network of female associations in *Mama Day*, indicates what happens to mainland women deprived of ties to a female community rooted in an African past. They are exiled from history, which in Linden Hills is told only in terms of male genealogies.

Thus, Naylor's other works—*The Women of Brewster Place, Linden Hills, Bailey's Cafe,* and *The Men of Brewster Place*—reinforce the importance of connections to an African model of female leadership, both directly and indirectly. Naylor makes this point in a unique fashion, but it is nevertheless an iteration of a theme Carolyn Cooper finds increasingly common in works by black women globally: "In all of these feminist fictions of the African Diaspora the central characters are challenged, however unwillingly, to reappropriate the 'discredited knowledge' of their collective history. The need of these women to remember their 'ancient properties' forces them, with varying degrees of success, to confront the contradiction of acculturation in societies where 'the press toward upward social mobility' represses Afrocentric cultural norms" (1992, 84). Naylor in particular values independence for women, rather than their being controlled by men. She privileges women's connections to other women and establishes a model of family continuity in distinct opposition to the broken African-American families found in many other novels. In this positive vision of maternity, two sides of womanhood—the wise, beneficent matriarch and the angry, jealous sexual female—are shown to be inextricably connected. One side acts for the other. Finally, in *Mama Day*, Naylor asks us to hear as our own voice (*MD*, 10) the mystical knowledge of that "other place" where the rationalistic laws of the mainland "don't apply" (*MD*, 5). Reading the secrets of Mama Day, we, too, are initiated into her wisdom, so that ultimately the text reaches out to us, replicating the relationship between Mama Day and Cocoa in the bond between author and reader.

Works Cited

Adams, Monni. *Designs for Living.* Cambridge, Mass.: Harvard University Press, 1982.

Boone, Sylvia Ardyn. *Radiance from the Waters: Ideals of Beauty in Mende Art.* New Haven, Conn.: Yale University Press, 1986.

Butt-Thompson, Captain F. W. *West African Secret Societies.* 1929; rpt. New York: Argosy Antiquarian, 1969.

Christian, Barbara. "An Angle of Seeing: Motherhood in Buchi Emecheta's *The Joys of Motherhood* and Alice Walker's *Meridian* (1984)." In *Black Feminist Criticism: Perspectives on Black Women Writers.* Ed. Barbara Christian. New York: Pergamon Press, 1985a. 211–52.

———. "Trajectories of Self-Definition: Placing Contemporary Afro-American Women's Fiction." In *Conjuring: Black Women, Fiction, and Literary Tradition.* Eds. Marjorie Pryse and Hortense J. Spillers. Bloomington: Indiana University Press, 1985b. 233–48.

Collins, Patricia Hill. *Black Feminist Thought.* New York: Routledge, 1991.

Cooper, Carolyn. "'Something Ancestral Recaptured': Spirit Possession as Trope in Selected Feminist Fictions of the African Diaspora." In *Motherlands: Black Women's Writing from Africa, the Caribbean, and South Asia.* Ed. Susheila Nasta. New Brunswick, N.J.: Rutgers University Press, 1992. 64–87.

Creel, Margaret Washington. *"A Peculiar People": Slave Religion and Community-Culture Among the Gullahs.* New York: New York University Press, 1988.

Fraser, Celeste. "Stealing B(l)ack Voices: The Myth of the Black Matriarchy and *The Women of Brewster Place.*" In *Gloria Naylor: Critical Perspectives Past and Present.* Eds. Henry Louis Gates, Jr., and K. A. Appiah. New York: Amistad, 1993. 90–105.

Gates, Henry Louis, Jr. *The Signifying Monkey: A Theory of African-American Literary Criticism.* New York: Oxford University Press, 1988.

Hirsch, Marianne. *The Mother/Daughter Plot: Narrative, Psychoanalysis, Feminism.* Bloomington: Indiana University Press, 1989.

Johnson, Charles. *Being & Race: Black Writing Since 1970.* Bloomington: Indiana University Press, 1988.

Morrison, Toni. *Beloved.* New York: Plume, 1987.

Naylor, Gloria. *Bailey's Cafe.* New York: Harcourt Brace Jovanovich, 1992.

———. *Linden Hills.* New York: Penguin, 1985.

———. *Mama Day.* New York: Vintage, 1989.

———. *The Men of Brewster Place.* New York: Hyperion, 1998.

———. *The Women of Brewster Place.* New York: Penguin, 1982.

Tucker, Lindsey. "Recovering the Conjure Woman: Texts and Contexts in Naylor's *Mama Day.*" *African American Review* 28 (1994): 173–88.

Africana Womanist Revision in Gloria Naylor's *Mama Day* and *Bailey's Cafe*

Dorothy Perry Thompson

In their attempts to analyze the texts in Gloria Naylor's complicated tetralogy—*The Women of Brewster Place, Linden Hills, Mama Day,* and *Bailey's Cafe*—critics have often appropriated Eurocentric approaches that run the gamut from finding Chaucerian and Shakespearean analogues to employing Derridean theories of absence. Feminists have seized Naylor's oeuvre eagerly, exploring its dense symbology for delineations of oppressed women prevalent in the texts, especially *Linden Hills* and *Bailey's Cafe.* Given Naylor's personal history, as it informs her work, such discursive authorities, or sites of meaning, seem valid. She's an American female with an ivy league education—a B.A. in English from Brooklyn College and an M.A. from Yale in African-American studies. She knows deconstruction and the tenets of feminism as well as she knows the Eurocentric canon, which revolves on its Shakespearean-and-the-like axis. However, in *Mama Day* and *Bailey's Cafe,* Naylor continues her efforts at an intertextuality that mandates consideration of how both novels participate in the discursive practices of an "Other" culture and a gendered ideology that does not separate itself from that culture so that it can be dubbed simply "feminist."

Jacquelyn de Weever notes that the voice of the African-American female writer changes the "traditional double-voicedness of the Black American experience into a triple-voiced enterprise, one based on a triangular culture" (1991, 26). Concluding that no writer in this century can escape prior texts, de Weever claims that this fact is especially true of the African-Americans whose work must include the dualities of this heritage (1991, 25). As "expressive culture texts," to use Houston Baker's term, that add the dimension of *woman* to race, *Mama Day* and *Bailey's Cafe* embody codes and modes of signification and figurations that must be examined in terms of a praxis that includes the identifying elements of race and gender.

In interviews, presentations, and most importantly, in her literary oeuvre, Naylor has aligned herself with what can be described best as Africana womanism.[1] She gives us figurations that are distinctly African in origin (especially in *Mama Day*), and female characters who are more *womanish* (to recapitulate the origin of Alice Walker's coinage) than their sisters/cousins in *The Color Purple,* the novel that spawned the genre of contemporary womanist fiction. Shug, for example, is *outrageous* and *audacious,* and Sofia, in her actions, is *courageous* and *willful,* all characteristics identified by Walker in her definition of womanist.[2] But Walker's women in the novel ultimately recede, somewhat, from the reactionary stances that make them womanish as they settle into traditional roles as mates for their men.[3] Celie and Shug end their lesbian relationship; Nettie marries Adam; and Celie gives Albert some notice in her last letters, as she sees that he is changing. Also, these women are more American in their construction than some of Naylor's women. Even Celie's self-development, for example, is rooted in Western materialism. Her discovery of self is equated with her emergence as property owner and business woman. Also, except for the connections that Nettie insinuates when she discovers similarities between African and African-American folktales, and the unusual spirituality that Shug intuits (reminiscent of African animism), these women are cut off from their cultural past. However, because the novel does culminate in a happy celebration of all of the selves of the text, Walker does succeed in presenting womanists, who, through their own methods of sisterly support, can promote healing, showing, to return again to Walker's definition, love of the folk.

I mention spirituality, distance from the cultural past, and materialism to mark them as iconic signposts—elements of consideration in Africana womanism. Additionally, other significant elements and methods appear that have what I call a spiralytic relationship with Walker's original definition. That is, they wind *around* that definition as a center or source; second, in their cyclical movement, they also move *away* from the center, becoming more inclusive/expansive; third, they move *upward,* attaining levels of revision and refiguration that rest above the source of their energy by the magnitude or power of their difference.

Walker's definition originates from the expressive culture of black folk. From the black vernacular she has chosen a word that every African-American female with spunk probably heard as a youngster from scolding adults: *womanish*. Additionally, the syntax of the culture is used in the rhetoric of the explanation of the word, and the public history of the culture is invoked with the allusion to Harriet Tubman and other female liberation figures. Nevertheless, Walker frames these cultural elements in the traditions of Western academic definition: etymology first, then identification of class (*feminist*), and, finally, differentiation, or explanation of how the womanist is unlike other things in her class (*black*).

I make these comments on the strategy of the definition because in its methodology and movement away from Western scholarship, it has a relationship to that scholarship that is similar to the relationship of Africana womanism to womanism. That is, the icons of Africana womanism operate in a triangular fashion with Walker's definition: around, away from, and finally, upward. For example, whereas one can see Shug, Celie, and Sofia moving in concentric circles around the core, in Walker's later fiction, especially *Temple of My Familiar,* characters transcend these boundaries in a triangularity that adds the dimensions of recession (going away from the center) and ascension. In receding from the womanist center, the Africana womanist widens the circle to be more inclusive of cultural elements that (re)member the past—Africa, creating a connectedness for diasporic women in their various secondary cultures. In ascension, the goal is to move beyond reflection and expansion, to create energy, tension enough to destabilize harmful historiography, to revise, and ultimately, to liberate.

The signposts of this triangular movement can be identified in the spiralytic figurations that recur in texts such as Walker's *Temple,* and in Toni Morrison's *Song of Solomon* and *Beloved.* Walker's Miss Lissie, for example, is a dreadlocked figure who knows she has had past lives in ancient Egypt and Atlantis. Her racial (re)membering includes the last thousand years of black womanhood, especially the horrors of the African slave trade. Additionally, Walker's revisionist history posits an ancient African matricentric form of worship (Walker 1989, 63–64), while she uses her narrative authority to meld Hispanic culture (the Carlotta and Zede figures) into her revisionism. Morrison's figurations are not quite as expansive, culturally, but in *Song of Solomon* and *Beloved,* both Pilate and Sethe fit the prototype of (re)visioned pariahs—women whose supposed sins or strangeness must be revisited so that they can be understood in terms of their personal histories and gendered existences.

Even more fully than the works of Morrison and Walker, Gloria Naylor's last two novels encapsulate the primary signposts of Africana womanist revision. Regarding content, these elements include the ancestor/goddess of African tradition, necromancy, ritual, spiritual exploration/investigation, communalism, and general celebration of culture. Regarding discursive strategy the characteristic elements are multiple-voiced narration, conflation of temporal and spatial realities (part of African worldview), linguistic appropriateness (frequently, a speakerly text), and a matricentric focus (deconstruction of the *kyriarchy*, a term used by Masenya [1995, 149] to mean domination by lord or master as opposed to *patriarchy*, domination by the father). Finally, regarding purpose, Africana womanist revision aims to liberate its subjects from oppressive histories through recursion and destabilization. Characters, situations, objects, and the like from traditional myth or history are revisited and refashioned in ways that weaken the belief systems that gave rise to disparaging images of women and freed them from general discrimination based on gender.

These elements in Naylor's two novels show her using Walker's womanist axis, but widening the spirals to include figurations that are more dimensional and that ascend to higher levels of liberation in the ways that they are constructed. In *Mama Day*, willful and courageous women (re)member cultural myth and revise Judeo-Christian history. Miranda Day has inherited powers of necromancy (from the Latin *nigromantia*, meaning black magic) from her ancestor Sapphira Wade. Her great-niece Cocoa appears first as pure womanist: a brave southern female willing to take on the other-worldliness of New York City. When she returns home with a husband steeped in the traditions of Western logic, literature, and history, the stage is set for Naylor to offer a complicated symbology of liminality and confluence. She gives us liminars (characters in cultural limbo): some are physically separated from their birth culture (George); others are rendered helpless by it (Cocoa). Also, she poses Mama Day's magic as the tool to effect a joining of cultures to bridge the gap between Western and African tradition. Naylor's strategy successfully revises/deconstructs Judeo-Christian myth by stripping it of male-centered power. Moreover, she joins to that myth a matricentric African spirituality characteristic of Africana womanism. Ultimately, her figurations transcend the boundaries of the text.

What Cocoa's husband, George, confronts in Willow Springs, a sea island off the coasts of both Georgia and South Carolina, is the power of matricentric cultural myth, necromancy, and a worldview that contradicts his own belief systems. The myth begins the novel: "Everybody knows but nobody talks about the legend of Sapphira Wade. A true conjure woman: satin black, biscuit cream, red as Georgia clay: depending upon which of us takes a mind to her. She could walk through a lightning storm without being touched; grab a bolt of lightning in the palm of her hand; use the heat of lightning to start the kindling going under her medicine pot; depending upon which of us takes a mind to her" (*MD*, 3). The ensuing lines explain that Sapphira was an African slave who married her master in 1823, bore him seven sons in a thousand days, persuaded him to deed all of Willow Springs to his slaves, then killed him. Exactly how Sapphira caused Bascombe Wade's death depends, as do the details of her powers of conjure, upon "which of [the narrators] takes a mind to her." These repeated words become more significant when the listener/reader is told at the end of this first paragraph of the novel that "Sapphira don't live in the part of our memory we can use to form words" (*MD*, 4).

Naylor's discursive strategy at the novel's inception accomplishes several things. First, she establishes the collective voice of Willow Springs as having discursive authority. In the tradition of the speakerly text, which recalls African oral tradition, the reader becomes a listener, a participant in the discourse community. Second, Naylor effects (re)membrance—a recall of the cultural past that achieves its reality/validity as the individual mind envisions it. Karla Holloway explains that in the work of black women writers, (re)membrance is an "activation in the face of stasis, a restoration of fluidity, translucence and movement to the traditions of memory" (1992, 68). If memories of Sapphira are not spoken, she does not become static and one-dimensional. She may be as liminal or fractured as need be for a people whose history is not characterized by wholeness or one-dimensionality. Finally, what Naylor effects with the Sapphira story is a destabilization of traditional notions of myth. Once this is accomplished, then revision of a new order becomes possible.

Sapphira's and Miranda's powers of conjure are an element of spiralytic recession/expansion in Africana womanism. In their figurations, the two women move away from the womanist (black American feminist) tradition toward models that reflect the African past. Sapphira is the ancestor/goddess, a recurring figure in the fiction of African and African-American women writers. She is the conflation of the need for a new woman-centered spirituality and ancient African ancestor worship. Historian John Hope Franklin writes that members of early African societies devoutly believed in the continuance of the spirits of deceased family members. Deified at death, these spirits became more powerful as time passed, and more able to exert influence over the lives of their relatives (Franklin 1969, 32). Dona Marimba Richards explains that in the African worldview, the African family includes the dead, the living, and the "yet unborn," and the ritual of ancestor communion is emblematic of the interdependence of its parts (Richards 1980, 7). To make the dead more powerful, the living offer sacrifices; in return, the ancestors strengthen the *force vitale* of the living, thereby promoting their general health (Richards 1980, 7). Thus, Miranda has to confront the spirit of Peace in the well, dream Sapphira's name, and place herself at the ancestral home before she can help Cocoa, for all three efforts are symbolic gestures of ancestor communion.

Additionally, ancestor communion, as Richards explains it, symbolizes the African concept of Sacred Time (1980, 7). The living can communicate with the dead because the latter do not exist in a simple "past." In African spirituality, time is not linear; it is cyclical. Therefore, ideas of past, present, and future are eliminated (Richards 1980, 7). (Recall that Cocoa visits her dead husband's grave site and they talk easily about their lives together. George shows no "remorse" that he is separated from his beloved because in the African worldview, he is still with her.) As Cocoa begins the conversation in the first chapter, her trivial reminiscences and George's implied response indicate a comfortable relationship, though he is dead and she is remarried: "You were picking your teeth with a plastic straw—I know, I know, it wasn't really a straw, it was a coffee stirrer. But George, let's be fair, there are two little openings in those things that you could possibly suck liquid through if you were desperate enough" (*MD*, 13).

Sapphira and Miranda also spiral away from earlier womanist figurations in the texts of black women writers in the ways in which they are rooted in African traditions and beliefs. For example, Sophia and Squeak in Walker's *The Color Purple* are decidedly more Western in their sources of power and in their methods of using that power. Sofia resorts to physical force when she is threatened by her husband and the mayor. When the other women devise a plan to get Sofia out of jail, they use a power based on a premise embraced by contributors to the Western tradition from the Hellenic epics to *The Great Gatsby*: they presume that it is feminine beauty/guile that moves men. On the other hand, Sapphira, using African necromancy, defies Western temporality, enfranchises an entire island of slaves, and disappears, in one version of the story, "laughing in a burst of flames" (*MD*, 3).[4] Sapphira Wade's power deconstructs a kyriarchal structure and empowers the previous underclass in that structure. As a result,

"18 & 23" becomes a symbol for the collective memory of the people of Willow Springs—specifically for their belief in the necromancy of their ancestor/goddess and her continued presence in their lives.

When Miranda's family is threatened (Ruby's hex on Cocoa), Miranda relies on conjure to save her great-niece. First, she concocts a salve to counteract the effects of the mixture Ruby has put in Cocoa's hair. Then in a scene that recalls African tribal ritual of marking the house of a criminal (described in Olaudah Equiano's *Narrative,* for example), Miranda hits Ruby's house with a serpent-cane, causing the lightning to destroy it. However, saving Cocoa will entail still more. The African tradition of sacrifice becomes necessary.

The death of Cocoa's husband, George, creates the spiral movement in Naylor's text that is the most violent. There is enough energy in the resultant tension to destabilize the most pervasive and significant of all Western myths. George, posited as Judeo-Christian hero, dies so that the Days can be saved. The death of the Christ-figure in Naylor's revisionism is undergirded with motives that move it beyond a general redemption. Naylor adds another element as she infuses signs from expressive cultures. Redemption becomes qualified, or contingent, for Naylor sets these conditions: if George (born of a virgin mother in *Bailey's Cafe*) must die to save the last of the Days, then that death must effect a confluence of cultures so that the nature of life will change. The former kyriarchy (master-dominated society)—à la the Bascombe Wades of the world—must not be reestablished as superior to the cultures of women, of Africa, or of the diaspora. Therefore, even though George might be a Christ-figure, this Western logician is not posited as offering a belief system that is superior to the African matri-centric spirituality of Miranda Day. To convey this refigured relationship between the two worldviews, Naylor "lowers" the status of her "Christ" by making him, seemingly, the son of a whore. Then, in spite of his intellect and talents, George is rendered helpless in the face of the power of African voodoo. Nevertheless, Miranda's powers alone cannot save Cocoa; they must be coupled with George's beliefs. In this symbiotic relationship, Naylor insinuates an equality of cultures devoid of gendered prejudice and of the traditional Western domination.

One of the cultural signs of confluence that is the most significant (there are many in Naylor's dense symbology) is Miranda's prayer. Once she knows that a sacrifice has to be made, Miranda begins preliminary rites by going to the ancestral home, pointedly called the "other place" to connote the seat of a culture that is other than Western. There, she finds a water-damaged bill of sale that gives her only the first two letters of her ancestor's name. After a day of trying to guess the name, she "get[s] down on her stiffened knees and pray[s] to the Father and Son as she'd been taught. But she falls asleep, murmuring the names of women. And in her dreams she finally meets Sapphira" (*MD*, 280).

In this quick scene, Naylor merges elements of Judeo-Christian tradition, womanism, and African myth. First, she has a matriarch who has inherited powers of conjure from her African ancestor and performs a Christian ritual: kneeling and praying to the "Father and Son." Then, she subordinates that ritual to Miranda's concentration on women. Lastly, and most significantly, she adds to the idea of the "mal(e)formed" Trinity the idea of "woman"—specifically, an African ancestor/goddess who replaces the Holy Ghost. This is Africana womanist revision at its highest level: generative ascension results in the creation of a new myth characterized by a confluence of cultures.

Another important sign of confluence is the joining of hands. This act will serve as the symbolic joining of Miranda's and Cocoa's culture with George's. Naylor presents George's hands as metonyms of Western tradition when she has him speak the logic that that tradition has taught him. First, he believes that his helping hand as architectural engineer will hasten the repair of the bridge. When that effort fails, he decides what he needs to save his wife: a pair of oars in his *hands* to row across the Sound for help. He says: "I'm going to put the oars into the oarlocks and begin to row across the sound. That much I can do for her. And at that point in time when I can feel those oars between my hands, whether I make it or not won't be the issue. And if the boat begins to sink—I looked at my hands lit up by the moonlight—I'll place them in the water and start to swim" (*MD*, 282–83). Miranda, however, realizes that she needs George's hands in a different way: "[S]he needs that belief buried in George. Of his own accord he has to *hand* it over to her. She needs his hand in hers—his very hand—so she can connect it up with all the believing that had gone before. A single moment was all she asked, even a fingertip to touch hers here at the other place. So together they could be the bridge for Baby Girl to walk over" (*MD*, 285).

As well as pointing to a merger of African and Western belief systems, this passage resonates with an iconic element in African-American spirituality: the "laying on of hands." Particularly visible in black sanctified and charismatic churches, it is a ritual of African origin. The act recalls the belief in ancestor communion and spiritual continuity effected through what Richards calls a "diviner," or medium (1980, 43). Serving as diviner when Ruby puts a hex on Cocoa, Abigail uses her hands to quiet the worms in her granddaughter's body. Cocoa recalls "She sat on the bed, gathered me in her arms, and with the flat of her hand, she began to stroke—my back, my arms, my chest. . . . they would remain still until she went on to another part of my body. . . . Her one hand against so many of them. If only there was a way to bring me this kind of peace forever" (*MD*, 290).

Gary Storhoff, offering a Jungian analysis, reads the signs of the first hands (Miranda's and George's) section as symbolic of Miranda's getting in touch with her animus, and George with his anima, for psychic wholeness. Thus, John-Paul's cane becomes a phallic symbol, and the chicken coop where George is to take the cane becomes the anima since it houses eggs, the symbol of female reproductive power (Storhoff 1995, 40–41). Though Storhoff's reading is valid in its Jungian context, these symbols take on entirely different meanings in the expressive culture: chickens are ever-present in ritual drama of the diaspora. As noted by Zora Neale Hurston, they are especially important in sacrificial rites of the Hoo Doo culture of the American south and in the Caribbean. When Hurston studied under Luke Turner, a descendant of Marie Leveau, the high priestess of New Orleans Hoo Doo, she learned that chickens were sacrificed so that their spirits could be instructed by the medium to carry out the wishes of the living (Hurston 1990, 202–5).

All of these signs of confluence use icons indigenous to the culture of the narrative authority, that is—of the author, employing them. They are characteristic of what de Weever calls the "hybrid blossom" that results from the three-pronged tradition in which most American writers work (de Weever 1991, 21). For African-American writers those prongs are the Attic-Hebraic-Christian European culture, which became the foundation of the dominant culture transplanted to the Americas, African culture, and the African-American blended experience. "The triangulated tradition," de Weever notes, "testifies to the fragmented ontology of every American" (1991, 21–22).

In presenting fragments of African-American ontology, Naylor destabilizes the pieces of Western myth, then begins a revision that adds African elements. She wrenches the novel's temporal axis (that is as it exists as textual entity), moving the reader, in African cyclical fashion, first forward to the next novel in the series, *Bailey's Cafe,* then back to *Mama Day.* We cannot see the whole figure of George unless we move backward/forward to *Bailey's Cafe.* This intertextuality embraces/reinforces her themes and purpose. In order to liberate her figures and her readers from Western tradition, Naylor defies spatial and temporal expectation, creating a new story that exists above and beyond its origins, but which (at the same time) recalls those origins.

In her act of (re)membering/revising Judeo-Christian myth in *Bailey's Cafe,* Naylor uses African history and culture framed with the perspective of Africana womanism. The reader leaves the text feeling that she has visited a host of characters who, as biblical (re)figurations, may, indeed, be the threshold of a new beginning for humankind. For her (re)figuring and revising, Naylor chooses some of the most well-known women in Christian history, including Eve, Mary, Jezebel, and Esther. Other characters, including Nadine, Sadie, and Miss Maple, also become important in the author's complex symbology. Here, in addition to Africana womanism, Naylor adds signs of liminality that are even more evident than those in *Mama Day* (the portrayal of Cocoa being, perhaps, the exception).

Liminality is an appropriate description of the African-American experience as it applies to characters caught between very different cultures. Though the stages of the liminal process may apply to others, the experience of the African-American is easily translated into the language of liminality because of the unique history of the "burden of dual consciousness" (Du Bois 1909, 3). As long ago as 1902, sociologists such as W. E. B. Du Bois described the mental schism that exists for American blacks wrenched from one culture (African) and deposited into another (Western). This schism also has been examined by psychologists such as Kobi Kambon, who uses a comparative worldviews schematic to chart psycho-behavioral differences between African-Americans and European Americans (Kambon 1992, 11). Adjustments for African-Americans resulted in various rituals that blend African and European elements. These rituals have become recognized, historically, as indigenous to the culture of Africans in America.

In his analysis of ritualized experience, Arnold Van Gennep has identified three phases of the liminal process. The first is *separation,* or preliminary rites characterized by death symbols, sacrifice, journeys, and other signs of distance between the general population and the liminar. The second phase is *marge,* or liminal (threshold) rites. Indeterminacy symbols are common at this stage: namelessness, inertness (mock death), dislocation, humility, acceptance of pain, transvestitism, and loss of identifiers such as rank, clothing, and property. The third stage, *aggregation,* involves postliminal incorporation rites such as feasting, dancing, exchanging of gifts, oaths, hand clasps, and sexual mating (in Woodbridge and Anderson 1993,

579). Liminality also includes signs of rebirth, camaraderie, and the invoking of mystical powers.

Each of Naylor's major figures is at some stage of the liminal process, and there is a direct relationship between the characters' survival through aggregation and the trajectory of Naylor's revision. In this context, the purpose of her (re)figurations of the biblical women is twofold: first, they make a place for African-descended women in the central myth of Western tradition; and, second, her rewriting of that myth purges women of thousands of years of blame and shame.

Naylor's method of infusing African historiography into Judeo-Christian myth follows the same pattern of spiralytic movement she uses in *Mama Day*. However, instead of beginning with the womanist axis, Naylor roots each female's story in biblical history. The figure changes as it recedes from Western tradition and expands to include explanations, histories, and signs related to Africa or the diaspora. As ascension happens, Naylor reaches forward into contemporary reality to the African-descended female in America. The positions that modern society boxes black female outcasts into are posited: madam, whore, addict, nymphomaniac, wino. The derogatory labels descriptive of the positions the women find themselves in are signs of the first stage of liminality—separation. With the exception of Nadine, all of the women have been cut off from their communities.

Naylor's refigured Eve, for example, is cast out of her community for the "original" sin of discovering the connection between her body's natural urges and the vibrations of the earth. Eve explains: "The earth showed me what my body was for. Sometimes I'd break my fingernails from clawing them into the dirt or bite my arm to keep from crying out. And Billy Boy stomping up dust as I humped myself into the ground—him sweating and baying at the clouds" (*BC,* 87). While Billy Boy is portrayed as an idiot only doing the bidding of his playmate, his "Adam's apple straining, head thrown back to the sky" (*BC,* 87–88), Eve is treated by Godfather (read *God, the Father*) as purposefully evil, deserving of excommunication. Before he banishes her, he already has tried to quell her natural inquisitiveness and spunk with pulpit words that "resembled rounds of thunder" and with angry laughter like "lightning vibrations" (*BC,* 84).

Naylor's revision of the expulsion myth juxtaposes the logic of Eve's natural urges with the illogical wrath of God. Additionally, she highlights Adam's complicity: he may have been an idiot, but he, too, enjoyed the game. For her act, Eve is sent out of Pilottown, alienated from the only human contact she's ever had. As a black female outcast, she suffers through a process that many African-American women writers describe in their fiction.

Susan Willis comments on Toni Morrison's handling of the alienated black woman:

> Morrison's aim in writing is very often to disrupt alienation with what she calls eruptions of "funk." Dismayed by the tremendous influence of bourgeois society on young black women newly arrived from deep south cities . . . , Morrison describes the women's loss of spontaneity and sensuality. They learn how to behave. The careful development of thrift, patience, high morals, and good manners. In short, how to get rid of the funkiness. The dreadful funkiness of passion, the funkiness of nature, the funkiness of the wide range of human emotions. (Willis 1987, 87)

Naylor's (re)figured Eve, set in juxtaposition to the "de-funked" Sister Carrie, carries only a symbolic residue of the "funkiness of passion . . . [and] nature": she cannot get rid of the dirt beneath her fingernails. She sets up her own code of behavior, which does include morality (she sets up rules for herself and her tenants), thrift (she's an expert business woman), and patience (she's endured a thousand-year trek and has learned how to instruct her tenants, then wait for their personal self-evolutions). The stages of her own liminality have been marked by a separation and marge that eradicated her sense of humor and her sensuality. She says, "I'd already clearly seen enough of the world to know there was little I needed to laugh about. And the only road that lay open to me was the one ahead, and the only way I could walk it was the way I was. I had no choice but to walk into New Orleans neither male nor female — mud. But I could right then and there choose what I was going to be when I walked back out" (*BC,* 91).

Having begun the liminal process half-naked, nearly blind, and ignorant of the ways of the world, she emerges educated, poised on the threshold (at marge), ready to be married to the highest levels of society that her experience and potential will allow. Unfortunately, it is the early 1900s, and for a bright woman, in spite of her three trunks of silk suits and more than fifty-seven thousand dollars, society will not offer her the aggregation rites reserved for her male baccalaureate counterparts: no diploma, no graduation ceremony, no congratulatory handshakes.

Thus, in spite of her self-designed transformation, Eve still ends up near Bailey's edge of the world cafe. However, as she promised, she has made her own decisions about what she wants to be; moreover, she is *in charge* (like Walker's womanist) of negotiating the inclusivity or exclusivity of her space. Her brownstone becomes the reification of the "home" for the alienated as described by womanist bell hooks: "At times home is nowhere. At times one knows only extreme estrangement and alienation. Then home is no longer just one place. . . . Home is that place that enables and promotes varied and ever-changing perspectives, a place where one discovers new ways of seeing reality, frontiers of difference" (hooks 1990, 148). Naylor's Eve has the power to give such a home to women who have suffered a range of abuses in the oppressive systems they have come from.

In "Mary (Take One)" the abused woman is a (re)figuration of Mary Magdalene, the whore who washed the feet of Jesus with her hair. In a mocking inversion of Mary Magdalene's act of humility, the refigured Mary humbles herself to all men to rid herself of the whore she sees reflected in their eyes: "*I* was free as I gave them her. Over and over they became my saviors from her" (*BC*, 105). After Mary scars her face to destroy the beauty that makes men want her, she ends up at the brownstone. Symbolically enabling her to change her perspective, Eve lifts Mary's veil and says "Beautiful" (*BC*, 112). What Naylor's womanist perspective describes here is not the scar itself, but Mary's act of making it. The self-inflicted pain, a commonality in the liminal process, becomes a catalyst for change. Eve, recognizing the import of the act, welcomes Mary as she has so many other liminars. She is a womanist who, to use Michael Awkward's term, fosters "(comm)unity" for her suffering sisters in a setting that mocks the hypocritical values of their pre-separation communities (1989, 135).

Eve also helps one of the most maligned of all biblical women, Jezebel, (re)figured here as Jesse Bell, divorcee, bisexual, and drug addict. Through a long and complex symbology, Naylor effectively revises Jezebel's story so that her motivations become natural and understandable, and her general character simply "womanish": willful and committed to survival and wholeness for entire people. Also, in keeping with the vernacular tone of Walker's definition, Jesse is a working-class woman who "loves the folk" — her family. However, as Jezebel is beaten by the power of Elijah's more "organized" and patricentric religion (the catered picnic paralleling the biblical showdown at Mount Carmel), Jesse Bell's more fragmented and woman-centered rituals — seduction, cooking, putting on makeup — do not save her from being symbolically thrown to the dogs as Jezebel literally was. Explaining how she seduced her husband, Jesse boasts, "I got him the same way I kept him — with the best poon tang east of the Mississippi" (*BC*, 122). Later she says, "He loved everything about women . . . how I managed to get the seams in my stockings straight or how I penciled in the beauty mark over the right side of my lips. He'd watch me trying to arch my eyebrows for a whole hour, just fascinated, you know?" (BC, 123). Though these actions may seem trivial to others, Jesse knows their power. She warns, "You gotta keep tight reins on a man like that, cause Maybelline made a whole lot of those pencils. So Mama went where Papa went, or Papa didn't go out that night" (BC, 123).

The most effective description of feminine ritual appears later. Jesse describes her skill in combining her cooking and sexual talents:

> The next night I baked three sweet potato pies. I mean the heavy kind with lard in the crust and Alaga syrup bubbling all through them. And while my pies are cooling and he's in the bedroom reading his newspaper, I run me a warm bath and throw a whole bottle of vanilla extract in the water. So I'm soaking in the vanilla, the pies are cooling, and we're all ready about the same time. I go into our bedroom, carrying one of my pies, dressed the same way I stepped out of that tub. I made sure it was sliced real nice—six even pieces. And he's looking at me like I've gone out of my mind, but I still take it all real slow. I laid back on the pillows. Took out a slice, without disturbing a crumb, mind you. And wedged it right between my legs. It was time for the first lesson. Husband, I said, pointing, this is sweet potato pie. Didn't have a bit of trouble after that. Except it was all the man wanted for dinner for the next month. (BC, 124)

In spite of her power over her husband, Jesse loses him to the masculine traditions and ideas of Uncle Eli. Most of Eli's suggestions for how the family should operate are based on the power of money, whereas Jesse's are connected to family bonding. For example, when Jesse suggests her son be cared for by her mother, Eli says he should have a nanny. Instead of spending his summers fishing with Jesse's brothers, the boy goes to camp. Ultimately, Eli wins and Jesse turns to drugs and back to her lesbian lover.

Naylor invokes the Africana womanist element of necromancy in devising a method of salvation for Jesse Bell. Eve has the magical power to reconstruct Jesse's girlhood bedroom in the void in back of Bailey's Cafe. The symbols in the scene add up to an indictment of the Western images and ideals that destroy little black girls who cannot mirror and attain them. Jesse grew up with pictures of Bette Davis and Joan Crawford on her walls, and dreamed of having a luxury bathroom, probably like the ones she'd seen in the movies. Eve repeatedly tempts her with the same images—and the heroin that parallels them—so that she can effectively wean her. Eve's magic has to help Jesse (re)vision the images and ideals as the real enemies that intoxicated her, that have destroyed her selfhood. However, Eve's powers are limited. She can help Jesse only if Jesse uses her own willpower to help herself. Because self-healing in Naylor's revision involves seeing the past from a different perspective, the (re)figured character, though placed there by Eve, must (re)create her own view of herself in that past. In other words, Eve creates only the possibility for change.[5] If Jesse is going to be saved from elements that kill her self-esteem and confidence, she must be emotionally involved in the process.

Jesse's intoxication will probably end; Sadie's will not. Naylor's figuration of the prostitute-wino is the reification of the results of the American dream on a black female psyche already damaged by the absence of family bonding. The daughter of a prostitute who introduced her to the profession, Sadie has tried to make owning a home her salvation. When Iceman Jones, a man from a poor but functional family, takes Sadie to the void—the place of possibility or nihilism—she cannot accept the life he offers because she is still drunk with dreams of the picket fence, Martha Washingtons in her yard, and Waterford goblets on her table (*BC*, 72–74). Sadie's liminal state—she is caught between her daydreams of being a fine lady and her actual existence as wino/whore—leaves her short of the aggregation that Eve's brownstone offers: a (comm)unity of sisters (same profession) who have the advantage of ritual (rules and tradition) and a cultural mother-necromancer.

Naylor's revision highlights Eve's status as sociocultural figure. Her acts of saving are in line with characteristics of African-descended people as identified in African historian Cheikh Anta Diop's two-cradle theory of European and African worldview/cultural differences and sociologist Kobi Kambon's comparative worldviews schematic (Kambon 1992, 10–11). For example, Eve believes in harmony with nature as opposed to mastery over it, in communalism over individualism, and (as is evident in her general characterization) in privileging of matrilineal over patrilineal descent.[6] Though Eve is a madam who exercises control over the women in her brownstone, what she represents is not a system wherein those women are treated as chattel. They are allowed to make their own decisions about how they will operate in the spaces that Eve creates for them. Though Naylor posits Eve as a matriarch, she is not a reproduction of the male figurehead who owns women in the patrilineal system.

In her Esther (re)figuration, Naylor offers a microcosm of the evils of patrilineal ownership. Like property, Esther is given by her brother, in return for higher wages, to a man who uses her to satisfy his unusual sexual fantasies. Commenting on the metonymics that signify Esther's status and her self-concept, Maxine Montgomery notes, "he chooses to be intimate with her only in the cellar of his home. The pink and lace-trimmed bed where she must sleep alone reveals her confinement to a socially prescribed gender role. Her monologues point to a profound self-hatred in a world that evolves no terms for her existence" (1995, 31).

Eve helps Esther construct an inversion of her status, ironically imitating the physicality of her former abuse. She removes the lightbulbs from the basement of the brownstone and lets Esther meet her customers there. However, because this time Esther sets the rules—what the men will pay, how they will address her—she has passed from the liminal stages of separation from her family and marge (ignorance and helplessness) to a place of control and self-definition. Moreover, in her portrayal, Naylor has revised the biblical Esther, whose reputation rested mainly on the beauty that attracted the king and on her saving the Jewish people. In the biblical story, Esther's cousin Mordecai carefully prepares her for her "duties" to the king, and his eunuch Hegai trains her in court protocol. In Naylor's text, Esther's brother tells her nothing, and the revised Hegai becomes the farmer's "hag" who washes Esther but leaves her in her ignorance. Naylor has Eve reproduce a version of the farmer's cellar for Esther to operate in so that the self-sacrificing Esther is *recalled,* but *revised* with a new sense of self intact. The replication of historical circumstances is necessary for effective destabilization of the images of the "ignorant" Esther. Thus, revisiting the scene of oppression and abuse becomes liberating rather than traumatic.

The most traumatic story in Naylor's text is also its most complex and significant revision. "Mary (Take Two)" is a womanist tale so anchored in the source of historical female pain that Naylor must switch the narrative voice from male (Bailey) to female (Nadine). Nadine's is the more appropriate voice as hers is the perspective that has the most distance from Western ideology, the plus of gender identification, and the advantage of collective (re)membering that that gender identification and her cultural rootedness allow. Also, she has an emotional distance not possible for Mother Eve. (Nadine notices that Eve cries softly after she hears the story of Mariam, whose name means "little Mary.")

Mariam's story is based on the Mariology of Judeo-Christian history. That history includes the dignity and human fallibility of the Holy Virgin, the Immaculate Conception, the virgin birth, and the Assumption. To spiral away from and above this history—that is, to effectively revise it, Naylor first "revisits" it. She gives the reader a starting place that is recognizable because it is similar to biblical history: a young pregnant woman appears, claiming that no man has touched her. Then, the author adds to the biblical story of the Holy Virgin a cultural history from modern times: the young woman's "virginity" is related to tribal clitoridectomy rites. Her mutilation attests to her claim that she is a virgin, thus attesting to her dignity. The modern history Naylor chooses allows her to recede from the biblical one, then ascend to a startling Africana womanist (re)figuration: Mary is a slow-witted child who has suffered gender oppression in a male-dominated society. In order for her to "rise above" her oppressive past (achieve Assumption), she seeks Mother Eve and the community of the brownstone.

First, Naylor locates her figure, Mariam, in a geography and genealogy that would account historically and culturally for her condition, her inno-cence, and her humility. She is an outcast from the Beta Israel (Falasha) of Ethiopia, who claim to be descendants of Menelik I, alleged son of King Solomon and the Queen of Sheba. Of the Jewish faith, they are a tribe adhering to strict ritual and laws, especially regarding females and their purity. These rituals and laws clearly relegate women to a lower status, insinuating their supposed inferiority even in birth rites. Wolf Leslau ex-plains that if a Falasha woman gives birth to a male, the village gives twelve shouts, circumcises the male after the eighth day, then releases the mother from the *yamargam gogo* (hut of blood) to the child-bed hut for a stay of thirty-two days. However, if the woman gives birth to a female, the villag-ers give only nine shouts, and the mother is confined to the hut of blood for two weeks, and to the child-bed hut for a period of sixty-six days. The birthing process, and the mother herself, are considered so unclean that the hut is burned and the mother is allowed to return only under the cover of darkness, and only after she shaves her head and goes through thorough washings (Leslau 1969, xiv–xv). To preserve their virginity until marriage, the females undergo clitoridectomies. Pedersen explains that prior to the "simple clitoridectomy," the usual practice in some African tribes was to remove the entire external genitalia (1991, 647).

Naylor closely follows the details of these tribal traditions, as reported by anthropologists, even regarding the daily routines of the people. She writes: "All prayers turn toward Jerusalem as they spin linen, shape iron, and bake pottery outside their broken hovels" (*BC*, 146). The Falasha are iron smiths and weavers, and they engage in daily prayers performed by a high priest; the accuracy of these historical details is important to highlight in order to show them as effective elements in Naylor's revisionism. They lend believability to her (re)figurations and facilitate the destabilization she desires as she recalls Western myth.

For linguistic accuracy, Naylor's recursive strategy is to have Mariam paraphrase the words of the Holy Virgin. In an eastern, apocryphal "Book of James" tale that "deeply influenced the cult of the Virgin in the west," Mary is reported to have said, "I am pure before Him [God] and know not a man" (15:3) (Warner 1983, 26–7). In the Gospel of Luke, she says, "How shall this be, seeing I know not a man?" (Luke 1:34, AV). Naylor's Mariam says repeatedly, "*No man has ever touched me*" (*BC*, 143–46 passim). When Eve bathes Mariam, she concludes, "No man has even tried" (*BC*, 152).

One of the most effective elements of Naylor's revisionism is that the genealogy she gives her (re)figured Mary resonates with the historical Black madonna figures. Lucia Birnbaum, commenting on the appearance of the figure in many cultures, points out that images appear, almost always, near archaeological evidence of a pre-Christian woman divinity, and that in all of these cultures, the belief is that the divinity is black (Birnbaum 1993, 3). She hypothesizes that "veneration of the indigenous goddess of Old Europe merged with African, Middle Eastern, and Asian dark goddesses and persisted in the christian era in vernacular beliefs and rituals associated with black madonnas." Also, she believes that black madonnas "may be considered a metaphor for a memory of the time when the earth was believed to be the body of a woman and all cultures were equal, a memory transmitted in vernacular traditions of earth-bonded cultures" (Birnbaum 1993, 3–4).

Seemingly, Naylor capitalizes on the tradition of this metaphor in her Africana womanist (re)membering of the Madonna. This strategy adds believability to Naylor's (re)figured Mary. Subtly recalling occurrences of black madonnas in vernacular cultures makes Naylor's Mariam more a historical possibility for the reader. That Gabe the pawnshop owner is sympathetic to Mariam's situation adds another level of validity. He is a member of the Jewish faith who does not *question* the girl's condition; therefore, the reader sees Mariam through the eyes of a learned member of her spiritual community. If Gabe can accept her, given his knowledge of Jewish history, then the reader can accept her as a madonna. However, Naylor spirals away from the historical/cultural elements as she adds a five hundred mile trek to Mariam's separation process and posits her as a liminar, born slow-witted, who ends up at Eve's whorehouse a frightened and confused child. It takes a male from her own faith, Gabe , to guide her to the brownstone. After a symbolic reenactment/inversion of Mariam's clitoral mutilation (she uses a plum), Eve knows that she must employ her most potent powers of necromancy to help her, especially since Mariam herself seems to have no real understanding of what has happened to her, nor any means of helping herself.

Mariam's slow-wittedness, when juxtaposed with Eve's symbolic recalling of her clitoridectomy, becomes a serious indictment of Mariam's native community. Her feeble-mindedness is a metaphor for the mental immaturity of young girls who suffer, in an African society, irreversible damage to their psyches and their physical persons because of tribal "customs." Naylor's revisionism, which should end in liberation for all of her (re)figured women, does not stop short of aggregation for Mariam. After Eve the necromancer re-creates an Ethiopian village in the void, the baby is born and Mariam disappears in a flood of water. In traditional Mariology, there is no mention of Mary's "death." No body is found, and she is believed to have been "translated to heaven" (Warner 1983, 84). Thus, Naylor constructs her own plausible "transitus" or assumption. Mariam's aggregation, then, is to become a part of the collective memory of a people who will have specifics for a new Mariology. The first people to believe in and proclaim Mariology are the motley crew from Eve's brownstone and Bailey's Cafe, and Gabe. Evidently prostitutes, a madam, a "transvestite," a pawnshop owner, and the proprietors of a diner are not a believable group to others. Or, perhaps, something simply gets lost in their translation of Mariam's story. Whatever happens, Naylor shows in *Mama Day* that George's attitude toward and knowledge of his mother include no spiritual reverence, no inkling of her "assumption." She insinuates that George, steeped in Western traditions, has no room in the circle of those traditions to know about an African madonna, especially one who lived in a whorehouse.

Naylor's discursive strategies in *Bailey's Cafe* effectively reverse what Judith Baskins notes is a traditional representation of biblical women only in terms of their relationships to men (Baskins 1994, 211). However, labeling the author's accomplishment as simple revision from patricentric to matricentric focus would be relegating it to something reminiscent of early Anglo-American feminism. As an Africana womanist, Naylor constructs her text, her (re)figurations, with recursions that pay homage to the history and expressive culture of Africa and the diaspora. Mere reflection is not a stopping place for her. As she ascends to make new models, she not only revises Western tradition, but also liberates her listener/reader.

In *Mama Day*, her discursive implications are that liberation/salvation for African-descended people must entail a belief in their own ancient traditions, their voices, their rituals, their spirituality, their worldview. Nevertheless, the distinct delineation's in the novel, the intersections of cultures, and the added element of gender embrace and acknowledge the structure of the African-American consciousness—its history of fragmentation, and most of all, its tendency to prevail.

Afterword

In an atmosphere of Western scholarship, which for most of the last half-century has "taken a stand" (allusion to the Fugitives intended) against writers promoting ideologies in their texts and deconstructed authorial ownership of meaning, black women writers are constructing texts that pointedly call for a reversal of that trend. Alice Walker's definition of womanist deliberately *prefaces* her collection of essays that explore who she is as a writer, black woman, critic, and human being. Accurately locating her work, she signals with her prefatory definition, means understanding her critical theory and its origins in the vernacular tradition (her life) that underscores her discourse. Her womanist theory has been appropriated by factions such as South African women still struggling for equality in post-apartheid society (see M. Masenya, for example) and American female theologians (see Sanders and Williams) attempting to change the male-centered traditions that do not address their concerns or take advantage of their talents. This appropriation indicates their understanding of the necessary connection between the personal narrative of the writer—her background, politics, and so forth—and the intent of her discourse.

Recursion and refiguration must result in revisionism that enlightens, that alters oppressive trends, and that spurs iconic action. Walker's act of placing a headstone over the unmarked grave of Zora Neale Hurston was such an action, an outgrowth of intertextuality that mandates recursion to Hurston as the literary foremother. Gloria Naylor's brand of Africana womanism, in demanding critical praxes that collapse the distance between discursive authority and text, is a parallel spurring of iconic action. As Walker's public homage to Hurston caused critics to "rediscover" Hurston, to look at her as subtext in the work of contemporary African-American women, Naylor's work asks them to consider the Africana womanist as subtext, as negotiator of meaning in her own work.

Notes

1. Hudson-Weems, who coined the term in 1987, uses it to "identif[y] the ethnicity of the woman being considered . . . her ancestry and land base—Africa" and differentiates between Africana womanism and Walker's womanism by defining the latter as a black version of feminism, a movement founded by middle-class white females, and the former as an ideology "grounded in African culture, and therefore one that focuses on the unique experiences, struggles, needs, desires of Africana women" (1995, 22–23, 24).

2. Walker's full definition is as follows:

Womanist

1. From *womanish*. (Opp. of "girlish," i.e., irresponsible, not serious.) A black feminist or feminist of color. From the black folk expression "You acting womanish," i.e. like a woman. Usually referring to outrageous, audacious, courageous or *willful* behavior. Wanting to know more and in greater depth than is considered "good" for one. Interested in grown-up doings. Acting grown up. Interchangeable with another black folk expression: "You trying to be grown." Responsible. In charge. *Serious*.

2. *Also*: A woman who loves other women, sexually and/or nonsexually. Appreciates and prefers women's culture, women's emotional flexibility (values tears as natural counterbalances of laughter), and women's strength. Sometimes loves individual men, sexually and/or nonsexually. Committed to survival and wholeness of entire people, male *and* female. Not a separatist, except periodically, for health. Traditionally universalist, as in: "Mama, why are we brown, pink and yellow, and our cousins white, beige and black?" Ans.: "Well, you know the colored race is just like a flower garden, with every flower represented." Traditionally capable, as in: "Mama, I'm walking to Canada and I'm taking you and a bunch of other slaves with me." Reply: "It wouldn't be the first time."

3. Loves music. Loves dance. Loves the moon. *Loves* the Spirit. Loves love and food and roundness. Loves struggle. *Loves* the folk. Loves herself. *Regardless*.

4. Womanist is to feminist as purple to lavender. (Walker 1983, xi–xii)

3. Mary Agnes may be the exception.

4. Also, it is worthwhile to note here that Sapphira, as Africana womanist figuration, spirals above her African-American cousin Sapphire of Amos and Andy fame. The former revises the latter so that Sapphire's comedic jabs and threatening body stances (hands akimbo) become ridiculous emblems of power. Naylor's name choice for this figure is deliberate—aimed at revision of one of the most damaging images of the African-American female.

5. Naylor shows that other characters also have the power to create change for themselves. For Sadie, Iceman Jones transforms the void, and Stanley makes it snow there. Both men can create possibilities for themselves because they are in touch with the realities of their lives.

6. Kambon's chart of worldview differences attributes harmony with nature, communalism to Africans, and mastery over nature and individualism to Europeans. Also, in his work, the psychologist, espousing Diop's description, attributes matrilineal descent to Africans and patrilineage to Europeans. To support his claims, Kambon uses the cultural data of more than a dozen scholars who have done research on worldview differences, including Cheikh Anta Diop's "Two Cradle Theory of African and European Worldview/Cultural Differences" table in Kambon's book.

Works Cited

Awkward, Michael. *Inspiriting Influences: Tradition, Revision, and Afro-American Women's Novels.* New York: Columbia University Press, 1989.

Baker, Houston. *Blues, Ideology, and Afro-American Literature: A Vernacular Theory.* Chicago: University of Chicago Press, 1984.

Baskins, Judith. "Women at Odds: Biblical Paradigms." In *Feminist Nightmares: Women at Odds: Feminism and the Problem of Sisterhood.* New York: New York University Press, 1994.

Birnbaum, Lucia. *Black Madonnas: Feminism, Religion, and Politics in Italy.* Boston: Northeastern University Press, 1993.

de Weever, Jacquelyn. *Mythmaking and Metaphor in Black Women's Fiction.* New York: St. Martin's Press, 1991.

Du Bois, W. E. B. *The Souls of Black Folk.* 1902. Chicago: McClurg, 1909.

Equiano, Olaudah. "The Interesting Narrative of the Life of Olaudah Equiano or Gustavus Vassa, the African." In *Black Writers of America.* Eds. Richard Barksdale and Kenneth Kinnamon. New York: Macmillan, 1972. 5–38.

Franklin, John Hope. *From Slavery to Freedom (1947).* New York: Vintage Books, 1969.

Holloway, Karla. *Moorings and Metaphors: Figures of Culture and Gender in Black Women's Literature.* New Brunswick, N.J.: Rutgers University Press, 1992.

hooks, bell. *Yearning: race, gender, and cultural politics.* Boston: South End Press, 1990.

Hudson-Weems, Clenora. *Africana Womanism: Reclaiming Ourselves.* Troy, Mich.: Bedford Publishers, 1993.

Hurston, Zora Neale. *Mules and Men (1935).* New York: Harper and Row, 1990.

Kambon, Kobi. *The African Personality in America: An African-Centered Framework.* Tallahassee, Fla.: Nubian Nations Publications, 1992.

Leslau, Wolf. *Falasha Anthology: The Black Jews of Ethiopia (1951).* New York: Schocken Books, 1969.

Masenya, Madipoane. "African Womanist Hermeneutics: A Suppressed Voice from South Africa Speaks." *Journal of Feminist Studies in Religion* (Spring 1995): 149–55.

Montgomery, Maxine Lavon. "Authority, Multivocality, and the New World Order in Gloria Naylor's *Bailey's Cafe.*" *African American Review* 29 (Spring 1995): 27–33.

Morrison, Toni. *Beloved.* New York: New American Library, 1987.

———. *Song of Solomon.* New York: New American Library, 1977.

Naylor, Gloria. *Bailey's Cafe.* New York: Harcourt Brace Jovanovich, 1992.

———. *Mama Day.* New York: Vintage Books, 1993.

Pedersen, Susan. "National Bodies, Unspeakable Acts: The Sexual Politics of Colonial Policy-Making." *Journal of Modern History* 63 (1991): 647–80.

Richards, Dona Marimba. *Let the Circle Be Unbroken: The Implications of African Spirituality in the Diaspora.* Trenton, N.J.: Red Sea Press, 1980.

Sanders, Cheryl. "Afrocentrism and Womanism in the Seminary." *Christianity and Crisis* 52 (April 1992): 123–26.

Storhoff, Gary. "'The Only Voice Is Your Own': Gloria Naylor's Revision of *The Tempest.*" *African American Review* 29 (Spring 1995): 35–45.

Walker, Alice. *In Search of Our Mother's Gardens.* New York: Harcourt Brace Jovanovich, 1983.

———. *The Color Purple.* New York: Pocket Books, 1982.

———. *The Temple of My Familiar.* New York: Pocket Books, 1989.

Warner, Marina. *Alone of All Her Sex: The Myth and the Cult of the Virgin Mary.* New York: Vintage Books, 1983.

Williams, Delores. "Womanist Theology: Black Women's Voices." *Christianity and Crisis* 47 (March 1987): 66–70.

Willis, Susan. *Specifying: Black Women Writing the American Experience.* Madison: University of Wisconsin Press, 1987.

Woodbridge, Linda, and Roland Anderson. "Liminality." In *Encyclopedia of Contemporary Literary Theory.* Ed. Irena R. Makaryk. Toronto: University of Toronto Press, 1993.

"Into the Midst of Nothing"

Gloria Naylor and the *Différance*

Philip Page

In Toni Morrison's *Jazz,* the imagery of wells is significant. Because Violet Trace's mother committed suicide by jumping into a well, Violet's severe depression and near suicide are centered on her fears of wells: "the well sucked her sleep" (Morrison 1992, 102). The well is an image of death—enclosed, dark, and final, much like a grave or a coffin. It is a fixed point, a closed circle, where variation, alternatives, movement, play, indeed life, all cease. Violet's recovery is couched in terms of her acceptance of the well as a salutary fact of life: when she and her husband, Joe, are spiritually reunited at the end of the novel, "she rests her hand on his chest as though it were the sunlit rim of a well" (Morrison 1992, 225). Morrison's narrator reaches the same position when she "dream[s] a nice dream" for Golden Grey, placing him "next to a well," "standing there in shapely light," "not aware of its mossy, unpleasant odor, or the little life that hovers at its rim, but to stand there next to it and from down in it, where the light does not reach, a collection of leftover smiles stirs, some brief benevolent love rises from the darkness" (Morrison 1992, 161). The choice is not whether to plunge into the death-hole or to try to avoid it; instead, mental health is found *next to* the well, where the play between light and dark, life and death, self and other can be welcomed.

Jacques Derrida, meditating on the ontology of books, describes "the unnameable bottomless well" as "the abyss," an image of the center that is "the absence of play and difference, another name for death." Any book, as a completed, enclosed entity, "was to have insinuated itself into the dangerous hole, was to have furtively penetrated into the menacing dwelling place." For Derrida, only by repetition does one escape from this well/trap. If we return to the book, to the hole, we attain a "strange serenity" and we are "fulfilled . . . by remaining open, by pronouncing nonclosure" (Derrida 1978, 296, 297, 298). As for Morrison, the well is a potentially dangerous opening but at the same time an opportunity for discovery, peace, and self-development. The well is destructive if taken as a fixed, monologic entity; but it is beneficial if taken as part of a fluid and multivalent orientation toward the open-endedness of being.

The well and ordinary space are thus a traditional binary; but, as with all other binaries, Derrida argues that their relationship is infinitely complex. In one sense, the rim of the well represents the Derridean acceptance of all such possibilities in the relationship between well and non-well. Yet the well itself is double-edged, thereby, like the rim, suggestive of the *différance.* Taken singly, the well represents the forces that drive characters into closed, monologic reliance on originary selves, as well as the very condition of an illusionary self-presence. In this sense, the well is the absence of play, repetition, and life. Simultaneously, the well, including its rim, is the unspeakable différance that allows for life. As long as we return to it, as long as we incorporate it into a larger and more complex multiplicity, the well—a womb as well as a tomb—is that which allows us to live. The well symbolizes the shift from a monologic, either/or perspective to an open, both/and stance in which the attention is focused not on fixed entities but on the différance, the endless flux within and between entities. Presence *and* absence, self *and* other, ordinary space *and* the well are equally acknowledged. Such thinking thus shifts from the traditional Western emphasis on fixed entities and the irreconcilable separations between binary opposites to a blurring of boundaries and an embrace of inclusiveness.[1]

A similar shift is often advocated by those who have been historically excluded from mainstream Western culture. Feminist theorists, for example, have welcomed the doubled perspective afforded by women's insider/outsider status.[2] Similarly, the ambiguous status of African-Americans within but outside mainstream American culture has necessitated a "double-consciousness," to use W. E. B Du Bois's famous term. The doubleness is a curse and a blessing, for it leads to "second-sight" (Du Bois 1989, 5) and a "special perspective" (Ellison 1972, 131), which allows for openness, the embrace of contradiction and paradox, and a broad inclusiveness, even of one's deepest fears.[3] Black feminist theorists have emphasized the unique perspective of black women as the other in American culture, a perspective that especially enables them to incorporate a multiplicity of perspectives.[4]

Like Morrison's fiction, Gloria Naylor's novels are empowered by her ability to carry readers into the bittersweet conditions of contemporary life. By depicting the complex and paradoxical mixtures of tragedy and joy in African-American characters' lives, Naylor leads her characters and readers into the ambiguous but strangely satisfying realm of the différance, into life not in avoidance of the abyss but at its edge.

The symbol for this theme in Naylor's fiction is wells and well-like images such as basements, alleys, and walls. These physical images suggest both the psychological dead ends into which characters are driven and the social and psychological forces that pressure them into such conditions. Concurrently, Naylor's fiction posits other characters symbolically placed on the rims of wells. Such characters model the Derridean stance of accepting play, open-endedness, and plurality. Not locked into the logocentrism of insistence on a unitary self, on bipolar opposites, or on the well as a death trap, they are able to return to the well, to defer and to differ, in short to comprehend and accept the différance. Wells in Naylor's fiction thus have multiple values.

Naylor's only literal image of a well occurs in the crucial scene in *Mama Day* in which Miranda Day overcomes her fears and opens the well where her sister Peace killed herself. Prior to this moment, Miranda "ha[d] evaded the symbolic truth of the well" (Storhoff 1995, 42), fearing to face her family's tragedy. She had only sensed the loss felt by Peace's mother, ignoring the loss and grief also borne by her father. As for Violet Trace, opening the well enables Miranda to reconnect with the past, in her case to identify with her father's pain: "looking past the losing was to feel for the man who built this house and the one who nailed this well shut" (*MD*, 285). This opening at the edge of the well gives Miranda access to her paternal ancestry, which heretofore had been overshadowed by her reliance on her female ancestors, especially the Days' legendary foremother, Sapphira Wade. Opening herself to her father's grief not only contributes to the community's ongoing reinterpretations of its history and its identity, but it leads Miranda to an understanding of George's strength of will and to her discovery of the means of saving her niece Cocoa.[5]

For Miranda, as for Violet, the well symbolizes the tragic familial past and the grief that cannot be borne or even admitted but must be acknowledged. To prevent future family tragedy, she must return to and accept the past tragedy. She must "look past the pain" (*MD*, 283)—hers as well as her father's. To do so constitutes a reawakening: "She sleeps within her sleep. To wake from one is to be given back ears as the steady heart tells her—look past the pain; to wake from the other is to stare up at the ceiling from the mahogany bed and to know that she must go out and uncover the well where Peace died" (*MD*, 283). Because the closed well is a site of destructive repression, it is an image of death and decay: "a bottomless pit," full of "foul air," the surface of the water "slimy and covered with floating pools of fungus" (*MD*, 284). At first Miranda feels nothing, but "refusing to let go of the edge," she closes her eyes and then viscerally feels the repressed pain: "And when it comes, it comes with a force that almost knocks her on her knees. She wants to run from all that screaming" (284). The mythic power of the closed well has the potential to kill, yet Miranda—like the narrator of *Jazz*, Violet, Naylor, and Morrison, and by implication all human beings—must risk that danger in order to live fully.

In such proximity, that Other is no longer a fixed or originary entity inflated out of proportion because of its inaccessibility; instead, one can learn to know it by returning to it, consumed neither by its presence nor by a futile attempt to decree its absence. At the rim of the well, Miranda experiences the *différance*—the ever-present but unrealizable principle that creates difference and hence meaning, in Derrida's words, "the non-full, non-simple, structured and differentiating origin of differences" (1982, 11). Her act is both a spatial differentiation and a temporal deferral. By entering the Other of space and time, she returns to the site of her father's—and the family's—deepest pain and innermost being. This essential truth had been repressed, buried in Miranda's and the family's unconsciousness, because the entire family had privileged consciousness and presence in their acceptance of the ancestry of Sapphira Wade and their denial of the family's tragedies.[6] Miranda cannot return fully to her father's grief, but at the well she encounters its trace, a substitute for the absent present, a "simulacrum of a presence that dislocates, displaces, refers to itself" (Derrida 1982, 24). The well and Miranda's epiphany there are also analogous to Derrida's concept of the breach, the gap between oppositions that "opens up a conducting path" (Derrida 1978, 200). Like Derrida's breach, Miranda's encounter with the previously unacknowledged and inconceivable Other stuns her but also creates new dimensions of consciousness for her.

Naylor constructs her first two novels, *The Women of Brewster Place* and *Linden Hills*, in settings that serve as symbolic wells. Like the literal well in *Mama Day*, the neighborhoods of the first two novels symbolically mark the communities' repressions. Both Brewster Place and Linden Hills are physically shaped like wells: the former is an urban block, closed off from the bustling city by a high brick wall; the latter is a V-shaped hill whose circular drives wend downward to the Nedeed house. As Barbara Christian argues, both communities are "self-enclosed," cut off from the rest of American society, much like African-Americans throughout American history (1990, 352). For most of the characters, life in these wells/traps is hellish, in Brewster Place primarily because of the impositions of white power, and in Linden Hills primarily because of the greed, envy, and social ambitions of the residents.

Most of the characters in both novels are trapped in the spiritual death of their monologic perspectives with the well; unlike Miranda, they are unable to open the closed lid to gain a new perspective. In *The Women of Brewster Place,* only Kiswana Browne provides an outside perspective, but her effectiveness is severely limited by her struggles to find her own identity. As opposed to the residents of Linden Hills, Willie and the Andersons (living outside the "well") do provide a viable alternative to the enclosed community. For them, generosity, empathy, and love outweigh status and economic success; their perspectives, outside Linden Hills, and symbolically on the rim of the well, allow them to nurture their own and others' souls rather than to lose their souls.[7]

In both novels, other well-like images reinforce the negativity. In the first novel, the alley is a dead end within the dead end of Brewster Place, the domain of C. C. Baker's macho gang. It stands in strict opposition to the female-dominated street. Hence, when the fragile Lorraine, who had futilely sought accommodation between her lesbianism and the community of heterosexual women, mistakenly enters the alley, it literally becomes her tomb. In this novel, there's no fusing of the two genders, no accommodations, no play, no unraveling of binaries, no awareness of the différance — there are only dead ends.

In *Linden Hills,* each house becomes a well/tomb for the African-American inmates, who have given up their souls to gain supposed status and "have turned away from their past and from their deepest sense of who they are" (Ward 1993, 182). Laurel Dumont's empty swimming pool is literally her death/trap when she dives into it, but the house as tomb is most graphic for the generations of Nedeed women. Each is trapped and/or allows herself to be trapped in the house and the obsessions of her husband. The series comes to its macabre conclusion with the last woman, Willa Prescott Nedeed, who is locked in the basement, a former morgue, "entombed in 'otherness'" like all black women (Werner 1987, 51). Anticipating Miranda's discovery of her ancestors' pain when she opens the well, Willa discovers in her symbolic well traces of the myriad sufferings of the former Mrs. Nedeeds—in their journals, their recipes, their photograph albums. What she finds is not full representations but fragments, suggestive of the fragmented lives to which the women and Willa herself were reduced. According to Margaret Homans, Willa finds "a record simply of effacement and silencing" (1993, 159), not presence but presence of absence, a pattern repeated once again in Willa's own life (160). Through her research in the well, Willa returns to the past—to the book—and thereby experiences the spatial difference and the temporal deferral of the différance, so that she can achieve "the strange serenity of such a return" (Derrida 1978, 298). Forced in her captivity to confront herself, her history, and the histories of her predecessors, Willa awakens to her responsibilities for her own life (Ward 1993, 192). But Willa's rebirth comes too late, so she can return to life only momentarily, only long enough to reorder her life—symbolized by her cleaning the kitchen—and to settle accounts with her husband. Despite the brevity of her return, the self-awareness she achieves in her agony indicates the power of such confrontation with the past and the hidden self, power that Miranda Day is able to marshal more fully after she opens the well.

In *The Women of Brewster Place,* Mattie mothers other women with her intuitive compassion but is powerless to prevent Lorraine's death, and the residents are unable to prevent the disintegration of the neighborhood. The only recourse to oppression is to try to obliterate the opposite term, to tear down the obstructing wall, to annihilate the well. This dreamlike attempt brings momentary relief and the "miracle" (*WBP,* 188) of returning sunshine but no lasting satisfaction. In *Linden Hills,* the community's failure is even worse, especially since it is self-imposed, although the momentary awakening of Willa and the potential of Willie are promising signs. Linked to Willa by their names and by his empathy for her, Willie holds the promise of a deferred fruition. Such deferral is achieved in Miranda's extension of the preliminary work accomplished by Mattie and Willa.

Like Naylor's first two novels, *Mama Day* is replete with examples of characters' harmful fixations on narrow objectives, obsessions that limit them metaphorically to the closed unity of the well. The Day family history is marked by suicides; Frances and Ruby exhaust themselves in their single-minded pursuit of Junior Lee; and George kills himself in his determination to save Cocoa. As Meisenhelder (1993) argues, characters who try to achieve their purposes in isolation always fail, but success comes to those who perceive the quiltlike pattern of life in which everything and everyone is independent—a distinct piece of the fabric—but joined in harmony with all the other pieces.

In *Mama Day* and *Bailey's Cafe,* the settings are again isolated communities, but the isolation is not a trap but rather a site for entering the différance. Willow Springs, a place outside history and geography, allows for a new perspective, not limited to the racial stereotypes and cultural restrictions of ordinary places. Through the islanders' spiritual power and especially Miranda's reconciliation of mainstream American and island values, Naylor suggests that the island is in the différance, simultaneously present and absent, existing and not existing: "Willow Springs ain't in no state. Georgia and South Carolina done tried, though—been trying since right after the Civil War to prove that Willow Springs belong to one or the other of them" (*MD,* 4–5).

In *Bailey's Cafe* Naylor creates a complex dynamic between the crushing stories of the characters who have drifted into the mystical neighborhood and the neighborhood itself, presided over by "Bailey," Nadine, Eve, and Gabriel. The lives of the visitors have been marred by their horrific encounters with racial and gender discrimination. That monologic power has been inflicted implacably, brutally, without question or hesitation; it has transformed the visitors into victims, into emphatically disprivileged terms of traditional binaries. Psychologically, they are in the well, unable to imagine any alternative to their victimhood.

Sadie, never desired or loved, "f[e]ll through the cracks of the upswings and downswings" (*BC,* 41). Innately possessing a sense of beauty, "*class*" (*BC,* 68) and elegance, she is driven deeper and deeper into her private sorrow, forced into a debilitating absorption in her defeated self-presence. She tries to make a home with Daniel, but his drinking and the thunderous trains drive her further inward. All her dreams must be infinitely deferred, as in Langston Hughes's poem that Naylor uses as the epigraph to *The Women of Brewster Place.* Liquor bottles become her personal well, as she finds solace only in the "stars" printed on them (*BC,* 65). After years of psychological deprivation, she internalizes the well, "the endless space of the black hole waiting to open in her heart" (*BC,* 64). Her dreams of a house, a picket fence, geraniums, laughter, Waterford crystal, and a good meal (*BC,* 72–77) are so disconnected from reality that she cannot accept Iceman Jones's offer of a shared life. She cannot escape the well/trap of her preoccupying struggle and her victimized self.

Esther, another victim of male subjugation, is driven even further into the psychological well. Directed at age twelve by her older brother to have sex in the dark basement with a man he calls her husband, she develops a psychosis that allows her to exist only in the dark basement of Eve's board-inghouse and the symbolic well of her mind. Aside from the johns who must bring her white roses and call her "little sister," her only companions are the spiders and a radio hero called The Shadow. Because her "hus-band" cautioned her, "*We won't speak about this, Esther,*" silence becomes her mode, as she can never find "a word for what happens between us in the cellar" (*BC*, 97). Lacking language, she cannot sense the différance; she has no play, only absolutes. She is at the bottom of the well, isolated in the dark, lacking Willa Nedeed's contacts with any predecessors, lacking the trace, and therefore unable to reclaim her life.

For other lost souls, the well takes other forms. For Mary/Peaches it starts as the wall her father builds around their house to keep boys out and becomes the internal wall she builds between her repressed self and her whore self that she sees reflected in every man's lustful eyes. She disfigures her face in a futile attempt to eliminate that lust and thereby to integrate her two selves. For Jesse Bell, the well is the alcohol and the heroin that she uses to blot out her history of mistreatment and loss. Her only sustaining hope is to return to her childhood bedroom, which becomes the image she dreams of.

Each of these female visitors to the neighborhood has been driven even more deeply into the symbolic well than were the characters in Naylor's first three novels. In *The Women of Brewster Place,* the women at least have the temporary comfort of the community and of each other. This support offsets their spiritual entrapment and enables them to collaborate in their brief vision of escape. In *Linden Hills,* the female, and male, victims of spiritual death at least have the comforts of wealth and status. In *Mama Day,* the residents of Willow Springs—despite their difficulties—are advan-tageously placed in the différance, where they can offset the debilitating effects of racial oppression and enjoy the psychic freedom and spiritual integration of their community. George's deep commitments to a mono-logic, rationalistic methodology do not allow him to join this community, but Cocoa appears to do so.

In the metaphysical gap between these unfortunate visitors to the neigh-borhood and the four proprietors of *Bailey's Cafe* is Miss Maple. He expe-riences the monologic insistence on an absolute white/black polarity at Stanford, in prison, and in his unsuccessful job search. But he is spared the extreme brutality that the women experience and, perhaps as a result, de-velops a more integrated and multiple response characterized by his female persona, his job as Eve's bouncer and janitor, his plans for his own com-pany, and his success in jingle contests. This multiplicity is rooted in his radically diverse genealogy that includes African-American, Native American, and Mexican ancestors. That mixed ethnicity translates into his non-binary mixing of genders, when he sensibly yields to sexual aggression in prison and later chooses comfortable female clothing. These accommodations allow Miss Maple to find his own identity, to "be my own man" (BC, 173) and to be free, "one of the freest men I know" (BC, 216).

Miss Maple thus shares many of the characteristics of the four proprietors and of Miranda, Willie, the Andersons, and Mattie. They offer acceptance and solace based on a hard-nosed acknowledgment of life's brutalities, on a relativistic incorporation of multiplicity, on a gritty compromise at the rim of the well. They have learned the futility of endorsing any fixed or originary value; in short, they are comfortable with the différance.

The neighborhood in *Bailey's Cafe*, in particular the cafe itself, is a metaphysical crossroads. Existing nowhere and everywhere, it is in the différance. Like Derrida's writing, which "is always explicitly inscribed in the margins of some preexisting text" (Johnson 1981, x), it is "right on the margin between the edge of the world and infinite possibility" (BC, 76). Like Willow Springs, it is not on any map, and yet "you can find [it] in any town" (BC, 112). It is a spiritual "way station" (BC, 221), a place "to take a breather for a while" (BC, 28), a place you must know in your soul in order to find it: "If they can't figure out that we're only here when they need us, they don't need to figure it out" (BC, 28). As suggested by the epigraph and the musical terminology in the chapter titles ("The Jam," "Mary [Take One]," "Miss Maple's Blues," "The Wrap"), it is an incarnation of the blues (Montgomery 1995, 30). Like the blues, the neighborhood simultaneously accepts hardship and mourns the associated loss. As Derrida (1982) advocates, the neighborhood returns—infinitely—to the past, not in a futile attempt to erase it but to re-realize it, to retrace it, to unravel the oppositions.[8] The philosophy is tough love: you are neither hassled nor coddled; you follow the "routine" at the cafe or you don't eat; you play by Eve's "house rules" or you don't play (BC, 92).

Behind the cafe is the well. It is a "void" (BC, 76), an "endless plunge" (BC, 76), a "black empty space" (BC, 137), where many visitors come to commit suicide (BC, 162). But, like Naylor's other wells, it is double-edged. Once the well is accepted—that is, once the implacable harshness of life, including death, is accepted and once one frees oneself from the narrow constraints of binary opposites—out back is where deferred dreams come true. Sadie and Jones "dance under the stars" (BC, 40); Jesse Bell sees her dream of "the simple bedroom she'd had as a girl" (BC, 138); Mariam finds "exactly what her childlike mind called up: endless water" (*BC*, 228); and Miss Maple "steps off boldly into the midst of nothing and is suspended midair by a gentle wind that starts to swirl his cape around his knees" (*BC*, 216).

The abyss is not threatening to Miss Maple or the four proprietors because they have accepted it and all it represents. At the edge of the well, they perpetually return to it and hence are not bound by it; it is absorbed into their stoic acceptance of life. Privileged by Naylor, the four proprietors are clear-sighted, straightforward, and direct: Bailey claims "I call 'em the way I see 'em" (*BC*, 32) and praises Nadine for the same quality: "like me, she calls 'em as she sees 'em" (*BC*, 116). Like Miranda and Abigail in *Mama Day*, they are realists trying to be honest but not necessarily nice. Despite their sometimes rough exteriors, they are compassionate and tolerant, helping others endure the pain or pass beyond it. They have no illusions about life, expecting little from it: Gabe knows that "the world, it still waits to commit suicide" (*BC*, 219), and Bailey accepts that "the brotherhood of man . . . is a crock of bull" (*BC*, 220) and that "life is [not] supposed to make you feel good, or to make you feel miserable either. Life is just supposed to make you feel" (*BC*, 219).

Like Miranda and Abigail, these four proprietors have extraordinary strength of character, which has prevented them from becoming victims. Nadine confines her letters to Bailey to "short short" ones, but with "perfect timing" (*BC*, 13); and unlike most people, she "doesn't bother" to "translate [her] feelings for the general population" (*BC*, 19). When banished by her tyrannical father, Eve treks through the delta and eventually establishes her rigidly run boardinghouse and her beloved garden (*BC*, 92). These characters are larger than life, possessing almost superhuman powers: Gabe is able to rescue Mariam; Bailey "can get inside a lot of heads around here" (*BC*, 165); and Nadine "look[s] like an African goddess" (*BC*, 13). Eve is the most mythical, becoming one with the delta dust (*BC*, 86) and walking across the delta for "a thousand years" (*BC*, 82). She knows the cafe routine before she arrives (*BC*, 80), "already knew" Esther's story (*BC*, 99), and sets up Mariam's dreamscape (*BC*, 224). She is a dream-maker, a tough *griot*, reminiscent in name and personality of the biblical Eve and Eva Peace in Toni Morrison's *Sula*. Like the other three proprietors, she was relegated to the margins: "it seemed there was nowhere on earth for a woman like me" (*BC*, 91). She and Nadine are the kind of women Naylor admires, women who have "turned their backs on the world" and who have "been selfish to some degree" (Naylor 1985a,

572). They, like Miranda, Abigail, Bailey, Gabriel, and Naylor, have said, "*I am here*. That *I* contains myriad realities—not all of them pretty, but not all of them ugly, either" (Naylor 1988–89, 31).

Through her four presiding figures, and often through Bailey as their principal spokesperson, Naylor creates a worldview that privileges tolerance, open-endedness, and complexity, all of which become possible when one has transcended Brewster Place and Linden Hills, has acknowledged and accepted the abyss, and (like Miranda) has had the courage to open the well. The neighborhood accepts all comers, all who have suffered and who need relief. Customs from all over the world are welcomed: Miss Maple admires the loose-fitting business clothes of non-Westerners (*BC*, 201), and Bailey enjoys the music of many cultures (*BC*, 162). At the end of the novel, the ritual performance of George's circumcision brings the community together in a celebration of cross-cultural harmony. This valuing of tolerance contrasts sharply with the novel's refrain of intolerance and bigotry. As Karen Joy Fowler comments, the book's "abundance plays against the particular pains contained in the various characters' stories" (1993, 27).

The neighborhood's *ethos* of tolerance is reinforced by the belief that everything always remains open. Emancipated from the constraints of monologism, the neighborhood has no beginning, no end, no fixed points; it exists in the pure play of the nontemporal and nonspatial. Bailey expresses the apparently shared views that life has "more questions than answers" (*BC*, 229) and that "no life is perfect" (*BC*, 228). Instead of desiring answers or perfection, Bailey relishes endless flux: "If life is truly a song, then what we've got here is just snatches of a few melodies. All these folks are in transition; they come midway in their stories and go on" (*BC*, 219). Everything remains open partly because everything is more complex than it may appear: Iceman Jones knows "that most things aren't what they seem" (*BC*, 70), and Bailey warns readers "if you're expecting to get the answer in a few notes, you're mistaken" (*BC*, 4).

This insistence on complexity is expressed in the metaphor of going under the surface. Bailey, listening closely to the stereotyped opinions of Sister Carrie and Sugar Man, warns readers not to oversimplify: "If you don't listen below the surface, they're both one-note players" (*BC*, 33). Hearing only that one note is insufficient, for everyone in this novel—and, Naylor implies, every human being—has a complex story: "But nobody comes in here with a simple story. Every one-liner's got a life underneath it. Every point's got a counterpoint" (*BC*, 34). Bailey's advice for readers is that "Anything really worth hearing in this greasy spoon happens under the surface. You need to know that if you plan to stick around here and listen while we play it all out" (*BC*, 35). Readers must learn what the four proprietors have learned and what the victimized visitors are struggling to learn—how to go below the surface, to "take 'em one key down" (*BC*, 34). Characters and readers must learn not only tolerance for others but tolerance and understanding of the multiple layers of meanings. All must move beyond monologism into multiplicity.

The form of this novel itself exhibits these values of openness and depth. The musical metaphors around which the narrative is structured push the written medium toward a nondiscursive, nonprescriptive mode, a mode that suggests rather than defines, that opens rather than narrows. Similarly, the point of view is not restricted to one voice or one perspective. Although Bailey is the principal narrator, usually introducing and concluding each character's story, his voice is not sufficient. Maxine Lavon Montgomery argues that this multiplicity is necessary because "the male voice is severely limited in its ability to decode the very private experiences the women relate" (1995, 28). But the larger point is that no single voice is adequate to convey the characters' experiences. A single voice would metaphorically place the text in the well, in a confining monologism; therefore, a multiplicity of voices is necessary to convey the multiplicity of life, to ensure that life and the novel keep their play. For this reason, when Bailey's voice is insufficient to narrate Mariam's story, two additional voices—Nadine's and Eve's—are required.

To avoid the constrictions of a single perspective, Naylor includes the voices of nearly every character: direct transcription of Sadie's thoughts alternate with Bailey's narration (*BC*, 72–78); Eve (81–91), Mary/Peaches (102–12), Esther (95–99), and Miss Maple (165–213) all take over the telling of their stories; Jesse Bell's first-person narration is interpolated into Bailey's narration (137–41); and Nadine and Eve narrate Mariam's life story (143–60). Naylor even includes the direct words of minor characters, such as the anonymous soldiers and their officer, who shout their determination to "kill Japs" (21), the unnamed customers with whom Bailey argues (31), the stereotyped religious zealot Sister Carrie and the equally stereotyped hipster Sugar Man (32–34), Esther's miscellaneous customers (95), Esther's "husband" (95), and Miss Maple's father (185).

Naylor also underscores and extends the plural and oral-like narration by unexpectedly shifting one character's indirect discourse to another character's language. For example, Miss Maple's narration is interrupted by a direct transcription of the Gatlin boys' thought: "What they couldn't tear apart, they stomped—*My God, look, it ain't got a tail after all*" (*BC*,

180, emphasis added). Similarly, Bailey's narration is interrupted by Gabe's thought: "And banging down old radios and flinging used overcoats into boxes and sweeping up a dust storm. *Puppy, cover your ears, a goy shouldn't be hearing these things*" (221, emphasis added). With this doubling of free indirect discourse, Naylor implies that no single voice suffices, even within a single sentence.

In addition to creating a communal narration, Naylor's narrative technique tends to transform the written text into oral performance. On one level, the entire text carries the sense of being spoken directly to the reader. From beginning to end, Bailey's language sounds more spoken than written, with its contractions, its informality, its casualness: the novel starts with "I can't say I've had much education. Book education" (*BC,* 3) and ends with "And that's how we wrap it, folks" (*BC,* 229). As in the latter sentence, Bailey frequently addresses readers directly: we are customers at his cafe ("And if you've got a problem with how I feel, well, there are other cafes" [12]); we are recipients of his lessons ("If you don't listen below the surface, they're both one-note players" [33]); we are taken under his wing ("But I think you've got the drift" [35]); we hear his complaints ("I want you to know right off that Nadine lied on me" [161]); and we receive his hints ("And what I heard is too ignorant to believe. And just guess who I heard it from? [Sister Carrie and Sugar Man, in case you need a hint]" [223]). The sense that readers are listening directly to the novel is sustained when both Nadine and Miss Maple also address us. Nadine begins her narration with "You already know that my name is Nadine" (*BC,* 143), and Miss Maple interjects a "dialogue" with readers in which the latter's presumed questions are posed and then answered by Miss Maple: "And now I'm going to hold a conversation with what I assume are some of your more troubling thoughts about this whole endeavor" (*BC,* 203).

On another level, the language of the text is addressed to and heard by the other characters. Several times Bailey directs asides to Nadine, implying that she is listening to his narration, for example "Nadine, nobody asked you" (*BC,* 4). Nadine acknowledges that she has heard Bailey's long address to the reader: "You already know that my name is Nadine, and my husband's told you that I don't like to talk" (143). This mutual participation in the narrative peaks during the circumcision of the new infant, George. Everyone is there, even Esther, who "wonder of wonders . . . smiled" (225). Peaches begins to sing a spiritual and soon everyone is singing: "One voice joined in. Another voice joined. And another" (225). They sing of their assertions of identity ("Anybody ask you who I am? Tell him— you're the child of God") and of the harmony of human beings and God, of

"Peace on earth" (226). The three males share the male roles appropriate for the ritual: Gabriel is the father and rabbi, Bailey is the godfather, and Miss Maple "took the role of the other male guests to help [Bailey] respond to the blessing" (226).

This overlay of oral qualities within the written novel suggests Derrida's insistent argument in *Of Grammatology* against the traditional Western privileging of speech over writing. Just as Derrida argues that spoken language is not more accurate or truthful than written language, Naylor also unravels the apparent dichotomy between the two. Derrida reconfigures perceptions of language by undermining the traditional values placed on the immediate presence of speaker and auditor in speech, while Naylor (like many fiction writers) works from the opposite direction to nudge her necessarily written text toward the domain of speech. The effects are complementary: each reduces the traditional valuing of preset suppositions and instead slips into the unexplored but exhilarating gaps between and among them.

Just as Bailey is impressed with the Jewish communal ritual ("And that's what I like the most about Gabe's faith; nothing important can happen unless they're all in it together as a community" [*BC*, 227]), Naylor structures her novel so that this most important event—the first birth on the block—brings this community together. Individuals may, and will, be trapped in their well-like tragedies, but communities, as in the brick-throwing demonstration in *The Women of Brewster Place* and in the annual Candle Walk in *Mama Day*, can gain at least momentary relief by singing, by performing time-honored rituals, by telling and hearing each other's stories, and by embracing each other and each other's cultures. Multiple voices can create communities and thereby help characters avoid the isolation of the well.

As the novel's multiple narrations and its orality increase the connections among characters and readers, the shifts in point of view often enact the principle of going beneath the surface. Bailey uses the metaphor of going "one key down" (*BC*, 34) to indicate the deeper layer(s) of meaning beneath the surface meaning. Bailey illustrates this strategy in his transcriptions of Sister Carrie's and Sugar Man's actual words and then in his translations of what the two really mean (*BC*, 33–35). After presenting their actual words, he tells us what they are really saying "one key down" and on "even a lower key" (*BC*, 34). Through Bailey, Naylor thus creates an explicit model for readers of this and of all of her novels: the stories of Naylor's characters must be read as Bailey reads the words of Sister Carrie and Sugar Man, not merely for their surface meaning but for the layers of deeper meanings. Naylor structures her stories to encourage such a reading strategy. In "Mood: Indigo," the narration of Sadie's story goes one key down when it shifts from Bailey's point of view to the italicized paragraphs directly depicting Sadie's dream of middle-class comfort (*BC*, 72–77). Similarly, the narration goes beneath the surface when it shifts from Bailey's voice to the voices of Eve (*BC*, 81–91), Esther (95–99), Mary/ Peaches (102–12), Jesse Bell (117–32), and Miss Maple (165–213).

In "Jesse Bell" the narration descends even lower when Sister Carrie and Eve duel with contrasting biblical passages as commentaries on Jesse (*BC*, 134–36). During this exchange Eve sarcastically signifies on Carrie when she calls out "somebody in here likes Ezekiel. Somebody even likes the *sixteenth chapter* of Ezekiel" (*BC*, 135). Eve subdues Carrie with this and similar counter-passages that emphasize divine love for the fallen. Naylor invites the reader to play the biblical game by quoting Ezekiel 16:6 without identifying it, letting it stand as a concluding, and tolerating, comment on Jesse: *"And when I passed by thee, and saw polluted in thine own blood, I said unto thee when thou wast in thy blood, Live; yea, I said unto thee when thou was in thy blood, Live"* (*BC*, 136).

The narration continues to push the usual limits when Jesse's indirect discourse is frequently interpolated, without warnings or transitions, into Bailey's narration. For example, when Bailey narrates "Jesse didn't quite know what it meant, but this weird mama-jama was beginning to really scare her" (*BC*, 137), "weird mama-jama" is Jesse's term for Eve, not Bailey's. The technique is most obvious in the following paragraph, in which the first person shifts abruptly from Bailey to Jesse: "Jesse has never tried to describe for me what it was like that second time around. She says there are no words for the experience. I can only tell you this, Bailey, I sincerely prayed to die" (*BC*, 141).

Besides drawing characters and readers closer together, the multiple, shifting, and oral narration of this novel reflects the creation of a stable and supportive community, unlike the broken one in *The Women of Brewster Place,* the absent one in *Linden Hills,* and the questionable one in *Mama Day.* By embodying such a community in *Bailey's Cafe,* the narration reinforces the connections among the participants and all human beings. Since the point of view can flow back and forth among the characters, and since the characters can overhear each other's narrations to the reader, the physical and psychological distances among them are metaphorically eliminated. All can join in each other's dream fantasies; all can participate in the celebration of George's birth. One passage in particular, a one-key-down passage, suggests such metaphysical interconnections. As Bailey recalls his experiences in World War II, his identity expands to incorporate all American soldiers in the Pacific. This merger begins cryptically with the refrain, *"We weren't getting into Tokyo"* (*BC*, 21–23), and develops into a full-blown monologue within Bailey's narration. As "The Soldier," Bailey has been present at every Pacific battle, imagines that "the end of the world is blue" (23), feels the horror of Japanese civilians caught in the war, participates in the atomic bombings of Hiroshima and Nagasaki, and worries about the "unborn children" and the "new age" (26) to follow. Bailey encompasses not only every soldier but also every victim and even the unborn victims because he transcends the barriers that usually isolate individuals. Entering the différance, he floats free of any limiting self-presence, just as the novel's narration allows the characters and its readers to escape theirs.

Characters in this novel are able to cross such boundaries because, unlike in Naylor's first three novels, here the characters are not enmeshed in limiting stereotypes. The residents of Linden Hills are trapped in logocentrism by their own conformity to white values of economic success and social status. George and Cocoa in *Mama Day* must struggle with their preconceived absolutes, in particular, with white values of love, courtship, and life.[9] But *Bailey's Cafe* culminates with the cross-cultural, communal celebration of the birth of Mariam's son. This birth is the occasion for the neighborhood's coming together, but, in keeping with Naylor's and the privileged characters' tough realism, it will not change the world: "Life will go on. Still, I do understand the point this little fella is making as he wakes up in the basket: When you have to face it with more questions than answers, it can be a crying shame" (*BC*, 229).

For Naylor to end this novel with a birth is particularly significant because throughout her fiction births are rare and associated with extreme hardship. In *The Women of Brewster Place*, Lucielia's first child is electrocuted and her second one aborted. In *Linden Hills*, Willa Nedeed must watch the corpse of her son as she struggles toward her own psychic rebirth and physical death. In *Mama Day*, Bernice Duvall first develops cysts instead of a baby and then her baby dies, and pregnancy for Cocoa Day almost kills her. Given this context of difficult pregnancies and births, George's birth is especially miraculous. Not only is he the first child born in this neighborhood, but he is born to a woman whose vagina had been ritually sewn shut. His conception is thus a mystery and a miracle, which strengthens the sense in this novel that he is a Christ-like figure. Mariam's sealed vagina is another well image, in this case a closed well, a well like a tomb, but a double-edged well, a well of death transformed into a source of life.

At the other end of life, deaths in Naylor's novels are also traumatic. Many characters meet violent deaths: Serena, Lorraine, and Ben in *The Women of Brewster Place*; Laurel Dumont and the three Mrs. Nedeeds in *Linden Hills*; Little Caesar and George in *Mama Day*; and numerous, unnamed suicides in *Bailey's Cafe*.

That birth and death should be so difficult is predicted by the womb/tomb image of the well. Well, birth, and death are mysterious and unavoidable. As Derrida (1978), Morrison (1992), and Naylor intimate, the temptation to ignore such abysses must be resisted and their inevitability acknowledged. In *Bailey's Cafe,* Naylor establishes a community of privileged characters who have done just that, who are comfortable with the abysses of a devastating world and therefore are secure in their identities and roles. They endure because they have learned to accept the brutality of African-American life in a racialized society, because they have transformed their double-consciousness into an advantage, because they have absorbed the différance.

In one sense the occasion of George's birth restores a sense of cosmic harmony to the novel's characters, establishes for them a living and livable African-American space, and thereby restores a sense of the past and provides hope for the present if not the future. At the same time the event strengthens the secure identities of the four privileged characters and offers a basis for positive identity formation for the others. All this can happen because all the characters, and now the participating reader, have learned to accept the abyss. Like the inhabitants of the Bottom in Morrison's *Sula,* they have learned that "the presence of evil was something to be first recognized, then dealt with, survived, outwitted, triumphed over" (Morrison 1975, 118).

In another sense, however, such triumphant implications of George's birth are called into question. In *Mama Day,* the male protagonist is the same George, born to a fifteen-year-old mother across the street from Bailey's Cafe and raised in an orphanage (*MD,* 130–31). In that novel, George is less clearly a Christ-figure, bound up in his rigid self-presence. Although his birth unites the community in *Bailey's Cafe,* that miraculous moment is only a moment.

For Naylor, as for Derrida, there can be no ultimate solutions; instead, life is a continuous process of difference and deferral. Naylor's novels begin with the notion of deferral in her use of Hughes's "What Happens to a Dream Deferred?" as the epigraph to *The Women of Brewster Place.* Ongoing deferral is evident throughout her novels in the explicit links among their settings and characters, for example in the geographic, economic, and social connections between Linden Hills and Brewster Place and in the implicit developmental progressions from Willa to Willie, and from Mattie and Willa to Miranda, Nadine, and Eve. Reading *Bailey's Cafe* and *Mama Day* in reverse order, the bright promise of George's birth at the end of *Bailey's Cafe* is deferred to the birth of Cocoa's son, also named George, at the end of *Mama Day*. With that repetition, Naylor returns to the symbolic event of the first George's birth, defers its promise, and leaves open and alive the potential of the second George.

Naylor's exploration of the différance reflects broad cultural concerns. The synthesis of cultures, individuals, genders, and generations at the end of *Bailey's Cafe* projects the cosmic harmony that characterizes West African religions and philosophies. This worldview, in contrast to the Euro-American emphasis on differences and "dissent," as Miss Maple calls it (*BC,* 192), stresses the integration of individual, community, nature, and the supernatural.[10] This novel and the celebration in which it culminates also depict the founding, acceptance of, and consecration of a meaningful African-American place and time. African-Americans' assigned places have been in the well at the bottom of American society; as Houston Baker, Jr., contends, African-Americans have been consigned to the holds of slavers, then rural cabins, and later urban kitchenettes (1989, 136–41). The refugees in *Bailey's Cafe* have been denied not only a place but any meaningful past, just as African-Americans have historically been denied a past. As a result of such difficulties, the characters are plagued by the problem of establishing and maintaining viable identities: Ellison contends that "Negro Americans are in desperate search for identity" (1972, 297), and Barbara Christian urges black women "to define and express [their] totality rather than being defined by others" (1985, 159). Pursuing a sense of identity in the face of such displacements, Naylor's characters are forced to confront the false illusions of traditional binaries and instead must adopt the survival strategies of deferral, flexibility, and multiplicity.

Notes

1. Elsewhere, I have discussed some connections between deconstruction and African-American culture (Page 1996, 3–25) and some relationships between Derrida and Morrison (Page 1995, 55–56; 1996, 159–76).

2. For example, Luce Irigaray exults in women's "disruptive excess" (1991), and Rachel DuPlessis celebrates the "both/and vision" of the female aesthetic (1985, 276).

3. Examples of such formulations by African-American male theorists include that of Robert Stepto, who praises African-American culture for espousing the both/and, or what he calls "modal," perspective (1979, xiii) and that of Houston

Baker, Jr., who attests that "This historic condition outside mainstream American culture forced African Americans to deconstruct, defamiliarize, and signify within the master discourse" (1989, 136–41).

4. For example, Mae Henderson welcomes "the deconstructive function of black women's writing" and the black woman writer's ability "to see the other, but also to see what the other cannot see" (1990, 135, 137), and Valerie Smith argues that black feminists are ideally situated to ensure that the radical discourses of blacks and feminists are not diluted (1989, 40–43).

5. Susan Meisenhelder points out that Miranda's contribution to the community's quiltlike interpretations of itself is to appreciate the male perspective of Sapphira's owner, Bascombe Wade (1993, 415).

6. Following Freud, Derrida argues that humans tend to privilege the conscious over the unconscious and that recognition of the différance and the consequent unraveling of the binary opposition between consciousness and unconsciousness allows for the recovery of what has been repressed (1978, 16–22).

7. Catherine C. Ward emphasizes that Ruth Anderson represents a perspective characterized by pure human love (1993, 186).

8. As Derrida puts it, "Thus one could reconsider all the pairs of opposites on which philosophy is constructed and on which our discourse lives, not in order to see opposition erase itself but to see what indicates that each of the terms must appear as the différance of the other" (1982, 17).

9. Meisenhelder demonstrates that George and Cocoa try unsuccessfully to understand each other and Willow Springs in terms of white myths (1993, 405–12).

10. For commentaries on traditional West African world views, see Jahn (1961) and Mbiti (1989).

Works Cited

Baker, Houston A., Jr. "There Is No More Beautiful Way: Theory and the Poetics of Afro-American Women's Writing." *Afro-American Literary Study in the 1990s.* Eds. Houston Baker and Patricia Redmond. Chicago: University of Chicago Press, 1989. 135–55.

Christian, Barbara. *Black Feminist Criticism: Perspectives on Black Women Writers.* New York: Pergamon Press, 1985.

———. "Gloria Naylor's Geography: Community, Class, and Patriarchy in *The Women of Brewster Place* and *Linden Hills*." In *Reading Black, Reading Feminist: A Critical Anthology.* Ed. Henry Louis Gates, Jr. New York: Penguin, 1990. 348–73.

Derrida, Jacques. *Margins of Philosophy.* Trans. Alan Bass. Chicago: University of Chicago Press, 1982.

———. *Of Grammatology.* Trans. Gayatri Chakravorty Spivak. Baltimore: Johns Hopkins University Press, 1974.

———. *Writing and Difference.* Trans. Alan Bass. Chicago: University of Chicago Press, 1978.

Du Bois, W. E. B. *The Souls of Black Folk.* New York: Penguin, 1989.

DuPlessis, Rachel Blau. "For the Etruscans." In *The New Feminist Criticism.* Ed. Elaine Showalter. New York: Pantheon, 1985. 271–91.

Ellison, Ralph. *Shadow and Act.* New York: Vintage, 1972.

Fowler, Karen Joy. Review of *Bailey's Cafe. Chicago Tribune,* Oct. 4, 1992. In *Gloria Naylor: Critical Perspectives Past and Present.* Eds. Henry Louis Gates, Jr., and K. A. Appiah. New York: Amistad, 1993. 26–28.

Henderson, Mae Gwendolyn. "Speaking in Tongues: Dialogics, Dialectics, and the Black Woman Writer's Literary Tradition." In *Reading Black, Reading Feminist: A Critical Anthology.* Ed. Henry Louis Gates, Jr. New York: Penguin, 1990. 116–42.

Homans, Margaret. "The Woman in the Cave." In *Gloria Naylor: Critical Perspectives Past and Present.* Eds. Henry Louis Gates, Jr., and K. A. Appiah. New York: Amistad, 1993. 152–81.

Irigaray, Luce. "The Power of Discourse and the Subordination of the Feminine." *The Irigaray Reader.* Ed. Margaret Whitford. Oxford: Basil Blackwell, 1991. 118–27.

Jahn, Janheinz. *Muntu: An Outline of the New African Culture.* Trans. Marjorie Grene. New York: Grove, 1961.

Johnson, Barbara. Translator's Introduction. *Dissemination.* By Jacques Derrida. Chicago: University of Chicago Press, 1981.

Mbiti, John. *African Religions and Philosophy.* 2nd ed. Oxford: Heinemann, 1989.

Meisenhelder, Susan. "'The Whole Picture' in Gloria Naylor's *Mama Day." African American Review* 27 no. 3 (1993): 405–19.

Montgomery, Maxine Lavon. "Authority, Multivocality, and the New World Order in Gloria Naylor's *Bailey's Cafe." African American Review* 29 (1995): 27–33.

Morrison, Toni. *Jazz.* New York: Knopf, 1992.

———. *Sula.* New York: Bantam, 1975.

Naylor, Gloria. *Bailey's Cafe.* New York: Vintage, 1993.

———. *Linden Hills.* New York: Penguin, 1985b.

———. "Love and Sex in the Afro-American Novel." *Yale Review* 78 (1988–89): 19–31.

———. *Mama Day.* New York: Vintage, 1989.

———. *The Women of Brewster Place.* New York: Penguin, 1982.

Naylor, Gloria, and Toni Morrison. "Gloria Naylor and Toni Morrison: A Conversation." *Southern Review* 21 no. 3 (1985a): 567–93.

Page, Philip. *Dangerous Freedom: Fusion and Fragmentation in Toni Morrison's Novels.* Jackson: University Press of Mississippi, 1996.

———. "Traces of Derrida in Toni Morrison's *Jazz." African American Review* 29 (1995): 55–66.

Smith, Valerie. "Black Feminist Theory and the Representation of the 'Other'." In *Changing Our Own Words: Essays on Criticism, Theory, and Writing by Black Women.* Ed. Cheryl A. Wall. New Brunswick, N.J.: Rutgers University Press, 1989. 38–57.

Stepto, Robert B. *From Behind the Veil: A Study of Afro-American Narrative.* Urbana: University of Illinois Press, 1979.

Storhoff, Gary. "'The Only Voice Is Your Own': Gloria Naylor's Revision of *The Tempest.*" *African American Review* 29 (1995): 35–45.

Ward, Catherine C. "*Linden Hills*: A Modern *Inferno.*" In *Gloria Naylor: Critical Perspectives Past and Present.* Eds. Henry Louis Gates, Jr., and K. A. Appiah. New York: Amistad, 1993. 182–94.

Werner, Craig. "Minstrel Nightmares and Black Dreams of Faulkner's Dreams of Blacks." In *Faulkner and Race: Faulkner and Yoknapatawpha, 1986.* Eds. Doreen Fowler and Ann J. Abadie. Jackson: University Press of Mississippi, 1987. 35–57.

Framing the Possibilities

Collective Agency and the Novels of Gloria Naylor

Margot Anne Kelley

In *Borders, Boundaries, and Frames,* Mae Henderson observes that a "frame generates meaning through its internal arrangement of space as well as through its definition of the boundary between images" (1995, 21). The framing may reinforce or undermine prevailing assumptions about boundaries and about both that which is framed and that which is un-framed. However, the frame exists not as an entity that can be separated entirely from either the object it frames—the painting or literary text, for instance, or from the objects that are rendered external to it—like the wall or the world. Rather, the frame is, as Derrida explains in *Glas,* "a *parergon,* a composite of inside and outside, but a composite which is not an amal-gam or half-and-half but an outside which is called outside the inside to constitute it as inside" (Culler 1982, 195). Clarifying the function of the parergon, Jonathan Culler notes that "at the very moment that it is playing an essential, constitutive, enshrining and protecting role . . . it undermines this role by leading itself to be defined as subsidiary ornamentation" (1982, 195). Therefore, he adds, the logic of the parergon can be regarded as akin to that of the *supplement,* for in both cases "the marginal becomes central by virtue of its own marginality" (Culler 1982, 196).

Given this capacity for challenging the boundaries between inside and outside, as well as for redefining the relationship between central and marginal, the frame is a potentially useful device for writers working to deconstruct narrative and/or cultural assumptions that have relegated them to the literary or social periphery. As a technique for destabilizing narrative, frames have been used in a variety of postmodern fictions. Further, the notion of framing, as a way to imaginatively intertwine the competing realities that lay claim to the (now-fragmentary) individual, has become a common trope in postmodern theory. Fredric Jameson, for instance, has argued that the postmodern dilemma involves "our insertion as individual subjects into a multidimensional set of radically discontinuous realities, whose frames range from the still surviving spaces of bourgeois private life all the way to the unimaginable decentering of global capital itself. Not even Einsteinian relativity, or the multiple subjective worlds of the older modernists, is capable of giving any kind of adequate figuration to this process" (1991, 413). Homi Bhabha extends this image, describing the "the *in-between* spaces of double-frames" as the site where a "new historical subject" can emerge (1994, 216, 217).

To see what this new historical subject might look like, and what, precisely, are the conditions for its emergence, we do well to turn from theoretical articulations to literary ones. In each of her novels, Gloria Naylor calls attention to borders and boundaries; and in her fourth, *Bailey's Cafe,* she explores the political, social, and aesthetic possibilities that become available when one reconceives existing identities, as well as social and economic institutions, through different frames. In this text, she uses two intertwined "spatial" frames and one "temporal" frame to organize the stories of the women who live at Eve's place, a boardinghouse that the locals think of as both whorehouse and convent. As readers quickly realize, these women are likened to the biblical characters whose names they share (Eve, Esther, Jezebel, Mary Magdalene, and the Virgin Mary); and they are all transgressors of socially constructed borders, of the frames that others establish to circumscribe their lives. Naylor has explained that she offered these particular representations of women in order to reclaim the word "whore" and the sexuality that she believes has been demonized through the pejorative associations of that word within "the Judeo-Christian ethic" and tradition (Naylor 1992b).

Certainly she succeeds at this task, but this goal is achieved largely in the center of the text and this aim does not obviously require the use of any frames, much less three. Therefore, I believe that her decision to employ multiple frames must be investigated in its own right. Whereas in *The Women of Brewster Place* Naylor employed a very short, single frame, here she uses frames that, in their proliferation and their complexity, suggest that she is indeed making "the marginal become[] central." Using these frames helped her to create an "in-between" space where, as Bhabha argued, narrative attempts to "enjoin the global and the local" can be played out in order to make discernible postcolonial identities that had previously been unrepresentable (Bhabha 1994, 216). In the frames, and in the world they circumscribe, characters employ what the sociologist Michel deCerteau has termed "tactics" to deflect the most oppressive aspects of advanced capitalism, thereby enacting a partial alternative that lets characters have more agency and allows readers to imagine a different social order (deCerteau, 1984). The immensity of the struggle Naylor envisions is hinted at by the complexity of the frames. Within and between the frames she counterpoints and simultaneously destabilizes the simple binary relations between a variety of seemingly diametric factors, including space and time, African-American musical legacies and Western literary traditions, Judaic and Christian beliefs, male and female, birth and death, among many others. In short, she uses the frames to demarcate a zone of undecidability, for only in that sort of space will a thoroughgoing transformation of identity, and an associated emergence of a revitalized form of agency, be possible. Naylor repeats this construction across her first four novels, which work together as a quartet. Consequently, to recognize this space and the tasks being undertaken there, we need to attend to the ways that she uses intertextual links to unite the novels into a multivolume text, a "place" where she has been able to define an aesthetic and a cultural terrain that works both with and against the prevailing one(s).

Bailey's Cafe is a composite novel containing nine full-length stories and one very short piece that cannot readily stand alone ("The Vamp"). *Bailey's Cafe* begins with a fairly lengthy overture entitled "Maestro, if you please," which is followed by the brief section "The Vamp," where the counterpointing lines of Sister Carrie (a churchwoman) and Sugar Man (a pimp) emerge. With melody and harmony established in these opening pieces, the next seven sections—while discrete—are collectively subtitled "The Jam," and they form the heart of the improvisation. Here, individual voices proffer solos, and the group is followed by "The Wrap," an ensemble conclusion. In defining the frames that operate in this novel, I call the first frame "temporal" because it becomes apparent only as the reader discovers the related references interspersed throughout the text; that is, we experience it in time. In *A Dictionary of Narratology,* Gerald Prince calls this type simply a frame, and likens it to a "schema" in that it is serially ordered and is a "global semantic framework" that guides the reader's "perceptions and comprehensions" (1987, 84). This frame is composed through the references to musical constructions—both the names of the sections and the names of some of the stories within those sections, with titles like "Mood: Indigo" offering us the clearest examples. This musical construction at the level of story and section titles also encourages readers to look for musical patterns within the stories themselves—and specifically to expect these patterns to coincide with African-American jazz traditions.

The second and third frames are the sort I call "spatial," and that Gerald Prince calls "frame narratives." The two pieces that compose such a frame are positioned before and after an embedded narrative; this embedded narrative can—but doesn't need to—exist at a different diegetic level (Prince 1987, 33). The first spatial frame in *Bailey's Cafe* is created as a subset of the musical overlay. "Maestro, if you please" (plus "The Vamp") and "The Wrap" are set off from, and literally border, "The Jam." Because the reader most often becomes conscious of such a frame as part of a nesting strategy, when he or she regards an outline or schematic description of the book, we can say this type of frame exists more obviously in space than in time.

The third frame is slightly less obvious. Whereas the distinction between the beginning and ending stories in the novel (on the one hand) and the middle seven (on the other hand) is conspicuous, Naylor does not provide equally explicit clues to make us expect any of the sections of "The Jam" to be ontologically distinct from other sections. However, when we consider the seven stories in "The Jam"—"Mood: Indigo," "Eve's Song," "Sweet Esther," "Mary (Take One)," "Jesse Bell," "Mary (Take Two)," and "Miss Maple's Blues"—we begin to sense simply from their titles that the second through sixth "Jam" stories do form a discrete unit. They are the retellings of the stories of "classical women from the Bible" (Naylor 1992b). However, the first story and the seventh do not conform to that model. Thus, these two stories, another beginning and ending pair, form a spatial frame that is both a part of and also separate from the rest of "The Jam."

Actually, Naylor does provide a variety of connecting threads that encourage us to see "Mood: Indigo" (which is about Sadie) and "Miss Maple's Blues" (which is about Stanley) as counterpointing each other: not only are these two characters the only protagonists in "The Jam" who do not have biblical counterparts, but also they both work as housekeepers in "whorehouses," both have economic concerns that are paramount, and both are in stories with titles that conspicuously invoke jazz/blues tradition. "Mood: Indigo" is, of course, referring to Duke Ellington's famous piece (1930). In fact, while Naylor has often commented that the book is generally structured around jazz principles (Carabi 1992, 42; Perry 1993, 235), in an interview on National Public Radio she explained that Sadie's story is intended "actually to transliterate Duke Ellington's 'Mood Indigo'." Naylor said she chose that piece because she wanted to explore a call and response pattern in which the two instruments "never quite make it . . . you leave that piece of music feeling every sort of lack, every sort of 'might have been' imaginable" (Naylor 1992b). In contrast, the title "Miss Maple's Blues" likely plays off Scott Joplin's "Maple Leaf Rag," the first well-known ragtime piece (1899) and, as such, one of the first blues numbers to attain widespread public recognition. Like a rag, this story sets up two counterpointing melody lines (Stanley's exploration of what it is to be or to not be a man), followed by a trio (which occurs at his luncheon at Waco Glass and Tile), and a definitive finale (Stanley and Bailey toasting New Year's 1949). The connection between the two characters that is forged musically is playfully reinforced through their names. (The editor for many of the various standard reference books on music published by Grove Press is Stanley Sadie.)

As straightforward as this pairing might seem, we need to complicate our understanding of it, because Naylor claims that it is not Sadie and Stanley, but rather Bailey and Stanley, who are complementary figures. Naylor explained it this way to Virginia Fowler:

> [Stanley] and Bailey are bookends to a story that I'm telling about sexuality and sexual identity. . . . However, in order to talk about what is female sexuality and female sexual identity necessitates talking about what is male sexuality and male sexual identity, because you cannot have one without the other. . . . and Bailey and Miss Maple, if you take them apart, experience by experience—they are antithetical to each other. You know, Bailey went to war, Miss Maple didn't. Bailey was the typical—what would you call him?—man about town, preyer on women. Miss Maple was not. Their classes were different. Their take on history was very different. That's why Miss Maple served what he served to do. (Fowler 1996, 150)

The double-duty that "Miss Maple's Blues" performs, functioning both as the complement story to "Mood: Indigo" within "The Jam" and as a counter to the maestro's introduction, allows us to see that Naylor is not simply nesting her frames neatly around the centered tales, but also problematizing the act of framing itself. In particular, she shows here that the frame is both "inside and outside" that which is framed—and thus cannot be entirely distinguished from either the "content" or the "external world"—and that the tendency to spatialize knowledge can be usefully complemented by a temporalizing process.[1]

While it might be interesting simply to note that Naylor creates complicated frames, I am most interested in the ways in which she uses the frames
to perform certain tasks that enhance her ability to formulate a zone of
undecidability. The external spatial frame in *Bailey's Cafe* helps Naylor to
establish a narrative moment that is both in and out of time. The book
begins in late 1945, when the man-called-Bailey returns from World War II.
In a voice that seems to be both his own and that of every Allied soldier, he
has prayed not to have to fight with the Japanese on their own land, and
when this prayer is answered, it is by the United States's detonation of the
bombs Little Boy and Fat Man. Little Boy, he says, saved him "in exchange
for [his] soul," while the detonation of the second bomb "claim[ed] our
children. The unborn children," offering in their place "the earth melted
open and g[iving] birth . . . salvation [rising] like the head of a newborn"
(*BC*, 26). This sacrifice of "unborn children" seems to extend to its horrifying conclusion the pessimistic pattern that Naylor acknowledged when
she told Donna Perry that the "children die in my books" (Perry 1993,
225). The despair one feels about lost individuals is exponentially in-
creased in this nuclear disaster: both the present generation and the future
children of now-infertile men and women are lost. Amazingly, Naylor
manages to offer a counterimage that is hopeful in the concluding section.
There, she inverts the earlier death-in-birth moment by offering the impossible birth of George—the son of a virgin mother—whose arrival is eased
by Eve's fashioning a "world lit up with lights" (*BC*, 228). Because the
street is a limbo, a place that exists where it is needed (and hence is simultaneously everywhere and nowhere) and is also a site where time freezes
(*BC*, 219) until the inhabitants can make choices about their lives, Bailey
fears that this birth will cause the street to disappear. He cannot imagine
how "Life itself [can] ever begin here" (*BC*, 221). But it does; and so between the end and the beginning, between apocalypse and renewal, Naylor
has created an interzone, an "in-between" site that is not demarcated by
conventional understandings of space and time, where she reconsiders and
transforms not only the identity "whore," but a whole constellation of
identities.

Presenting the world of the text as couched between an apocalypse and
a miracle certainly establishes some narrative freedom for Naylor. And
within this narrative space, she constructs two frames that employ rhythms
offered by jazz and the blues. These frames can modulate the ways in which
we read the stories of the "biblical" women that they circumscribe, for this
musical legacy embodies two (among many) attitudes that are at odds with

the religious tradition. First, the blues manifest a "tension between innova-tion and tradition" (Barlow 1989, 9)—a tension that is diminished within a Christian religious context that overwhelmingly privileges tradition over innovation. Second, the musical tradition invites the reader to hold atti-tudes about female sexuality that are quite different from those fueled by an inimical biblical tradition. In sharp contrast to the Bible, where positive imagery is not routinely aligned with enthusiastic sexual impulses for women, sexual imagery is a staple of the blues; as Paul Oliver noted in *Blues Fell This Morning*, "sexual metaphors were used extensively in the blues, they were never evasive, but were used as figures of speech should be used: to amplify the meaning by analogy and comparison" (1990, 97). Moreover, these metaphors were not the sanitized tropes of the popular music industry, but "the language . . . used in everyday speech. To those only accustomed to the conventions of the printed and the recorded word, the blues sometimes seemed violent and coarse, but its expression was a natural and uninhibited one" (Oliver 1990, 102). Usually raw, sometimes aggressive, frequently boastful, the metaphors celebrate sexual intercourse, sexual freedom, and an eroticization of experience generally. This delight in sexuality seems precisely the sort of model Naylor needs to enhance her task of reclaiming "female sexuality and female sexual identity" from its debased position within Judeo-Christian tradition.[2]

However, we see in "Mary, Take One" that the breach between religious and musical traditions is not as easy to traverse as Shug makes it look in Spielberg's movie version of *The Color Purple*. Mary (Peaches) regards herself as psychically split—the good girl (Mary) and the sexual wanton ("her"); she tries unsuccessfully to save her "self" through good works (getting As, "join[ing] the Missionary Circle," rolling "bandages for the resistance," even singing "in the church choir") and finds that the only way to find temporary relief is by giving "her" to "any son of any man" (*BC*, 105), men she meets in blues clubs in "a part of town" filled with "fast music [and] fast women" (*BC*, 106). Through this contrast, Naylor con-nects the "Mary" side to church (and other "good") work and the "Mag-dalene" side to sexual freedom and hot music. Eventually made to see her hunger as potentially lethal, Peaches erases not her own desire but her desirability by literalizing the split she feels: she gouges her face with a beer opener, tearing a gash from her right cheekbone to the left side of her chin (111). Although Eve promises that she will "return [Peaches] . . . whole" to her father, this promise is deferred beyond the end of the text, leading us to wonder whether the woman can be healed, whether the asserted schism between a Mary and a Magdalene can be revealed to be smaller than tradition teaches, whether the religious and musical traditions can be conjoined.

Even when we move away from the stories in which musical and biblical ideology interact, and instead examine the stories of Sadie and Stanley, we encounter a problem with using the blues in an unselfconscious manner to provide characters with a liberating paradigm, one that works outside the confining strictures of linear narrative and the cultural logic it instantiates. Houston A. Baker, Henry Louis Gates, Jr., and many other critics have examined ways in which the blues structure is evident in African-American literature, and how this structure can modulate Western narrative structures. And Naylor is, certainly, employing this intertext in some of the ways that these critics describe as typical. However, she seems also to acknowledge that the blues, as a critical tool, needs to be historicized not only in terms of its liberating potential but also in terms of its stifling potential. As a highly popular musical form in the United States (and elsewhere), the blues became subjected to the same compromises and distortions that often occur when aesthetic and capitalist forces collide. The recording success of blueswomen, beginning as early as the 1920s, contributed to a transformation of the ostensibly freeing tradition: "savory sexual metaphors" were "often used to titillate prospective record buyers. . . . The end result was that the classic blues sometimes became a burlesque of African-American sexuality" (Barlow 1989, 142). Thus, while the blues offer a frame through which we can appreciate women's sexuality, it is a frame that has been compromised by—or at least complicated by—its own marketplace success. In this national, capitalist context, it has been transformed and has likely reinforced a dichotomized sexual stereotyping of African-American women, continuing the antebellum division of black women into the alternative figures of whore or mammy, and later (especially within the context we see in Peaches's story or in novels like *The Color Purple,* James Baldwin's *Go Tell It on the Mountain,* or Diane McKinney-Whetstone's *Tumbling*) into the bifurcation between churchwoman and whore, between saint and sinner.

Indeed, Sadie's story makes it quite clear that this dichotomy is alive and dangerous within the world of the text, and that women's identities continue to be limned by the sexual economics that underlie the word "whore" in the first place. Sadie tries—first as a girl-child, then as a helper in a brothel, and later as a wife—to use housecleaning and quiet, gentle ways as a means to survive without becoming a prostitute. Neither in her youth nor later, after her husband dies, though, is she able to rely on these nurturing attributes; instead, she works as a prostitute first to please her mother and later to earn twenty-five cents to buy enough wine to blot out her reality and replace it with a world in which she and Jones enjoy nicely prepared meals in a well-tended house. There, she is simultaneously "a lady" and a whore. Of course, seeing women as having split identities is not new, nor is seeing this split as related to economic necessity. Moreover, this dichotomy seems predicated on another common split, on distinguishing between "the woman, and the woman's body" (Glück, "Lamentations," l. 25). However, Naylor nuances this schism by having Sadie charge clients only as much as she needs to buy her wine each day. In that way, she defies the premise that one should charge as much for a product as the market will bear, and thereby that the split between the woman and the woman's body is a pure subject/object division. With a legacy of slavery further complicating Sadie's subjugation due to gender, though, the issue of self-ownership that this decision raises becomes especially problematic. Nevertheless, the choice not to charge more can be read as a "tactic" in deCerteau's sense, as a challenge to capitalism and to her own oppression, a notion I will explore shortly.

In Stanley's story, as in Sadie's, Naylor interleaves economic systems with concerns about sexual, gender, and racial identity, and allows us to infer that men, too, might be split into "the man and the man's body." As was true for Sadie, Stanley struggles to survive economically and to maintain a satisfying self-image within an environment that disallows his identity. While Sadie's compromise seems confusing primarily only to Jones, Stanley's is curious to nearly all the characters: he divides his identity over time and adopts female garb for a while. Although he is not cross-dressing to disguise himself or to remake himself in some simple fashion, Stanley seems to be inhabiting a different identity—to be a different person—when he is identified as Miss Maple. Therefore, we can say that, in some ways, he manifests three different identities, and that the past of Stanley inflects the present of Miss Maple, who is preparing for the reemergence, in the future, of Stanley.

Having familial money and a father who esteemed education, Stanley earned a Ph.D. in mathematics at Stanford. But rather than rely on inherited money, he tries to earn enough to start a business. At each job interview, he offers prospective employers incredibly detailed marketing projections—but he cannot get a job because of his race. Unwilling to give up his search, but feeling hot and uncomfortable in American menswear when at interviews during the summer, he decides to wear loose-fitting business attire to interviews. He opts for American-style women's dresses because he feels it is more appropriate to be consistent with his national identity than to wear men's African robes and pretend to a different nationality.

The choice to privilege national identity over gender identity is important and is intriguingly prepared for within the text during the fight between the redneck bullies, the Gatlin brothers, and Stanley's gentle, erudite father. During this fight, Stanley and his father are wearing the only clothes available to them—taffeta and lace crinoline—and Stanley helps a little but mostly watches as his father beats the shit out of the brothers. At last realizing what his father has long been trying to teach him about being a man, Stanley sees (among other things) that clothes certainly do not "make the man." Both during the fight scene and later when Stanley dons women's wear, the reader recognizes that Naylor is manipulating the signifying functions of attire to call attention to the near impossibility of Stanley inhabiting all of the identity positions he "should" within the existing environment. He *should* be able to be black and be a man. As a doctorate holder in a growing field, he *should* be able to get a job and to enter the economy he understands so well; unable to do so, he must try, instead, to enter through a side door.

And so he does. He writes product jingles that consistently win contests because, as Bailey reports, the "contests are more than a publicity gimmick; by reading [the entries], a company analyst can tell exactly what their customers want a product to do for them. And they use them to plan future strategies. The winning jingles have nothing to do with their being good; they're just the ones that can be used to spearhead the new marketing campaigns. And since he's already jump started a lot of these places, he already knows what the bulk of those entries from housewives are going to demonstrate" (*BC*, 215). Stanley manages to gain fifty thousand dollars in this way; but his need to do so by winning contests rather than by doing salaried work suggests, again, the injustice that creates such a poor fit between certain identities and the capitalist formation. And while Sadie's solution is troubling because it is debilitating, Stanley's solution is vexing both because it does not take advantage of his abilities and because it reminds readers of the false promise still offered to Americans of escaping poverty through winning contests and lotteries. However, if his jingle-writing is seen as a tactic, this way of making money takes on a new significance in the novel.

This internal frame (which I noted is the second spatial frame), then, introduces the problem of identity/ positionality in terms of race, sex, and gender, as inflected by a capitalist tradition, in order to indicate that the characters are schismed by their need to exist within this economy. By dealing with these issues in her blues-entitled stories, Naylor implies that even if we shift frames, seeing identities through the filters of the jazz and blues tradition, the characters still live in conditions that are debilitating. Moreover, because Sadie and Stanley counter each other in terms of a variety of identity attributes—female/male, poor/wealthy, poorly educated/well educated, uncaring family/nurturing family—we see that the economic and social conditions render life difficult for anyone, in principle, who is born black in the United States. When even a story entitled "Mood: Indigo" or "Miss Maple's Blues" offers so little promise for protagonists to exceed the system into which they were born, Naylor seems to indicate that the capitalist logic and the concomitant commodification of the blues has compromised the potential of the ideas and attitudes embodied in the musical traditions that African-American writers and critics most extol.

I noted above that both Sadie and Stanley are simultaneously participating in and challenging some aspects of capitalism, Sadie through her variable rates and Stanley through his astute jingle-writing. And while I am reluctant to endorse these acts fully or to see them as straightforward ways out of a disabling economic order, I do see their potential as "tactics" within the terms Michel deCerteau defines. In *The Practice of Everyday Life,* he notes that a "tactic" is "an art of being in between," an "art of the weak" (1984, 30, 37), available to and often pursued by people living in disempowering situations. In contrast to a "strategy," which uses actions and culture products in their intended fashion, and thus in concert with the prevailing power structures, tactics work because individuals "us[e] them with respect to ends and references foreign to the system they had no choice but to accept" (1984, xiii). DeCerteau emphasizes the role that tactics have in allowing one to evade conscription into a production/consumption economy, for he sees advanced capitalism as reinforcing a mode of consumption that is devoid of production, devoid of energizing and imaginative use of the product: "the television viewer," he writes, "cannot write anything on the screen of his set. He has been dislodged from the product" (1984, 31). Ranging from cooking and shopping to stealing time from one's employer to storytelling to maintaining a gift economy, what all of the varied tactics have in common is that they enable individuals to get what they want by "turning to their own ends forces alien to them" in order to seize the moment (1984, xix). Specifically, using a product in an unanticipated way allows one to reclaim the role of imaginative producer and to resist, albeit temporarily, the role into which one has been slotted by the economic paradigm. So when Sadie changes the rules of "the oldest profession" or when Stanley uses his knowledge that the contests are meant to jump-start advertising campaigns rather than to reward witticism, they are signifying on the rules, employing tactics for survival within inimical conditions. Such tactics are prevalent in Naylor's novels, and later I will look closely at the ways in which she contrasts Christmas and Candle Walk to show the communal potential tactics can have.

Before turning to the ways in which these tactics function in the middle texts of the quartet, however, let us turn briefly to the center of *Bailey's Cafe,* where Naylor has used her own tactics to make this interzone even more suitable for transformation. There, she continues her engagement with the Western literary tradition. Nearly all critical discussions of Naylor's novels include some acknowledgment of her use of Shakespeare, Dante, and other major canonical Western writers, with critics proposing different rationales for the sustained dialogue she establishes.[3] In "Rainbows of Darkness" Valerie Traub notes that Naylor displays a "structural ambivalence" in her relationship to "the Shakespearean repertoire—[a] mixture of admiration and resentment" that "maps the outlines of one possible strategy for negotiating the field of white Western aesthetic production" (1993, 161). We may extend Traub's claims when we regard Naylor's deployment of biblical stories in *Bailey's Cafe.* Not only is she addressing the field of aesthetic production, but also quite overtly the field of culture production itself. Using the frames to circumscribe the five biblical revisions, Naylor has been able to generate tensions between the frames and the individual stories that complicate our readings of each section, that allow us to regard her activity as a tactical "turning to [her] own ends" of a story tradition long used to disempower women and African-Americans. In doing so, Naylor fashions this environment as a site where one can work through revised understandings of the material presented in the stories and can develop some promising notions of collective agency.

Naylor begins by desacralizing, in a sense, the biblical stories that are the "basis" for her revisions. While her work has not engendered the angry protests that the religious revisions in *The Satanic Verses* prompted,[4] it is similarly "blasphemous" insofar as it "misrepresents" the sacred in a secular context. However, Naylor, unlike Rushdie, has managed to use this "blasphemy" in ways that readers are able to grasp, and to do so to create a moment when (in Homi Bhabha's words) "the subject-matter or the content of a cultural tradition is being overwhelmed, or alienated, in the act of translation. Into the asserted authenticity or continuity of tradition, [this] 'secular' blasphemy releases a temporality that reveals the contingencies, even the incommensurabilities, involved in the process of social transformation" (Bhabha 1994, 225–26). By transcoding the biblical stories,

Naylor "desacralizes the transparent assumptions of cultural supremacy, and in that very act, demands a contextual specificity, a historical differentiation *within* minority positions" (Bhabha 1994, 228). When we think about Naylor's act within the terms Bhabha provides, we see that she points out that the biblical stories are themselves historically contingent, and that their particularities need to be attended to. Once we can see these stories as contingent and not as culturally supreme, Naylor can suggest to us that the possibility of alternative stories exists. And finally, she can illustrate, through the specificity of her stories, and through their differences from one another, that the alternative stories must not be seen as a single, unified "alternative perspective" but must be regarded with attention to their radical specificity, an attribute often elided both by cultural tradition and by overly simplified understandings of difference.[5]

Equally as important as the desacralizing of the religious texts is the concurrent reintroduction of temporality. DeCerteau had argued that people who are displaced or colonized rely on tactics because they live in a place that is not their own, one that "belongs to the other," and so rather than resort to techniques that are indigenous, they employ these moves that instead "depend[] on time" (deCerteau 1984, xix). This emphasis on the moment, on taking advantage of shifting situations, of fleeting opportunities, is the political and economic equivalent of the musical improvisation that is so important to jazz and blues. Each depends upon the actor being simultaneously aware of the rules of the system and willing to work against or across those rules to achieve the desired effect; each depends upon the actor being able to create on the fly.

Perhaps an even more significant consequence of evoking the temporal is that it enables Naylor to locate *Bailey's Cafe* in a world both inside and outside of time. This setting is consonant with some of Bhabha's ideas about time as described in *The Location of Culture*. There, he links the notion of nation and the establishment of minority discourses and identities with both the remaking of boundaries and with a particular sense of time—a kind of time during which conventional causality no longer operates. He connects this sort of time to both the "psychoanalytic concept of *Nachtraglichkeit* (deferred action): 'a transferential function, whereby the past dissolves into the present, so that the future becomes (once again) an *open question,* instead of being specified by the fixity of the past" (Bhabha 1994, 219), and also to Walter Benjamin's notion of the "historical 'present,'" which is a "'present which is not a transition, but in which time stands still and has come to a stop.' *For this notion,*" he emphasizes, "*defines the present in which history is being written.* From this discursive space of struggle, the violence of the letter, the terror of the timeless, is negotiated . . . a collective agency" (Bhabha 1994, 233). In *Bailey's Cafe*, we visit a cafe that is located in Brooklyn, San Francisco, Addis Ababa, and so forth, and a time that is the period from 1945 to 1949, but one that also is entirely outside of space (the cafe "sits right on the margin between the edge of the world and infinite possibility, the back door opens out to a void" [*BC*, 76]) and outside of time ("we do nothing here but freeze time" [219]). This conjunction suggests that Naylor is concertedly employing the notion of a "historical present," providing her characters with a moment when time "has come to a stop" so that they have an opportunity, as the man-called-Bailey explains it, to "take a breather for a while" (28). They need this respite in order to make the future an "open question" in the ultimate sense: people who arrive at the cafe do so on their way to committing suicide. Taking "a breather" gives these folks a chance to decide whether they must head out the back door, into the void, or whether they can "eventually go back out and resume [their lives]—hopefully better off than when [they] found us" (221).

Like time, space here functions to guarantee new opportunities for the characters. Although readers sometime presume that Bailey's Cafe is in New York (where it is for George in *Mama Day*), it is in fact carefully presented as in no single place. By manipulating locales, Naylor reminds us of our tendency to ascribe significance based on geographical or national position, and she also reminds us of the problems inherent in that act in a transnational (postnational?) world. Further, the shifting foci created both by the variety of locations and by the multiple frames trope

> the performative nature of differential identities: the regulation and negotiation of those spaces that are continually, *contingently,* "opening out," remaking the boundaries, exposing the limits of any claim to a singular or autonomous sign of difference—be it class, gender, or race. Such assignations of social differences—where difference in neither One nor the Other but *something else besides, in-between*—find their agency in a form of the "future" where the past is not originary, where the present is not simply transitory. (Bhabha 1994, 219)

Just as we see that locations are demarcated by somewhat artificial boundaries, we see that the assignation of identity characteristics as the *defining* characteristics is inappropriately limiting. Rather than see Mariam as quite different from her American counterparts, for instance, we see all of the women as subject to many of the same limitations. And rather than seeing Stanley's identity as profoundly dissimilar to that of the women, we see that, like them, he also has his actions curtailed by the constructions imposed on him by his culture. To move beyond these boundaries entails opening the question of the future, making it less circumscribed by the exigencies of one attribute, be it race, or gender, or national history, for example.

Thus, for Naylor, as for Bhabha, creating new possibilities for future purposive action requires not only reconfiguring the environment within which such activity takes place, but also rethinking agency itself. I suggest that the sort of narrative space and time Naylor has fabricated is precisely the sort that allows us to model, to imagine, the emergence of a collective agency. And given the musical overlay, we ought not be surprised to find moments of collectivity in the ensemble conclusion, "The Wrap." The two most striking concern the birth and circumcision ceremony of George.

On the day of George's birth, "a lot of things didn't happen" (*BC*, 223). Clearing space for the impossible, Naylor writes "the sun didn't shine. The pilot light didn't catch. . . . The jukebox went totally on the blink. And not one person complained" (*BC*, 223). We might read this absence as akin to the generative nothing from which comes everything in Judeo-Christian terms, or as consistent with the American literary tradition of using negations to "cancel institutions and practices that have developed in society so that one might celebrate a genuine point of beginning—with its attendant hope and promise for the future" (Martin 1985, 5), or as simply a moment when conventional activity is set aside. Even if the last is the case, it is still a moment when a community gathers for a miracle: "besides the few customers, everyone who lived on the street was gathered inside. And I mean everyone, even strange little Esther" (*BC*, 224–25). At the sound of the baby's first cry, Peaches starts to sing, and "one voice joined in. Another voice joined. And another. . . . Soon we were all singing, a bit ragged and off-key. But all singing" (225–26). Having sung a Christian spiritual together, the customers have become a choir, the individuals an ensemble. Later, this rudimentary community gathers for the boy's circumcision. At that time, the man-called-Bailey points out that at this event, and at other Jewish ceremonies, everyone must be present because "nothing important can happen unless they're [the Jewish people] all in it together as a community" (227). Although only Gabe is Jewish, the others participate because they recognize the importance of the event, seeing it as a ceremony "about survival" (226). Thus, through the birth itself, and through the narrator's recognition that the circumcision ceremony is about a nation's (or more precisely, a diaspora people's) enduring, Naylor conflates her representation of renewal and of hope with her depiction of collective activity. In doing so, she implicitly opposes the optimism and sense of possibility gen-erated by this communal activity to the earlier depictions of near hopeless-ness of individuals constrained by capitalist logic.

Partha Chatterjee has argued that "'it is not so much the state-civil soci-ety opposition but rather the capital-community opposition that seems to be the great unsurpassed contradiction in Western social philosophy'" (in Bhabha 1994, 231). Picking up on this distinction, Homi Bhabha notes that Chatterjee is offering a reading of community that constitutes it as a category that simultaneously "enables a division between the private and the public, the civil and the familial; but [at the same time shows that] as a performative discourse it enacts the impossibility of drawing an objective line between the two" (Bhabha 1994, 231). In this way, community can cut across the categories that capital tends to reify, can "'seep through the interstices of the objectively constructed, contractually relegated structure of civil society,' class relations and national identities. Community disturbs the grand globalizing narrative of capital, displaces the emphasis on pro-duction in 'class' collectivity, and disrupts the homogeneity of the imagined community of the nation" (Bhabha 1994, 231). Obviously, community—as it is being articulated in this context—is not limited in the usual ways. To the contrary, community is being asserted to extend beyond such group definitions. And to understand this community, we must rethink our reli-ance on spatial metaphors and acknowledge its temporal dimension; we must recognize that "minority communities negotiate their collective iden-tifications" both in space and across time (Bhabha 1994, 231). Such a realization allows a better understanding of Naylor's complex narrative structure, of her doubled and involuted spatial frames and her musical, temporal one. Working through the Western narrative preoccupation with spatial logic, she manages to create a space that is neither "real" nor a simple utopia. Instead, she defines a realm within which she can begin to examine how community can sustain itself while, as is necessary at present, working within the world capitalism defines.

Particularly in this regard, what Naylor is accomplishing in *Bailey's Cafe* is analogous to one of the aims she is achieving in the quartet as a whole. Although she maintains that she did not know what her various books would be about much before she began each one, she has often commented that, from very early on, she intended *The Women of Brewster Place* to serve as the first book of a tetralogy. Her plan was that this quartet would "lay the basis or the foundation . . . for a career" (in Perry 1993, 224). In this quartet—*The Women of Brewster Place* (1982), *Linden Hills* (1985), *Mama Day* (1989), and *Bailey's Cafe* (1992)—she has used a variety of strategies to unify the novels including recurring characters (Kiswana Browne and George Andrews, among others) and references to locales (Linden Hills is mentioned in both *The Women of Brewster Place* and *Mama Day,* for instance). Further, all four novels participate in the oft-remarked intertextual relationship with classic Western narratives. These intertextual links within Naylor's canon, and within the Western canon more generally, contribute to a sense of cohesion; however, the narrative forms of the four novels seem rather disparate.

Upon close examination, though, one sees that across the four novels Naylor's pattern of framing a site within which to work out new para-digms, new possibilities, is again present: *The Women of Brewster Place* and *Bailey's Cafe,* the first and last novels in the series, are composite nov-els that themselves employ frames to circumscribe series of short stories that focus on different female characters. Both have a temporal overlay (the dawn to dusk and procreation metaphors in the *Brewster* frame), and both deploy deferral as a crucial narrative device. In contrast, *Linden Hills* and *Mama Day,* the middle two texts, are more conventionally shaped novels, and they are composed as fully interleaved stories rather than as successive stories. Both provide a higher degree of conventional closure and less reliance on deferral beyond the ending. Recalling Derrida's de-scription of a frame, we can say that *The Women of Brewster Place* and *Bailey's Cafe* form a frame that is "a composite of inside and outside"— both a part of the quartet and the boundary that defines the coherence of the set, which asserts its integrity. Given these parallels between the fram-ing novels, we can expect *The Women of Brewster Place* to share some thematic attributes with *Bailey's Cafe.* And indeed, in both we see an over-riding preoccupation with African-American women's survival under ad-verse economic and social conditions.

Moreover, we might expect to see explorations of the "community-capi-tal opposition" as crucial to the middle texts, and to see an exploration of collective agency as a technique for "disturb[ing] the grand globalizing narrative of capital" as one source of hope in this pair. If we focus on *Linden Hills* alone, we will readily see the community-capital opposition, but will probably feel pessimistic about the possibilities of collective agency. However, if we contrast *Linden Hills* with *Mama Day,* we can more easily see that Naylor's sustained analysis of the black middle class in the former is evoking the risks that are momentarily resolved in the latter.

In an interview with Angels Carabi, Naylor explained that in *Linden Hills* she wanted to "look at what happens to black Americans when they move up in America's society. They first lose family ties . . . then there are the community ties. You can create a whole different type of community around you—mostly of a mixture of other professional, middle-class people—but you lose the ties with your spiritual or religious values. And ultimately, the strongest and most difficult ties to let go of are your ties with your ethnocentric sense of self. You forget what it means to be an African American" (Carabi 1992, 41–42). And indeed, most of the characters do lose their communal ties and do forget what it means. But Willie and Lester, the itinerant poets wandering through the Dantesque circles of Linden Hills the week before Christmas, have not entirely forgotten. Willie still has enough perspective that he is able to tell Lester that the residents of Linden Hills "have lost [it]. . . . They've lost all touch with what it is to be them" (*LH*, 59). And in the verbal exchange about Christmas presents that establishes their motivation for working their way through the development, doing odd jobs, Lester suggests that their "losing it" is intertwined with finding a place for themselves within a capitalist framework.

When Willie compliments Lester on his warm gloves and boots, Lester dismissively describes them as "an early Christmas present from my mom and sister. Said they might as well give it to me now since it's so bitter and I'm too damned trifling to buy myself something to keep away frostbite" (*LH*, 30). Willie thinks their gesture shows they care, but Lester disagrees, and explains to Willie the role that Christmas has assumed in Linden Hills:

> "That ain't caring, White, that's showing off. See what we gave you? Now what you gonna give us, you no-good bum, you. They gave me this stuff and prayed it would burn my ass every time I wore it. . . . I'm telling ya, Willie, it's torment every time I have to wear this, 'cause it's less than a week till Christmas and I ain't got the money to buy them something expensive. You know those type of broads. I'd better not bring in no Woolworth's perfume and powder set. It's Chanel or nothing. And I ain't got no Chanel money, so it's nothing. And then I'm nothing and they've made their point again for another year. Merry Christmas, baby." (*LH*, 31)

More than adolescent whining or frustration, Lester's complaint in this scene illustrates the general transformation of Christmas into a holiday marked by consumerism at its worst, and shows that the materialism that commercialism encourages affects not only little children but also adults, destroying all the positive feelings of family and community that the day could, in principle, engender.

The bitterness is slightly attenuated in the succeeding scene, when Willie and Lester talk to Norm and Ruth, a couple who have virtually no material objects, but in whose home "love rules" (*LH*, 38). When Ruth suggests that the two could earn enough money to buy gifts by doing odd jobs, Willie finds it "a wonderful idea—colossal. Anything that put the music back in Ruth's voice as she spoke to him" (41) and plans to buy a gift for her and Norm with his earnings. In contrast to Willie's sweet and other-focused attitude, Lester thinks it's a good idea because at the same time that he earns money, he guarantees that his "mom would have a shit-fit knowing I was doing that to buy her a present. That alone would be worth it" (41). He uses his labor to get even with her as well as to get a gift for her.

In sharp contrast to this holiday is Candle Walk, the celebration that the residents of Willow Springs hold instead of Christmas in *Mama Day*. On December 22, "folks take to the road—strolling, laughing, and talking—holding some kind of light in their hands" (*MD*, 110). The tradition has been going on for longer than anyone can remember, and it was a way for everyone to help one another survive:

> Used to be when Willow Springs was mostly cotton and farming, by the end of the year it was common knowledge who done turned a profit and who didn't. . . . And them being short on cash and long on pride, Candle Walk was a way of getting help without feeling obliged. Since everybody said, "Come my way, Candle Walk," sort of as a season's greeting and expected a little something, them that needed a little more got it quiet-like from their neighbors. And it weren't no hardship giving something back—only had to be any bit of something, as long as it came from the earth and the work of your own hands . . . it all got accepted with the same grace. (*MD*, 110)

Of course, this holiday has changed over time, too, with pettiness entering into the exchanges sometimes or folks buying rather than making gifts. But Mama Day feels sure that "it'll take generations . . . for Willow Springs to stop doing it at all. And more generations again to stop talking about the time 'when there used to be some kinda 18 & 23 going-on near December twenty-second.' By then, she figures, it won't be the world as we know it no way—and so no need for the memory" (*MD*, 111).

Now, while there is still a need for memory, we see in Candle Walk a compelling alternative to the debased version of Christmas that exists in Linden Hills and in the United States more generally. Gifts continue to be gifts; and as such, they can be regarded as part of the type of gift economy deCerteau described. Gifts are part of a "style of social exchange" that, like a *potlatch,* establishes "an interplay of voluntary allowances that counts on reciprocity and organizes a social network articulated by the 'obligation to give.' . . . [This economy] survives in our economy, though on its margins or in its interstices. . . . Because of this, the politics of the 'gift' *also* becomes a diversionary tactic" (deCerteau 1984, 27). While gifts have become objects through which people enact power plays in *Linden Hills,* they continue to be a way individuals can make exchanges outside the system in which value is assigned "according to the code of generalized equivalence constituted by money" in *Mama Day* (deCerteau 1984, 27). Gifts can reinforce community by providing a quiet mechanism for those who have to share with those who need, thereby making welfare and other state-sponsored aid less necessary, as well as making the survival of the group more important than "making a point." In Willow Springs, Candle Walk continues in the present of the text, a time that is not some overly idealized preindustrial era but rather is close to our own era (much of it occurs during the 1980s), a time one would be hard pressed to associate with economic selflessness in this country.

Mama Day doesn't predict what the world will be like in the future, just that "it won't be the world as we know it no way" (*MD,* 111). Bailey, in contrast, is anxious; he reasons that "if the world outside is becoming such that life itself can be brought forth in limbo, then one day, much too soon, I'm gonna start seeing young children walk through that door. Children who have lost their futures" (*BC,* 227). His trepidation rings true for Americans today, making the social significance of Naylor's efforts that much more important for us to contemplate. Working through a careful narrative logic, Naylor has framed a space in which to present and to deconstruct the various forces that limit action and identity within advanced capitalism in the United States, a system that continues to be racist and sexist. She has indicated the peril and promise of both typically Western and particularly African-American paradigms—showing the ways in which both need to be nuanced, rather than entirely embraced or dismissed. And finally, she has depicted an image of collective agency emerging within this interzone, within a site that has been undecided. Akin to models being explored by sociologists and postcolonial theorists, this image of community is one that crosses boundaries, unmakes restrictions, and—with both work and luck—allows the future to become "(once again) an open question" (Bhabha 1994, 219), a time we can approach with "pure devilment and curiosity" (*MD,* 312).

Notes

1. We can extend this point to the quartet: while *The Women of Brewster Place* and *Bailey's Cafe* form a fairly unambiguous frame in that they are the only composite novels and are the first and last work in the quartet, the simple balance is complicated by the nonchronological position of *Bailey's Cafe*. As the earliest text in the characters' chronology, it redefines the quartet as a cycle, a shift that itself manipulates the act of framing and reintroduces time into the quartet in a particularly important way.

2. Larry Neal aligns the blues and the religious tradition, noting their shared origin and their important continuities. In "Any Day Now: Black Art and Black Liberation" he asserted that "even though they [the blues] primarily deal with the world as flesh, they are essentially religious. Because they finally celebrate life and the ability of man to control and shape his destiny" (quoted in Baker 1988, 157). Similarly, Portia K. Maultsby (1990) notes that blues and gospel music share the same origins and have cross-pollinated each other. While both critics are correct in making such links between musical and religious traditions, neither fully addresses the almost diametric ways in which the forms have come to signify within African-American (and American more generally) culture.

3. In addition to Traub, see especially Peter Erickson, "Shakespeare's Black? The Role of Shakespeare in Naylor's Novels"; Margaret Homans, "The Woman in the Cave: Recent Feminist Fictions and the Classical Underworld"; James Robert Saunders, "The Ornamentation of Old Ideas: Gloria Naylor's First Three Novels" (all reprinted in Gates and Appiah 1993).

4. The sample of reviews included in the Gates and Appiah collection suggests that her revisions engendered little negative comment.

5. For discussions of the biblical counterparts to these stories, see the essays in this volume by Karen Schneider and Dorothy Perry Thompson, as well as Virginia Fowler's *Gloria Naylor: In Search of Sanctuary* (1996).

Works Cited

Baker, Houston A., Jr. *Afro-American Poetics: Revisions of Harlem and the Black Aesthetic*. Madison: University of Wisconsin Press, 1988.

Barlow, William. *"Looking Up at Down": The Emergence of Blues Culture*. Philadelphia: Temple University Press, 1989.

Bhabha, Homi K. *The Location of Culture*. London: Routledge, 1994.

Carabi, Angels. "Belles Lettres Interview." *Belles Lettres* (Spring 1992): 36–42.

Culler, Jonathan. *On Deconstruction: Theory and Criticism after Structuralism*. Ithaca, N.Y.: Cornell University Press, 1982.

deCerteau. Michel. *The Practice of Everyday Life*. Trans. Steven Rendall. Berkeley: University of California Press, 1984.

Fowler, Virginia. *Gloria Naylor: In Search of Sanctuary*. Twayne's United States Author Series. New York: Twayne, 1996.

Gates, Henry Louis, Jr., and K. A. Appiah. *Gloria Naylor: Critical Perspectives Past and Present*. New York: Amistad, 1993.

Glück, Louise. *Descending Figure*. New York: Ecco Press, 1980.

Henderson, Mae. *Borders, Boundaries, and Frames: Cultural Criticism and Cultural Studies*. New York: Routledge, 1995.

Jameson, Fredric. *Postmodernism, or, the Cultural Logic of Late Capitalism*. Durham, N.C.: Duke University Press, 1991.

Martin, Terence. "The Negative Structures of American Literature." *American Literature* 57 no. 1 (March 1985): 1–22.

Maultsby, Portia K. "Africanisms in African-American Music." In *Africanisms in American Culture*. Ed. Joseph E. Holloway. Bloomington: Indiana University Press, 1990. 185–210.

Naylor, Gloria. *Bailey's Cafe*. New York: Harcourt Brace Jovanovich, 1992a.

———. Interview with Tom Vitale, National Public Radio, Sept. 22, 1992b.

———. *Linden Hills*. New York: Penguin, 1985.

———. *Mama Day*. New York: Vintage, 1989.

———. *The Women of Brewster Place*. New York: Penguin, 1983.

Oliver, Paul. *Blues Fell This Morning: Meaning in the Blues* (rev. ed.). New York: Cambridge University Press, 1990.

Perry, Donna. *Backtalk: Women Writers Speak Out*. New Brunswick, N.J.: Rutgers University Press, 1993.

Prince, Gerald. *A Dictionary of Narratology*. Lincoln: University of Nebraska Press, 1987.

Sadie, Stanley, ed. *The New Grove Dictionary of Music and Musicians*. Washington, D.C.: Distributed by Grove's Dictionaries of Music, 1980.

Traub, Valerie. "Rainbows of Darkness: Deconstructing Shakespeare in the Work of Gloria Naylor and Zora Neale Hurston." In *Cross-Cultural Performances: Differences in Women's Re-Visions of Shakespeare*. Ed. Marianne Novy. Urbana: University of Illinois Press, 1993. 150–64.

Selected Bibliography

Andrews, Larry. "Black Sisterhood in Gloria Naylor's Novels," *CLA Journal* 33.1 (Sept. 1989): 1–25.

Awkward, Michael. *Inspiriting Influences: Tradition, Revision, and Afro-American Women's Novels*. New York: Columbia University Press, 1989.

Baker, Houston A., Jr. *Afro-American Poetics: Revisions of Harlem and the Black Aesthetic*. Madison: University of Wisconsin Press, 1988.

———. *Blues, Ideology, and Afro-American Literature: A Vernacular Theory*. Chicago: University of Chicago Press, 1984.

———. "Caliban's Triple Play." *Critical Inquiry* 13 (Autumn 1986): 182–96.

———. *The Journey Back: Issues in Black Literature and Criticism*. Chicago: University of Chicago Press, 1980.

———. "There Is No More Beautiful Way: Theory and the Poetics of Afro-American Women's Writing." In *Afro-American Literary Study in the 1990s*. Eds. Houston Baker and Patricia Redmond. Chicago: University of Chicago Press, 1989. 135–55.

Bhabha, Homi K. *The Location of Culture*. London: Routledge, 1994.

Butler, Judith. "Imitation and Gender Insubordination." In *The Lesbian and Gay Studies Reader*. Eds. Henry Abelove, Michele Aina Barale, and David M. Halperin. New York: Routledge, 1993. 307–20.

Cannon, Katie Geneva. *Katie's Canon: Womanism and the Soul of the Black Community*. New York: Continuum, 1995.

Carabi, Angels. "Belles Lettres Interview." *Belles Lettres* (Spring 1992): 36–42.

Christian, Barbara. "Creating a Universal Literature: Afro-American Women Writers." In *Black Feminist Criticism: Perspectives on Black Women Writers*. New York: Pergamon Press, 1985. 159–64.

————. "Naylor's Geography: Community, Class and Patriarchy in *The Women of Brewster Place* and *Linden Hills*." In *Gloria Naylor: Critical Perspectives Past and Present*. Eds. Henry L. Gates, Jr., and K. A. Appiah. New York: Amistad Press, 1993. 106–25.

————. "Trajectories of Self-Definition: Placing Contemporary Afro-American Women's Fiction." In *Conjuring: Black Women, Fiction, and Literary Tradition*. Eds. Marjorie Pryse and Hortense J. Spillers. Bloomington: Indiana University Press, 1985. 233–48.

Collins, Patricia Hill. *Black Feminist Thought*. New York: Routledge, 1991.

Cooper, Carolyn. "'Something Ancestral Recaptured': Spirit Possession as Trope in Selected Feminist Fictions of the African Diaspora." In *Motherlands: Black Women's Writing from Africa, the Caribbean, and South Asia*. Ed. Susheila Nasta. New Brunswick, N.J.: Rutgers University Press, 1992. 64–87.

Dance, Daryl C. "Black Eve or Madonna?: A Study of the Antithetical Views of the Mother in Black American Literature." In *Sturdy Black Bridges: Visions of Black Women in Literature*. Eds. Roseann P. Bell, Bettye J. Parker, and Beverly Guy-Sheftall. New York: Anchor Press, 1979. 123–31.

de Weever, Jacquelyn. *Mythmaking and Metaphor in Black Women's Fiction*. New York: St. Martin's Press, 1991.

Du Bois, W. E. B. *The Souls of Black Folk*. New York: Penguin, 1989.

Erickson, Peter. "'Shakespeare's Black?': The Role of Shakespeare in Naylor's Novels." In *Gloria Naylor: Critical Perspectives Past and Present*. Eds. Henry Louis Gates, Jr., and K. A. Appiah. New York: Amistad Press, 1993. 231–48.

Fowler, Virginia. *Gloria Naylor: In Search of Sanctuary*. Twayne's United States Authors Series. New York: Twayne, 1996.

Fraser, Celeste. "Stealing B(l)ack Voices: The Myth of the Black Matriarchy and *The Women of Brewster Place*." Gloria Naylor: Critical Perspectives Past and Present. Eds. Henry Louis Gates, Jr., and K. A. Appiah. New York: Amistad, 1993. 90–105.

Gates, Henry Louis, Jr. "The Blackness of Blackness: A Critique of *The Sign* and *The Signifying Monkey*." In *Black Literature and Literary Theory*. Ed. Henry Louis Gates, Jr. New York: Routledge, 1984. 285–321.

————. "Canon Formation, Literary History, and the Afro-American Tradition." In *Afro-American Literary Study in the 1990s*. Eds. Houston Baker and Patricia Redmond. Chicago: University of Chicago Press, 1989. 14–39.

————. *Loose Canons: Notes on the Culture Wars*. New York: Oxford University Press, 1992.

————. "Significant Others." *Contemporary Literature* 29, no. 4 (1988): 606–23.

————. *The Signifying Monkey: A Theory of African-American Literary Criticism*. New York: Oxford University Press, 1988.

Gates, Henry Louis, Jr., and K. A. Appiah, eds. *Gloria Naylor: Critical Perspectives Past and Present*. New York: Amistad, 1993.

Goddu, Teresa. "Reconstructing History in *Linden Hills*." In *Gloria Naylor: Criti-*

cal Perspectives Past and Present. Eds. Henry Louis Gates, Jr., and K. A. Appiah. New York: Amistad Press, 1993. 215–30.

Henderson, Mae Gwendolyn. "Speaking in Tongues: Dialogics, Dialectics, and the Black Woman Writer's Literary Tradition." In *Reading Black, Reading Feminist: A Critical Anthology.* Ed. Henry Louis Gates, Jr. New York: Meridian, 1990. 116–42.

Henderson, Stephen. "Survival Motion: A Study of the Black Writer and the Black Revolution in America." In *The Militant Black Writer in Africa and the United States.* Eds. Mercer Cook and Stephen Henderson. Madison: University of Wisconsin Press, 1969. 65–129.

Holloway, Karla. *Moorings and Metaphors: Figures of Culture and Gender in Black Women's Literature.* New Brunswick, N.J.: Rutgers University Press, 1992.

Homans, Margaret. "The Woman in the Cave." In *Gloria Naylor: Critical Perspectives Past and Present.* Eds. Henry L. Gates, Jr., and K. A. Appiah. New York: Amistad Press, 1993. 152–79.

hooks, bell. *Yearning: race, gender, and cultural politics.* Boston: South End Press, 1990.

Johnson, Charles. *Being & Race: Black Writing Since 1970.* Bloomington: Indiana University Press, 1988.

Jones, Jacqueline. *Labor of Love, Labor of Sorrow: Black Women, Work and the Family, from Slavery to the Present.* New York: Random House, 1985.

Kambon, Kobi. *The African Personality in America: An African-Centered Framework.* Tallahassee, Fla.: Nubian Nations Publications, 1992.

Kubitschek, Missy Dehn. *Claiming the Heritage: African-American Women Novelists and History.* Jackson: University Press of Mississippi, 1991.

———. "Toward a New World Order: Shakespeare, Morrison and Gloria Naylor's *Mama Day.*" *MELUS* 19, no. 3 (1994): 75–90.

Levy, Helen Fiddyment. "Lead on with Light." In *Gloria Naylor: Critical Perspectives Past and Present.* Eds. Henry Louis Gates, Jr., and K. Anthony Appiah. New York: Amistad, 1993. 263–84.

Masenya, Madipoane. "African Womanist Hermeneutics: A Suppressed Voice from South Africa Speaks." *Journal of Feminist Studies in Religion* (Spring 1995): 149–55.

Matus, Jill. "Dream, Deferral, and Closure in *The Women of Brewster Place.*" In *Gloria Naylor: Critical Perspectives Past and Present.* Eds. Henry L. Gates, Jr., and K. A. Appiah. New York: Amistad, 1993. 126–39.

Maultsby, Portia K. "Africanisms in African-American Music." In *Africanisms in American Culture.* Ed. Joseph E. Holloway. Bloomington: Indiana University Press, 1990. 185–210.

McDowell, Deborah E. "Boundaries: Or Distant Relations and Close Kin." In *Afro-American Literary Study in the 1990s.* Eds. Houston A. Baker and Patricia Redmond. Chicago: University of Chicago Press, 1989. 51–70.

Meisenhelder, Susan. "'The Whole Picture' in Gloria Naylor's *Mama Day.*" *African American Review* 27, no. 3 (1993): 405–19.

Montgomery, Maxine Lavon. "Authority, Multivocality, and the New World Order in Gloria Naylor's *Bailey's Cafe*." *African American Review* 29 (1995): 27–33.

Naylor, Gloria. *Bailey's Cafe*. New York: Harcourt Brace Jovanovich, 1992.

———. "Dusk." Excerpt from *The Men of Brewster Place*. *Callaloo* 19 (1996): 789–91.

———. Interview with Tom Vitale. "Morning Edition." National Public Radio. New York. Sept. 22, 1992.

———. *Linden Hills*. New York: Viking Penguin, 1985.

———. "Love and Sex in the Afro-American Novel." *Yale Review* 78 (1988–89): 19–31.

———. "The Love of Books." In *The Writing Life*. Eds. Neil Baldwin and Diane Osen. New York: Random House, 1995. 167–75.

———. *Mama Day*. New York: Vintage, 1993.

———. *The Men of Brewster Place*. New York: Hyperion, 1998.

———. *The Women of Brewster Place*. New York: Viking Penguin, 1982.

Naylor, Gloria, and Toni Morrison. "A Conversation." *Southern Review* 21, no. 3 (1985): 567–93.

Neal, Larry. "Some Reflections on the Black Aesthetic." In *The Black Aesthetic*. Ed. Addison Gayle, Jr. Garden City, N.Y.: Doubleday (Anchor Books), 1972. 12–15.

Perry, Donna. *Backtalk: Women Writers Speak Out*. New Brunswick, N.J.: Rutgers University Press, 1993.

Romines, Ann. *The Home Plot: Women, Writing, and Domestic Ritual*. Amherst: University of Massachusetts Press, 1992.

Rowell, Charles H. "An Interview with Gloria Naylor." *Callaloo* 20 (1997): 179–92.

Saunders, James Robert. "The Ornamentation of Old Ideas: Naylor's First Three Novels." In *Gloria Naylor: Critical Perspectives Past and Present*. Eds. Henry L. Gates, Jr., and K. A. Appiah. New York: Amistad, 1993. 263–84.

Smith, Valerie. "Black Feminist Theory and the Representation of the 'Other'." In *Changing Our Own Words: Essays on Criticism, Theory, and Writing by Black Women*. Ed. Cheryl A. Wall. New Brunswick, N.J.: Rutgers University Press, 1989. 38–57.

Stepto, Robert B. *From Behind the Veil: A Study of Afro-American Narrative*. Urbana: University of Illinois Press, 1979.

Storhoff, Gary. "'The Only Voice Is Your Own': Gloria Naylor's Revision of *The Tempest*." *African American Review* 29 (1995): 35–45.

Traub, Valerie. "Rainbows of Darkness: Deconstructing Shakespeare in the Work of Gloria Naylor and Zora Neale Hurston." In *Cross-Cultural Performances: Differences in Women's Re-Vision of Shakespeare*. Ed. Marianne Novy. Urbana: University of Illinois Press, 1993. 150–64.

Tucker, Lindsey. "Recovering the Conjure Woman: Texts and Contexts in Naylor's *Mama Day*." *African American Review* 28 (1994): 173–88.

Walker, Alice. "In Search of Our Mother's Gardens." In *In Search of Our Mother's Gardens: Womanist Prose by Alice Walker.* New York: Harcourt Brace Jovanovich, 1983. 231–43.

Ward, Catherine C. "*Linden Hills*: A Modern *Inferno*." In *Gloria Naylor: Critical Perspectives Past and Present.* Ed. Henry L. Gates, Jr., and K. A. Appiah. New York: Amistad, 1993. 182–94.

Willis, Susan. *Specifying: Black Women Writing the American Experience.* Madison: University of Wisconsin Press, 1987.

Winsbro, Bonnie. *Supernatural Forces: Belief, Difference, and Power in Contemporary Works by Ethnic Women.* Amherst: University of Massachusetts Press, 1993.

Contributors

Jennifer Brantley teaches at the University of Wisconsin—River Falls. She earned her Ph.D. at the University of Nebraska—Lincoln. In addition to her critical work focusing on American women writers, Brantley has published poetry in a variety of journals.

Kimberly A. Costino is a doctoral student at the University of Massachusetts in Amherst. Her research interests include composition studies, ethnic American fiction, and queer theory.

Margot Anne Kelley is an associate professor of English and assistant dean at Ursinus College in Pennsylvania. She earned her Ph.D. at Indiana University. Her scholarly focus is on contemporary African-American women's writing and on continuities between American literature and other cultural productions.

Amy K. Levin is director of women's studies and associate professor of English at Northern Illinois University. She earned her Ph.D. at City University of New York. She is the author of *The Suppressed Sister: A Relationship in Novels by Nineteenth- and Twentieth-Century British Women* (Bucknell University Press, 1992) and of essays and poems.

Maxine Lavon Montgomery is an associate professor of English at Florida State University in Tallahassee. She is the author of *The Apocalypse in African-American Fiction* (University Press of Florida, 1996). Her recent critical work has been on Toni Morrison and Gloria Naylor.

Philip Page is an associate professor of English at California State University, San Bernardino. He earned his Ph.D. at Johns Hopkins University. His book *Dangerous Freedom: Fusion and Fragmentation in Toni Morrison's Novels* (University Press of Mississippi, 1995) won the Eudora Welty Prize.

Karen Schneider is an associate professor of English at Western Kentucky University. She earned her Ph.D. at Indiana University, and is the author of *Loving Arms: British Women Writing the Second World War* (University Press of Kentucky, 1996). Her critical works focus on World War II literature, African-American women's fiction, and film.

Dorothy Perry Thompson is an associate professor of English at Winthrop University in South Carolina. She earned her Ph.D. at the University of South Carolina, and her current teaching focus is African-American literature. She has published original poetry in a variety of collections and journals.

Index

Abigail (character), 31–32, 33, 64, 80, 97, 122

Abshu (character), 57, 59

Adams, Monni, 75

Africana womanist revision, xxii–xxiii, 89–111; in *Bailey's Cafe*, xxii, 89–90, 97–107; liminality in, 98–99, 100, 101, 103, 104; in *Mama Day*, xxii, 89–90, 92–98, 107–8; sacrifice in, 95, 97; time in, 94, 97

African influence, 70, 71–73, 81, 84, 86–87, 129. *See also* Africana womanist revision; Secret societies

Aggregation, 98

Ambush (character), 77

Anderson, Ruth (character), 130n.7, 150–51

Andrews, Larry, 63

"Angle of Seeing, An" (Christian), 72–73

Awkward, Michael, 5, 11, 101

"Axiomatic" (Kosofsky), 40

Bailey (character), 5, 35–37, 53, 84, 118, 121, 122–23, 124, 125, 126–27, 137, 138, 142, 146, 147, 152. *See also* Not/Bailey

Bailey's Cafe (Naylor), xvi, xvii–xviii, xxiii–xxiv, 79; Africana womanist revision in, xxii, 89–90, 97–107; community in, 126–27; compulsory heterosexuality and capitalism in, 42, 50–53; différance in, 118–29; domestic ritual in, 55–56, 64–67; emancipation in, 1–20; frames in, xxiii, 134, 135–49; literary allusions in, xiii; maternity in, 73, 84; screams and laughter in, xxi, 21–22, 23, 24, 35–37; sexual economy in, xx, 10–11

Baker, C. C. (character), 16, 28, 85, 116

Baker, Houston, Jr., 5, 9, 64, 90, 129–30n.3, 140

Baldwin, James, 140

Barbershop, 85–86

Barlow, William, 139

Bascombe Wade (character), 63, 77, 78, 82, 93

Basil (character), xix, 24, 25, 27, 57

Baskins, Judith, 107

Being & Race (Johnson), 71

Beloved (Morrison), 71, 91–92

Ben (character), xix, 28, 42, 84, 85, 128

Benjamin, Walter, 145

Bernice (character), 63, 78, 127

Bhabha, Homi, 134, 135, 144, 145–46, 147, 148, 152

Biblical allusions, xiii, xvi, xx, 126, 134; Africana womanist revision and, 98–107; emancipation from, 9–14; frames and, 138–40, 144–45

Billy Boy (character), 51–52, 99

Binarism, xxii, 40, 41, 46–47, 50, 53, 113, 135

Birnbaum, Lucia, 106

Birth, 78, 127. *See also* Virgin birth

Black Feminist Thought (Collins), 72

Blues, 5, 25, 120, 137, 138, 139, 140, 143, 145, 153n.2

Blues Fell This Morning (Oliver), 139

Bluest Eye, The (Morrison), xii, 4

Body in Pain, The (Scarry), 33

Boone, Sylvia Ardyn, 74, 75, 76

Borders, Boundaries, and Frames (Henderson), 133

Brother Jerome (character), 85

Brown Girl, Brownstones (Marshall), 71

Butch (character), 24–25

Butler, Judith, 54n.3

Caliban's curse, 2, 9, 16, 17n.1

Candle Walk, xix, 63, 64, 77, 82, 125, 144, 151–52

Cannon, Katie, 21

Canterbury Tales, The (Chaucer), xiii, 5

Capitalism, xxi, xxiii, 141–43; community vs., 148, 149–52; compulsory heterosexuality and, 39–54

"Capitalism and Gay Identity" (D'Emilio), 39

Capra, Frank, 14

Carabi, Angels, xii, xiii, xiv, 149–50

Celie (character), 90, 91

Chatterjee, Partha, 148

Chaucerian allusions, xiii, 5, 89

Chickens, 35, 64, 76, 79, 81–82, 97

Christ-figures, 95, 127

Christian, Barbara, 17n.2, 62, 68n.2, 71, 72–73, 116, 129

Christmas story revision, 66–67, 144, 150–51

Ciel (character), xxi, 21, 23–24, 25, 26–28, 29, 31, 58–59, 83

Cixous, Helene, 27

Claiming the Heritage (Kubitschek), 29

Clarissa (character; chicken), 76, 81, 82, 83

Cocoa/Ophelia (character), xi, xv, 4, 5–7, 15, 30–31, 63, 64, 81–83, 94, 95, 97, 98, 117; Africana womanist aspects of, 92; as community member, 119;

pregnancy of, 127; screams of, xxi, 32, 34–35; as successor to Mama Day, 76, 79

Collective agency, 146, 149. *See also* Frames

Collins, Patricia Hill, 72

Color Purple, The (film), 139

Color Purple, The (Walker), 90, 94, 140

Community, 119, 126–27, 147–48, 149–52

Compulsory heterosexuality, xxi, 39–54; in *Bailey's Cafe*, 42, 50–53; in *Linden Hills*, xxi, 43–47, 49–50, 53; in *The Women of Brewster Place*, 42–43, 47–49

"Compulsory Heterosexuality and Lesbian Existance" (Rich), xxi, 41

Cooking, 61–62, 64

Cooper, Carolyn, 86–87

Cora Lee (character), 57–58

Creel, Margaret, 73, 74

Cross-dressing. *See* Stanley/Miss Maple

Culler, Jonathan, 133

Dance, Daryl, 67

Daniel (character), 65–66, 118

Dantean allusions, xiii, 5, 144

David (character), 45–46, 47, 49, 50

Davis, Angela, 60

"Dawn" (book section), 23

Death, 26, 26–27, 31–32, 128

deCerteau, Michel, xxiii, 135, 141, 143, 145, 151–52

D'Emilio, John, 39, 40–41

Derrida, Jacques, xxiii, 113, 114, 115, 120, 125, 128, 130nn.6, 8, 133, 149

de Weever, Jacquelyn, 89–90, 97

Dictionary of Narratology, A (Prince), 135

Différance, xxiii, 112–32; in *Bailey's Cafe*, 118–29; in *Linden Hills*, 115–17, 119; in *Mama Day*, 114–15, 117–18, 119, 125; in *The Women of Brewster Place*, 115–16, 117, 118, 119, 125

Diop, Cheikh Anta, 103

Discursive indenture, 1, 3

Diviners, 97

Doctor Buzzard (character), 77, 84, 85

Doctor Smithfield (character), 78

Domestic ritual, xxi–xxii, 55–69; in *Bailey's*

Domestic ritual (*continued*)
Cafe, 55–56, 64–67; in *Linden Hills*, 60–
63; in *Mama Day*, 63–64; in *The Women
of Brewster Place*, 56–60
Double-consciousness, 113–14
Du Bois, W. E. B., 98, 113
Due, Tananarive, 68n.1
DuPlessis, Rachel, 129n.2
"Dusk" (book section), 23, 60

Eli (character), 11–12, 15, 51, 102
Elijah (biblical figure), 9, 11
Ellington, Duke, 136–37
Ellison, Ralph, 113, 129
Emancipation, 1–20; from biblical
influences, 9–14; from language
constraints, 1–2, 8–9, 12–13; from
literary influences, 2–3, 5, 6, 8–9
Epistemology of the Closet, 40
Erickson, Peter, 2, 9
Esther (biblical figure), 9, 10
Esther (character), xx, 10–11, 35–36, 37,
103–4, 118–19, 121, 123, 124, 126
Etta Mae (character), 23, 25–26, 28, 33,
46–47, 50, 83–84
Eugene (character), 26, 58–59, 85
Eve (biblical figure), 9
Eve (character), 35, 36, 118, 119, 120,
121, 123, 126, 129, 138, 139; Africana
womanist aspects of, 99–101, 102–3,
104, 106–7; domestic ritual and, 66; as
a maternal figure, 73, 84; midwifery
and, 67; sexuality of, 12–13, 50, 51–52,
53
Evelyn (character), 55, 62
"Everyday Use" (Walker), 64
"Eve's Song" (book section), 136

Facial mutilation, 36, 101, 119, 139
Falasha, 105
Fertility, 76, 78
Fowler, Karen Joy, 122
Fowler, Virginia, 26, 37, 137
Frames, 133–54; in *Bailey's Cafe*, xxiii,
134, 135–49; in *Linden Hills*, 148, 149–
52; in *Mama Day*, 148, 151–52; spatial,
134, 136, 138, 142, 146; temporal, 134,

135, 145–46; in *The Women of Brewster
Place*, 134–35, 148, 149
Frances (character), 117
Franklin, John Hope, 93–94
Fraser, Celeste, 71

Gabriel (character), 16, 35, 37, 106, 107,
118, 121, 122, 124, 125, 147
Gates, Henry Louis, Jr., xiii, xvi–xvii, 1, 5,
15, 17n.5, 49–50, 72, 140
Gatlin brothers (characters), 8, 9, 123, 142
Gender identity, xxi, 29, 30, 42, 53, 55, 66,
141–42
Genital mutilation, 13, 67, 68n.4, 84, 105,
106–7
George (character; Cocoa's husband), xi,
xvi, xviii, xix, xx, xxi, 4, 7, 14, 15, 30–
31, 55, 63, 65, 67, 107, 122, 124, 126,
128, 129, 138, 147, 149; as a Christ-
figure, 95, 127; laying on of hands and,
96–97; as masculine principle, 64;
maternal power vs., 79–80, 81–83;
matricentric culture and, 92–93;
posthumous communication with, 94;
rationalism of, 6, 35, 80, 119; screams
and laughter of, 21, 32–33, 34–35, 36–
37; as suicide, 117
George (character; Cocoa's son), 129
Gifts, 151–52
Glas (Derrida), 133
Goddu, Teresa, 3
God-the-Father, 9, 12, 27, 99
Gonde, 75–76, 80, 83
Go Tell It on the Mountain (Baldwin), 140
Grandma Tilson (character), 61
Greasy (character), 85–86

Hair braiding, 76, 81
Healing, 22, 23, 26, 28, 33, 37, 78
Henderson, Mae, 21, 130n.4, 133
Henderson, Stephen, 56
Heterosexuality. *See* Compulsory hetero-
sexuality
Hirsch, Marianne, 70
Holloway, Karla, 93
Homans, Margaret, 3, 17n.5, 117
Home, 58, 60, 67, 101, 103

Homosexuality, 11, 23, 28, 85; binarism between heterosexuality and, 40, 41, 46–47, 50, 53; compulsory heterosexuality and capitalism vs., xxi, 39–54; as différance, 116
Hoo Doo, 97. *See also* Voodoo
Howard (character), 45
Hudson-Weems, Clenora, 109n.1
Hughes, Langston, 118, 128
Hurston, Zora Neale, 56, 97, 108

Iceman Jones (character), 66, 103, 118, 120, 122, 141
Identity, 141–42, 146–47. *See also* Gender identity
"Imitation and Gender Subordination" (Butler), 54n.3
Inferno, The (Dante), xiii. *See also* Dantean allusions
Intimate Violence (Tanner), 28
Irigaray, Luce, 3, 129n.2
It's a Wonderful Life (film), 14

"Jam, The" (book section), xxiii, 120, 135, 136, 137
Jameson, Fredric, 134
Jazz, 136–37, 138, 143, 145
Jazz (Morrison), 112, 115
Jesse Bell (character), 11, 36, 50–51, 84, 119, 120, 123, 126; Africana womanist aspects of, 101–3; domestic ritual and, 55–56
Jewish faith, 105, 106, 125, 147
Jezebel (biblical figure), 9, 11, 101
Johnson, Barbara, 120
Johnson, Charles, 71
Jones, Jacqueline, 56
Joplin, Scott, 137
Junior Lee (character), 34, 77, 80, 117

Kambon, Kobi, 98, 103, 110n.6
King Lear (Shakespeare), xiii, 6
Kiswana (character), 4, 56, 57, 59, 84, 116, 149
Kitchen, 62, 117
Kochman, Thomas, xvii
Kristeva, Julia, 22–23, 24, 25

Kubitschek, Missy Dehn, 2, 17n.7, 29
Kyriarchy, 92, 94, 95

Language, 1–2, 8–9, 12–13, 23, 78
"Laugh of the Medusa, The" (Cixous), 27
Laughter. *See* Screams and laughter
Laurel (character), 45, 86, 116, 128
Laying on of hands, 96–97
"Lead on with Light" (Levy), 47
Leafy (character), 56
Lesbian continuum, xxi, 48, 49, 50
Lesbians. *See* Homosexuality
Leslau, Wolf, 105
Lester (character), 29–30, 47, 49–50, 61, 86, 150–51
Levy, Helen Fiddyment, 47, 60, 61
Liminality, 98–99, 100, 101, 103, 104
Linden Hills (Naylor), xiii, xvii–xviii, 15, 89, 127, 128; community in, 126; compulsory heterosexuality and capitalism in, xxi, 43–47, 49–50, 53; différance in, 115–17, 119; domestic ritual in, 60–63; frames in, 148, 149–52; maternity in, 86; mimicry in, 3; screams and laughter in, xxi, 23, 29–30, 31, 35
Literary allusions, xiii, xx, 2–3, 5, 6, 8–9, 57–58, 144. *See also* Biblical allusions
Little Caesar (character), 128
Location of Culture, The (Bhabha), 145
Loose Canons (Gates), xiii
Lorraine (character), 23, 28–29, 30, 42–43, 45, 46, 47–48, 49, 50, 56–57, 116, 117, 128
Lucielia (character), 55, 57, 58, 127
Luther (character), 29, 30, 44–45, 46, 60, 61, 62
Luwana (character), 60–61, 62

McDowell, Deborah, 2, 17n.2, 68n.2
Madonna figures, 67, 106
"Maestro, if you please" (book section), 135, 136
Magic/supernatural, 6, 65; Africana womanist revision and, 92, 95, 102–3; maternity and, 71, 81, 84, 86. *See also* Diviners; Hoo-Doo; Necromancy; Spirituality

Mama Day (Naylor), xi, xvi, xvii–xviii, xix, xx, 5–7, 9, 14, 15, 85, 128, 129, 146; Africana womanist revision in, xxii, 89–90, 92–98, 107–8; community in, 126; différance in, 114–15, 117–18, 119, 125; domestic ritual in, 63–64; frames in, 148, 151–52; literary allusions in, xiii, 2–3; maternity in, xxii, 70–84, 86, 87; preconceived notions in, 127; screams and laughter in, xxi, 21, 23, 24, 30–35

Mama/Miranda Day (character), xi, 6, 30–35, 61, 64, 84, 86, 114–15, 116, 117, 120, 122, 129, 151, 152; Africana womanist aspects of, 92–93, 94, 95–97; as a maternal figure, 70, 74–75, 76–77, 78–79, 80–83; midwifery and, 63, 78; as a trickster, 72

Manhood, 7–9, 85–86

Marge, 98

Mariam (character), 13–14, 36–37, 51, 55, 64, 67, 79, 84, 120–21, 123; Africana womanist aspects of, 104–7; identity issues and, 146

Marshall, Paule, 71

Mary Magdalene (biblical figure), 9, 13, 101

Mary/Peaches (character), 13, 14, 36, 67, 101, 119, 123, 124, 126, 139–40, 147

"Mary (Take One)" (book section), 13, 101, 120, 136, 139

"Mary (Take Two)" (book section), 13–14, 104, 136

Masenya, Madipoane, 92, 108

Maternity, xxii, 70–88; African influence and, 70, 71–73, 81, 84, 86–87; magic/supernatural and, 71, 81, 84, 86; secret societies and, 73–76, 78–79, 83

Matriarchy, 77

Matricentric culture, 92–93

Matrilineal descent, 103

Mattie (character), 21, 46–47, 50, 117, 120, 129; domestic ritual and, 57, 58, 59; as a maternal figure, 73, 83–84; screams and laughter of, 23–28

Matus, Jill, 59

Meisenhelder, Susan, 15, 64, 117, 130n.5

Mende society, 74

Men of Brewster Place, The (Naylor), xix, 18–19n.17, 73, 84–86

Midsummer Night's Dream, A (Shakespeare), xiii, 57

Midwifery, xxii, 63, 67, 78

Miss Eva (character), 25

Miss Maple (character). *See* Stanley/Miss Maple

"Miss Maple's Blues" (book section), 7–9, 12, 15, 120, 136, 137, 143

Moi, Toril, 23

Montgomery, Maxine Lavon, 103–4, 120, 123

"Mood: Indigo" (book section), 5, 126, 136–37, 143

Morrison, Toni, xii, xiii, 4, 62, 70, 71, 91–92, 100, 112, 114, 115, 121, 128

Mother/Daughter Plot, The (Hirsch), 70

Musical metaphors, 25, 26, 123, 135–40. *See also* Blues; Jazz

Mutilation. *See* Facial mutilation; Genital mutilation

Nadine (character), 36, 99, 104, 118, 121, 123, 124, 129

Narration, 123–27

Narrative (Equiano), 95

Neal, Larry, 1, 153n.2

Necromancy, 92, 93–95, 102–3, 106–7

Nettie (character), 90

Norman (character), 29, 150–51

Not/Bailey (character), 7, 8, 14, 15–16. *See also* Bailey

Of Grammatology (Derrida), 125

Oliver, Paul, 139

"Only Voice Is Your Own, The" (Storhoff), 17n.4

Ophelia (character). *See* Cocoa/Ophelia

Original sin, 12, 99

Other, 1, 2, 4, 7, 60, 63, 79, 89, 115

Pain, 22, 25, 26, 27, 33, 36. *See also* Screams and laughter

Parergon, 133

Paternalism, 47

Patriarchy, 3, 60, 66, 92

Peace (character), 31–32, 34, 94, 114–15
Peaches (character). *See* Mary/Peaches
Pearl (character), 77
Peculiar People, A (Creel), 73
Perry, Donna, xiv, 138, 148
Petry, Ann, xiii
Pilate (character), 91–92
Practice of Everyday Life, The (deCerteau), 143
Preverbal sounds, 22–23, 24, 25, 26, 27, 29, 32, 34, 35, 37
Prince, Gerald, 135, 136

Quilting, 64

Rabuzzi, Kathryn, 63
Radiance from the Waters (Boone), 74
"Rainbows of Darkness" (Traub), 144
Rape, 8, 23, 28–29, 52
Reema (character), 77
Repetition, xvi, xvii–xix, 3
Reversal, xvii–xviii
Revolution in Poetic Language (Kristeva), 22
Rich, Adrienne, xxi, 41, 48, 49, 50
Richards, Dona Marimba, 94, 97
"Role of Shakespeare in Naylor's Novels, The" (Erickson), 2
Ruby (character), 34, 64, 76, 80–81, 82, 83, 95, 97, 117
Ruth (character), 29, 150–51

Sacred Time, 94
Sacrifice, 64, 95, 97
Sadie (character), 36, 65–66, 103, 118, 120, 123, 126, 136–37, 140–41, 142, 143–44
Salvation, 22, 25, 26, 27, 28, 34–35, 102, 103
Sammy (character), 57–58
Sande society, 74–76, 77, 82, 84
Sapphira (character), xix, 6, 63, 77, 79, 92, 93–95, 109n.4, 114, 115
Satanic Verses, The (Rushdie), 144
Scarry, Elaine, xxi, 33
Screams and laughter, 21–38; in *Bailey's Cafe*, xxi, 21–22, 23, 24, 35–37; in *Linden Hills*, xxi, 23, 29–30, 31, 35; in *Mama Day*, xxi, 21, 23, 24, 30–35; in

The Women of Brewster Place, xxi, 21, 23–29, 32, 33
Secret societies, 73–76, 78–79, 83
Sedgwick, Eve Kosofsky, 40
Separation, 98
Serena (character), 26, 55, 128
Sethe (character), 71, 91–92
Sexual economy, xx, 10–11
Sexuality, 12–13, 139–41. *See also* Compulsory heterosexuality; Homosexuality
Shakespearean allusions, xiii, xx, 2–3, 5, 6, 8, 57–58, 89, 144
Shug (character), 90, 91, 139
"Significant Others" (Gates), 17n.5
Signifyin(g), xvi–xviii, 4
Signifying Monkey, The (Gates), 72
Silla (character), 71
Sister Carrie (character), 100, 122, 123, 124, 125, 126, 135
Smith, Barbara, 17n.2, 68n.2
Smith, Valerie, 130n.4
Snead, James, xvii, xviii
Sofia (character), 90, 91
Song of Solomon (Morrison), 91–92
Sophia (character), 94
Sowei, 74, 75, 76, 78–79, 80
Sowo mask, 75, 76, 79, 82
Soyinka, Wole, 1–2, 4, 5
Spatial frames, 134, 136, 138, 142, 146
Spiralytic movement, 90–91, 93, 99
Spirituality, 63–64, 90. *See also* Magic/supernatural
Stanley/Miss Maple (character), 7–9, 14, 15, 16, 36, 84, 119–20, 121, 122, 123, 124, 125, 126, 129, 136, 137, 140, 146–47; capitalism impact on, 141–42; domestic ritual and, 65, 66; sexuality of, 50, 52–53; tactics of, 143–44
Stepto, Robert, 129n.3
Storhoff, Gary, 2–3, 9, 17n.4, 97
Strategy, xxiii, 46, 143
Street, The (Petry), xiii
Sugar Man (character), 122, 123, 124, 125, 135
Suicide, 117, 128
Sula (Morrison), 121, 128
"Sweet Esther" (book section), 11, 136

"System and the Speaking Subject, The" (Kristeva), 23

Tactics, xxiii, 135, 143–44
Tanner, Laura E., 28
Tempest, The (Shakespeare), 8
Temporal frames, 134, 135, 145–46
Their Eyes Were Watching God (Hurston), 56
Theresa (character), 23, 28, 43, 45, 46, 47–48, 49, 50, 56–57
Time, 14, 94, 97
"Trajectories of Self-Definition" (Marshall), 71
Traub, Valerie, 2, 3, 144
Trinity, 27, 96
Tubman, Harriet, 91
Tucker, Lindsey, 72, 80
"Two, The" (book section), 23, 28
Two-cradle theory, 103

"Vamp, The" (book section), 5, 135, 136
Van Gennep, Arnold, 98
Verbal sounds, 22, 24, 32, 37. *See also* preverbal sounds
Violet (character), 112, 114, 115
Virgin birth, 13–14, 21, 36–37, 104–5, 138
Virgin/whore dichotomy, 13–14
Vonnegut, Kurt, xv
Voodoo, 73, 95. *See also* Hoo Doo

Walker, Alice, xxii, 64, 68n.4, 70, 90–91, 92, 94, 100, 101, 108, 109n.2
Walking stick, 78–79, 81, 82, 95
Ward, Catherine C., 117, 130n.7

Warner, Marina, 106, 107
Well imagery, 31–32, 112–13, 114–17, 118–19, 120–21, 127, 128
Werner, Craig, 116
White, Hayden, 11
Willa (character), 3, 4, 31, 86, 116–17, 119, 127, 129; domestic ritual and, 61, 62–63; screams of, xxi, 29–30, 32
Willie (character), 29–30, 47, 49–50, 116, 117, 120, 129, 150–51
Willis, Susan, 65, 100
Willow Springs (fictional location), 6, 30–31, 118
Winsbro, Bonnie, 32
Winston (character), 45–46, 47, 49, 50
Womb/tomb imagery, 113, 116, 128
Women of Brewster Place, The (Naylor), xiv, xvii–xviii, xix, 4, 15–16, 67, 89, 127, 128; community in, 126; compulsory heterosexuality and capitalism in, 42–43, 47–49; différance in, 115–16, 117, 118, 119, 125; domestic ritual in, 56–60; frames in, 134–35, 148, 149; literary allusions in, xiii; maternity in, 71, 73, 83–84; screams and laughter in, xxi, 21, 23–29, 32, 33
Woods, Reverend Moreland (character), 47, 85
"Wrap, The" (book section), 5, 120, 135, 136, 147

Xavier (character), 86

Yamargam gogo, 105